SARA SANFORD

INCLUSION, INC

HOW TO DESIGN INTERSECTIONAL EQUITY INTO THE WORKPLACE

WILEY

Published by John Wiley & Sons, Inc., Hoboken, New Jersey.
Published simultaneously in Canada.

For general information on our other products and services or for technical support, please contact our Customer Care Department within the United States at (800) 762-2974, outside the United States at (317) 572-3993 or fax (317) 572-4002.

Wiley also publishes its books in a variety of electronic formats. Some content that appears in print may not be available in electronic formats. For more information about Wiley products, visit our web site at www.wiley.com.

Library of Congress Cataloging-in-Publication Data

Names: Sanford, Sara, author.
Title: Inclusion, inc : how to design intersectional equity into the
  workplace / Sara Sanford.
Description: Hoboken, New Jersey : Wiley, [2022] | Includes bibliographical
  references and index.
Identifiers: LCCN 2021062103 (print) | LCCN 2021062104 (ebook) | ISBN
  9781119849766 (cloth) | ISBN 9781119850038 (adobe pdf) | ISBN
  9781119850021 (epub)
Subjects: LCSH: Intersectionality (Sociology) | Work environment.
Classification: LCC HM488.5 .S26 2022 (print) | LCC HM488.5 (ebook) | DDC
  305.3—dc23/eng/20220119
LC record available at https://lccn.loc.gov/2021062103
LC ebook record available at https://lccn.loc.gov/2021062104

Cover Image: Wiley
Cover Design: Wiley
SKY10033157_031122

For my parents, for always believing.
And for anyone who's ever been underestimated.

Contents

Language Guide

Readers will come to this book with varying levels of diversity, equity, and inclusion (DEI) vocabulary. The dialogue around DEI is continuously evolving, and words can have different meanings for different people. This brief guide provides a common language framework for the rest of the book. It is not intended as a glossary, but rather to clarify how DEI language is being used in *Inclusion, Inc.*

Black

Why is "Black" capitalized in this book, but not "white," when referring to race?

In July 2020, the *New York Times* announced that, after a month of discussion, they would capitalize *Black* when describing people and cultures of African descent.[1] Hundreds of news organizations, including the Associated Press, made the same choice in the spring and summer of 2020. Most news organizations have declined to capitalize "white" because it is an identifier of skin color, rather than of shared experience.

For the reasons stated by these organizations, I have chosen to capitalize "Black" and not "white" when referring to race in *Inclusion, Inc.*

DEI

The term "DEI" stands for diversity, equity, and inclusion. In this book, it is used to refer to the field of work that focuses on ensuring that employees of all backgrounds—especially underestimated backgrounds—are included, treated fairly, and given the same opportunities to advance as their peers.

Diversity. The presence of individuals who differ from one another in a range of ways, such as socioeconomic status, age, gender identity, ethnicity, race, language, and religion.

Equity. Fairness of treatment for employees of all backgrounds. The distinction between *equity* and *equality* is important: Equity does not mean equal treatment, but rather creating equal access to opportunities through equitable practices.

Inclusion. Moving beyond recruiting underestimated individuals to involving them in decision-making and valuing and rewarding their contributions. One of my favorite definitions of inclusion came from DEI expert Verna Myers: "Diversity is being asked to the party. Inclusion is being asked to dance."

Intersectionality

How class, race, age, gender, sexual orientation, and other aspects of identity "intersect" with one another or overlap. For example, the experiences of being Latinx *or* being a woman are not the same as being Latinx *and* a woman. Certain biases are only experienced when living at the intersection of these two identities.

Neurodivergent

Refers to individuals who experience different neurological functioning than the majority of the population. Neurodivergence may present as autism, attention deficit disorder, dyslexia, dyspraxia, Tourette syndrome, or in a number of other forms.

Underestimated

Why is the term "underestimated," rather than "underrepresented," used to refer to individuals and groups that experience bias in the workplace?

In 2015, Arlan Hamilton founded the Los Angeles–based venture capital firm, Backstage Capital, to invest in "underestimated founders," including founders of color, women, and those who identify as LGBTQ. She also used the term "underestimated" in the title of her book, *It's About Damn Time: How to Turn Being Underestimated into Your Greatest Advantage.*

I wanted to adopt this term because in many cases, I believe it is more accurate than "underrepresented." For example, "underrepresented" is not accurate when women make up over half of a group. Although they may not be *underrepresented*, they remain *underestimated*.

When you see the term "underestimated" throughout this book, I am using it to refer to groups that have historically experienced systemic bias toward a facet of their identity, such as race, gender, age, nationality, disability status, or other characteristic that is not considered the "default." I think this term better reflects the untapped potential of these groups.

I still use the term "underrepresented" occasionally, when it is a contextually accurate descriptor of the group or individuals being discussed.

PART 1

Equity—It's Not Personal, It's Systemic

CHAPTER 1

Beyond Good Intentions

I thought 2016 was going to be a year for the underdogs. The Cubs were having their moment. It had been 108 years since they had won a World Series.

Yes, Cleveland had home field advantage. Yes, the Cubs were coming back from a 3–1 deficit, and only five teams in history had come back from that far behind to win. But when I deplaned in O'Hare, I believed the fanaticism surrounding me could beat any odds. I hadn't felt that kind of energy since Seattle's "Refuse to Lose" euphoria in '95.

I wasn't in town specifically for the Series, but I came from a baseball-loving family, and my parents had Chicago roots, so I was going to soak it up while I had the chance. Everywhere I went, I was seeing either Cubs signs or Hillary signs. #ImWithHer banners peeked out from under *End the Curse!* flags. All around, history seemed to be in the making.

I was in Chicago for work, and at the time, I had what I thought was a corporate do-gooder's dream job, overseeing DEI programming for a large financial company. I had spent the first part of my career advocating for equity from the other side, either in nonprofits and international NGOs, or through the lens of public policy. I had seen the limits of working on systemic problems from the outside, and I wanted to drive change from within. So, I had made the leap to the financial sector, determined to diversify the original old boys' club.

At the time, I felt optimistic. My employer had invested both time and budget. Employees, including executives, had attended trainings. We made sure our website didn't feature only stock photos of white men, and we ramped up our recruiting efforts to diversify our candidate base for job openings.

We had also created affinity groups for people of color and women, to provide a sense of community and opportunities for networking. To support our women's affinity group, we decided to invite a dozen members to join our executive team at a major financial services conference in Chicago. They would have an opportunity to get to know our executives over an intimate dinner and learn how committed our leadership team was to our diversity initiatives.

The dinner fell on the seventh game of the Series. I caught the top half of the first inning in the hotel lobby before we all left together. At the restaurant, a mainly Black waitstaff showed us to our private dining room. Pseudo castle doors separated us from the rest of the restaurant. The waiters gripped the iron door handles with both hands, braced themselves, and heaved backward to unseal them and haul them open.

We had our own décor—mock Medieval. I imagined the instructions the waitstaff had probably been given to provide us with "exceptional" service in this finance-friendly steakhouse that resembled so many others.

For me, the dinner was a means to an end. I needed to see that our leadership team understood the promise of diversity initiatives as a business imperative. I wanted management to genuinely believe supporting inclusion was a good call.

Those hurdles had now been cleared. Our affinity group had made it to the castle. Around us hung wall art in powerful frames: out-of-period noblemen in braided coats on rearing steeds, both species puffing out exaggerated chests. These were no rough-shod ponies of the Wild West; flaxen manes cascaded over their elegantly rounded shoulders. Hooves glistened. These were proper equine trophies, symbols of their riders' net worth.

"Have you decided on your order?" A waiter interrupted my thoughts.

"The salmon, please. Thank you."

As he left the room, I overheard a snippet of the Cubs game broadcast in the restaurant. Bottom of the fourth. I couldn't hear who was ahead.

I was seated between the VP of Business Development and my boss, a woman I looked up to and had learned from. She was one of few female leaders in the industry. Glancing around the table, I felt a brief sense of pride. The women from our affinity group seated with the executive team made this the most gender-balanced financial dinner I had attended.

I had gotten to know one woman at the table a little better during the conference. I'll call her Irene. She had confided to me that she had waited for decades to launch her own career in finance because she felt that, as a woman, she wouldn't have been taken seriously until a few years ago. I had assured her that she was in the right place, that our affinity networks were created with her in mind.

As the night went on, I lost track of how long we had been there. I excused myself to use the restroom. As I pushed open the heavy door to reenter the main restaurant, I saw there were no guests left. Tables had been wiped and chairs were stacked against the walls. I cringed. The waitstaff were patiently standing by the walls, hands folded over their aprons, waiting for us.

We were already an hour over our time. We were the customers I had dreaded in a previous life. I apologized and said I'd try to get our group to wrap it up.

The kitchen radio blasted the game. They were headed into extra innings.

When I returned to our room, I told the group that we were the only ones keeping the place open and suggested we take the party back to the hotel bar. But the conversations carried on. After another 20 minutes, one of the Black waiters slipped in gingerly and asked if everyone was happy with their evening before they wrapped up for the night. He was ignored. He tried again. "I'm so sorry to put an end to what looks like such a fun night, but we are going to have to be closing up soon."

Irene cut him off. "Oh, honey, we pay your bills, so we'll be leaving when we're leaving."

Our server nodded and retreated. As the door was slowly closing, but still partially open, Irene exclaimed loudly, to the whole room, as if sharing a joke she needed everyone to hear the setup for, "You know what I miss? *Back in my day*, I could have called him 'boy' and no one would have had a problem with it. *Back in my day*, I could have had him fired for speaking to a white woman that way."

A moment later I found myself standing. I was on my feet, an involuntary reaction, irrepressible. I was not weighing questions of correctness; it was far more basic. Somehow I thought I could not be the only one, but around the table my colleagues were only staring, staying seated, saying nothing.

"Oh honey, sit down, don't get upset," Irene urged.

Nervous laughter rattled through the room.

My hands went cold. *How could I be the only one? They all said they cared. They made public statements. What are they doing? Why is nobody saying anything?*

A roar was audible from the kitchen. The Cubs had gone ahead.

When my voice came, it was shaking. "Back in your day," I reminded Irene, "you wouldn't be sitting at this table. *Back in your day*, you wouldn't have been taken seriously as a woman in this profession. We're all here tonight because we don't want to go back to that time."

An exec nervously pushed around chunks of his surf and turf. I picked up my purse and coat, gave the castle doors one last shove, and left.

I rushed past the servers waiting to clear our table, out of the restaurant, and into a lone taxi waiting like a lifeboat.

On the way back to the hotel, triumphal horns blared throughout the city. I wanted to rejoice with my euphoric driver, but I was stunned.

I was not a victim in this situation. Nor was I a hero—I was simply mistaken. I thought that because our company had invested in these inclusion initiatives, our culture had actually changed. I thought the executives sitting at that table who had stated their commitment to diversity and attended trainings would have stood with me. I didn't think I was going to be alone.

We had checked all the right boxes, but the unspoken code of conduct hadn't changed. We had had our moment of truth, and nobody stood up.

And by running the programs that let us think we were the good guys, I was complicit.

How had this happened?

≈

The following Monday, I got the call from HR: My position no longer existed in the organization. I was terminated, effective immediately. The reason given was a recent merger. I knew about that merger. I had helped coordinate the resulting reorg, and I knew that all staffing decisions had been made months ago, so I found this difficult to believe. Either way, we were happy to part ways.

A few months later, I attended a CEO panel at the top of Seattle's World Trade Center. The topic: *What Does It Mean to Be an Effective Leader?*

The year was 2017, and the #MeToo hashtag had turned into a rallying cry for millions. Social activist Tarana Burke had coined the phrase in 2006 to build solidarity among survivors of abuse. More than a decade later, Alyssa Milano retweeted the phrase one night, and by morning, a movement was born. Around the world, women were taking the secrets they had kept inside whisper networks out into the international spotlight. Hollywood's leading ladies founded Time's Up to cover legal costs for victims seeking justice. Everywhere I went, I heard "Me Too."

Tarana Burke held the movement accountable, continuing to speak out for women who weren't going to be protected and still had to show up to hostile workplaces every day. For the movement's legacy to have meaning, she argued, employers would need to take meaningful action. It was up to business leaders to take the next steps.

In the audience at the Trade Center, I was waiting to see which CEO was going to take that next step. The panelists spoke about managing growth in a quickly scaling business, retaining customers in the face of increasing competition, and the impact of artificial intelligence on their industries. For all these topics, they had best practices, data, evidence, key performance indicators, and actionable takeaways.

Then the moderator asked the question I had been waiting for: "What is your approach to diversity, equity, and inclusion?"

A silent pause. Chairs creaked as the panelists' postures changed, their legs uncrossed and recrossed, they leaned backward slightly, getting a little distance from the microphone. Women in the audience made eye contact with each other. I realized many of us were holding our breath.

Finally, one of the panelists took the mic. It was the first time I had heard hesitation in any of their voices. The brave volunteer paused after each word, as if looking for approval that he was on track. Like a spelling bee contestant, he was waiting for each syllable he spoke to be the one that would disqualify him:

"Honestly. . .my. . .my approach to DEI. . .Well, I. . .I lead with love."

The others followed:

"Everyone at our company knows that we care about diversity. We don't have an [air quotes] approach [end air quotes] as much as it's just in our DNA."

"Every day, I come in being my most authentic self, and I think that lets everyone else know they can be their authentic self, no matter their background or gender."

Polite applause.

These answers cited no data. No best practices. No KPIs. No plan.

No next steps.

≈

Fast-forward to three years later. In the summer of 2020, in the wake of George Floyd's murder, corporate statements of solidarity flooded LinkedIn feeds. CEOs publicly renewed their pledges of commitment to racial justice, to equity, to inclusion. The Black Lives Matter movement had gained unstoppable momentum, and business leaders felt the pressure to vocally reaffirm their support of Black communities.

I was living in Seattle's Capitol Hill neighborhood at the time, three blocks from the East Precinct that had become the movement's infamous ground zero. I think the zone's temporary residents in tents and makeshift shelters were still deciding whether they were occupying the Capitol Hill Autonomous Zone (CHAZ) or the Capitol Hill Organized Protest (CHOP). Clickbait-seeking helicopters had become my round-the-clock white noise reality. From my apartment balcony on the third floor, Seattle's downtown peaks floated above Puget Sound. The corporate trapezoids of the financial district cut the skyline in business-casual shades of blue and silver.

Down on the street, at metropolitan basecamp, Black lives mattered. "I'd rather repaint gray buildings than bury my Black friends!" a leader of the movement shouted across the street through a bullhorn. In the afternoons, teenagers marched—hundreds of middle school and high school students under my window together, singing, making sure everyone knew the words to the songs that drowned out the helicopters. I felt hopeful, knowing that this time, their voices hadn't just reached my windows and faded out. They had traveled beyond, to those downtown windows, to the top floors.

Employees and consumers were demanding a new level of accountability, and national publications held CEOs to account, to ensure that they were walking their talk. For the first time in years, business leaders were forced to revisit their diversity data.

An email showed up in my inbox from a colleague who had attended the CEO panel with me three years earlier. Subject line: "Lead with Love."

He had forwarded me an article calling out executives who had made very public statements over the previous few years that they valued diversity, that it was "baked in" to their companies' cultures. The feature was a two-page spread. On the left side, dossiers of the self-proclaimed Good Guys and their solidarity statements. On the right, diversity reports from the companies they oversaw. A decade of diversity data showed little to no progress, year after year, with some companies regressing. The CEO who proclaimed "I lead with love" as his guiding DEI philosophy had the largest photo. The caption below: "Leadership or Lip Service?"

Good Intentions, Few Results

These individual companies and leaders are not anomalies. While some strides have been made toward workplace equality over the last 50 years, over the last two decades progress has stalled. Looking beyond the wage gap, women and minorities are still underrepresented in leadership,[1] receive less access to senior leaders,[2] and are leaving the fastest-growing sectors, such as tech, at higher rates than white men,[3] citing "culture" as the primary reason. Women—especially women of color—are more likely to have been laid off during the COVID-19 crisis,[4] and experts estimate that decades of progress toward workplace equality have been erased by the pandemic.[5]

Despite the rise of MeToo and Black Lives Matter, many workplaces have taken a step backward: Men are less likely now to want to mentor women than they were before the MeToo movement.[6] Managers are less likely to advocate for employees of color than they are for white employees,[7] and employees are more receptive to constructive criticism from a male manager than from a female manager.[8]

In short, we're still stuck.

Despite this sobering snapshot of the status quo, when it comes to equity and inclusion, there is good news:

We've been doing it all wrong.

The DEI Overwhelm

I was asked during a recent interview to pick one word to describe how business leaders feel about DEI. I think they were looking for "committed" or "optimistic."

I chose "overwhelmed."

This feeling isn't limited to business leaders. I spend my days listening to employees across all levels of organizations talk about what diversity and inclusion mean to them. In these conversations, I hear a lot of recurring themes:

- White employees want to support their peers of color but don't know where to start.

- Employees of color are told over and over again, "We need to hear voices like yours. We need more people of color to speak up." Then, they do speak up and they hear, "You're making your peers uncomfortable. You should just focus on leading your team. You're pulling the race card." Some find, after speaking up, that they're suddenly left out of meetings and important projects.

- Men want to be allies, but they're worried they're going to say the wrong thing.

- Women take advice to "Lean In" and stand up for themselves or negotiate for a raise, only to be told they're too aggressive or arrogant. Other women see these consequences and avoid speaking up, and then are told it's their own fault that their careers aren't progressing.

- Managers and executives start to explore DEI strategies and become paralyzed by an ever-changing DEI vocabulary, contradictory messages, and seemingly endless nuance. If they do implement new inclusive policies, they find a new segment of their employee base is angry at them.

- Employees who feel their neurodivergent status, age, or caretaking responsibilities impact how they're treated at work aren't sure they have a "right" to speak up, because what they're experiencing doesn't seem as bad as overt racism or sexism.

This is just the beginning. Whatever the particular mix of overwhelm looks like in each organization, I see the same repeated outcomes: Underestimated employees eventually realize their only choices are to assimilate or leave, and the businesses and employees both miss out. (Arlan Hamilton coined the term "underestimated" to refer to groups that have historically experienced bias.) Even if businesses manage to hold on to these employees, employers won't get the benefits of their unique insights, since they will never feel comfortable showing up authentically.

Employees who do choose to leave find they don't know how to determine if another employer will be better. Many "Most Inclusive Workplaces" lists are sponsored, or their criteria are unclear or unsubstantiated. Large organizations that appear more diverse than others don't show their attrition numbers. They may just be in a continuous cycle of losing and rehiring employees to keep their diversity numbers up. Alternatively, they may have diverse overall numbers, but zooming in could reveal that none of that diversity shows up in leadership.

Employees don't know where to look. Employers don't know what to do. In general, there's a lack of clarity about what works—what behaviors, processes, and practices should be tracked to catalyze progress toward equity at work.

I wrote *Inclusion, Inc* to provide this clarity.

To get out from under the overwhelm, we have to start by understanding the status quo. What have businesses been doing to address DEI, and why isn't it working?

Stop the Trainings

American businesses spend $8 billion a year on diversity trainings.[9]

The quintessential diversity training came out of a 1960s workplace focused on compliance. Title VII of the Civil Rights Act of 1964 had made it illegal for employers to discriminate on the basis of race, religion, sex, or national origin, and a barrage of discrimination suits quickly followed. One of the most common remedies was a court-ordered mandate for the organization to train all employees in anti-discriminatory behavior. Many companies wanted to avoid costly and embarrassing lawsuits and preemptively implemented trainings, collecting signatures from employees afterward, acknowledging that employees understood the consequences of noncompliance.

Over decades, trainings expanded to accommodate LGBTQ employees, as well as other groups, and many workplaces now prefer to call them "unconscious bias" trainings. Even as they've evolved, one aspect of trainings hasn't changed: their ineffectiveness.

Morgan Stanley had trainings, before they shelled out $100 million to settle high-profile sex discrimination lawsuits. Bank of America's trainings didn't keep them from paying $160 million in racial discrimination settlements. Uber had trainings before paying millions to settle a class action suit brought by 420 female and minority engineers alleging gender and racial discrimination. These totals don't take into account the enduring costs of tarnished brands.

Multiple studies published in the *Harvard Business Review* conclude that diversity trainings don't work and often backfire. These studies found that white men who were asked to attend diversity trainings were actually less likely to hire and promote women and minorities.[10] In general, participants who attend trainings in which they're told that we all hold biases leave those trainings believing that they are the exception, and their actions become *more* rooted in bias, not less.[11]

One of the reasons that biases are so insidious is that learning about them doesn't actually rid us of them. While becoming more aware of them can increase our ability to identify bias in others, it does not increase our ability to recognize it in ourselves. In fact, the stronger our biases are, the worse we are at seeing them, and the more neutral we believe we are. When this phenomenon is scaled, the more meritocratic we believe we are as an organization, the more biased our systems may be.

Chapter 3 describes in greater depth why trainings and other common approaches to DEI, such as affinity groups and the *Lean In* prescription, fall short. It also introduces new perspectives that can give businesses a competitive DEI advantage. For now, a quick preview: The difference between businesses that break the DEI inertia and those who stay stuck is defined by one key perspective shift: Equity *isn't personal*. It's systemic.

A Perspective Shift: From Changing Mindsets to Changing Mechanics

In a 1972 interview with *Playboy* magazine, the visionary architect, inventor, and philosopher Buckminster Fuller introduced the timeless wisdom of the trim tab—a small mechanism that helps stabilize an enormous ship or aircraft—which would become a central metaphor in his philosophy:

> *Something hit me very hard once, thinking about what one little man could do. Think of the Queen Elizabeth—the whole ship goes by and then comes the rudder. And there's a tiny thing at the edge of the rudder called a trim tab. It's a miniature rudder. Just moving the trim tab builds a low pressure that pulls the rudder around. Takes almost no effort at all. So I said that the little individual can be a trim tab. Society thinks that's it going right by you, that it's left you altogether. But if you're doing dynamic things mentally, the fact is that you can just put your foot out like that and the whole big ship of state is going to go. So I said, "Call me trim tab."*
>
> *The truth is that you get the low pressure to do things, rather than getting on the other side and trying to push the bow of the ship around. And you build that low pressure by getting rid of a little nonsense, getting rid of things that don't work and aren't true until you start to get that trim-tab motion.*

To reorient our businesses toward a more inclusive future, we need to stop asking employees to push harder against the bow of the ship, and instead, decrease the resistance employees face. We need trim tabs. The environmentalist movement gives us a good example of what this looks like.

Let's say you're an environmentalist who's traveled out of town to present your findings at a conference. While you're prepping for your presentation and running back and forth to networking events, your values don't change, but your focus and your actions might. You may be distracted and less vigilant about turning the lights or AC off in your hotel room every time you leave. Despite your environmentalist moral core, you're accidentally wasting energy.

European hotels figured out a behavioral design hack that reduces their energy bills and makes it easier for their environmentally conscious guests to act in alignment with their values.[12] Hotel guests must place a room key into a slot on the wall to activate the lights and temperature control system in their rooms. When they leave the room and take their key with them, they don't have to think about turning off the lights or the air conditioning. They just turn off when the key card is absent. By adding a trim tab, the design of the room has taken thinking (and willpower) out of the equation.

The human brain carries at least 200 unconscious biases that cognitive science has recognized.[13] Scientists estimate that unconscious biases drive between 75 and 90 percent of our decision-making, without our even realizing it.[14] Current approaches to DEI rely on employees to stay vigilant against incursions of unconscious biases that they're probably not even aware of, while performing well at challenging jobs. We're asking employees to push against the front of a very, very large ship, and we've seen how it's played out. We've plateaued. We've made all the progress we can make under the "try your best" model.

We still have a chance to change course. We can either ask employees to keep pushing against the front of the ship, or we can adjust our equity trim tabs and focus on correcting mechanics rather than mindsets.

GEN Certification: Discovering the Equity Trim Tabs

When Ford needed to improve quality in the 1980s, they plotted defect rates on charts that were visible to everyone in their factories. In today's automotive marketplace, Tesla has refocused the measurement spotlight on a new metric that matters: Delivery Performance—the percentage of fulfilled deliveries that meet the customer-promised delivery date. Any employee can log on to Tesla's KPI dashboard, at any time, to see the company's progress toward its 90 percent Delivery Performance goal. Digital dashboards that track business-critical function data provide a clear, quantifiable standard for employees to aspire to.

Employers, however, have never had such a measurable standard for equity in the US workplace. This has left them to take "best guesses" in an area that already feels fraught with complexity. Maybe moving networking events to work hours will get more women to participate, but without measurement, who knows? Maybe stating that leadership supports Black employees is enough to make them feel included, but without measurement, who knows?

Employees and employers both want clear benchmarks that go beyond good intentions. The LEED certification gave businesses this clarity around environmental stewardship by outlining the exact steps they need to take for certification. Our DEI-focused organization, GEN, wanted businesses to have this kind of playbook for workplace equity.

Seeing the impact other standards have made, we partnered with the University of Washington to create the first standardized certification for intersectional equity in US businesses: the GEN Certification.

Creating this certification meant finding the equity trim tabs. We found hundreds. We refer to them as "cultural levers" that can be adjusted to design bias out and equity in. Like the wall holder for the hotel key card, these simple redesigns take resistance out of the equation. As Fuller would say, we're "getting the low pressure to do things. . .getting rid of a little nonsense, getting rid of things that don't work and aren't true," making it easier for everyone to make decisions based on merit, rather than bias.

Over years, we beta tested these cultural levers, certified companies, and tracked their progress. We found out what works and what doesn't. Those findings form the blueprint for this book.

Is This Book for Me?

This is not a women's empowerment book (though women may feel empowered after reading it) or a book on racist behaviors in the workplace. This is a book about designing workplace environments that counter the impact of bias to become truly merit-based. It acknowledges that we all have bias but does not exhort individuals to just try harder to prevent themselves from being influenced by it. Instead, it shifts the challenge from the employee to "be better" to the organization, to do better, and provides concrete steps and design elements that businesses can use to meet it.

While the solutions presented in this book will not rid the workplace of sexist or racist individuals, they will provide systemic designs that are more likely to discourage those perspectives and minimize their impact. *Inclusion, Inc* offers a "trim tab" approach: simple, purposeful redesigns that amplify the effects of process optimizations, turning them into agents of transformational change.

We all come to the workplace with varying levels of DEI understanding and experience. This book is meant for anyone who wants to build, and work in, inclusive workplace systems. If you identify with any of the following groups, this book is for you!

Business Leaders: Expectations on managers and executives to champion DEI continue to rise. Many are finding themselves overwhelmed by the amount of complicated, highly nuanced information surrounding diversity and inclusion in the workplace. This book distills the profusion of DEI research and theory into accessible, actionable takeaways for identifying flawed processes and creating inclusive cultures.

HR Professionals and DEI Leaders: HR leaders are now expected to understand DEI in ways they haven't before. This book will serve as a basic reference for understanding DEI concepts and provide a roadmap for streamlining DEI initiatives. Not only will HR professionals be introduced to new knowledge, they'll be given language to advocate for implementing inclusive practices in their organizations.

Underestimated Employees: This book is also for anyone who has had to leave behind who they are to function successfully where they work. For individuals who have felt that their only two options as employees were to assimilate or leave, this book breaks down the systemic barriers they've faced, gives language to their experiences, and provides evidence-backed solutions for which they can advocate.

Allies: Supporters of equity in principle often ask, "What can I do?" Anyone looking to improve their understanding of DEI concepts can use this book to become better allies and advocate for effective solutions.

Job Seekers: Job candidates want clear benchmarks to know if a potential employer has gone beyond talk to meaningful action. Anyone who wants to know if an employer is truly inclusive can use *Inclusion, Inc* as a "checklist" to assess whether an employer has gone beyond recruiting to authentic inclusion.

Beyond Good Intentions to Meaningful Impact

The methods in this book can take business culture to the next level.

- *Beyond Recruiting*: While representation matters, companies need to do more than just recruit. If employees continue to be recruited into organizations that do not have the mechanisms in place to reduce the impact of bias, both the company and the employees lose out. For example, in the tech sector, the highest percentage of women who leave their employer exit at midcareer—the point at which it is most expensive for the company to replace them.[15] *Inclusion, Inc* addresses the pain points that cause underestimated employees to leave, saving employers the costs of attrition and turnover.

- *Beyond the Binary*: Simply looking at gender as the difference between women and men does not give a complete picture of gender equity. In addition, simply looking at DEI in terms of race and gender ignores the intersections of many other facets of individual identity. Understanding these intersections is essential to ensuring that efforts to foster equity benefit everyone, not just the dominant group. *Inclusion, Inc* offers solutions that address inequities faced by communities of color, those who do not identify with the binary definitions of gender, caretakers, minimum wage workers, those who have a disability, those who may experience ageism, and workers of underrepresented nationalities and religions.

- *Beyond Compliance*: Not being harassed or blatantly discriminated against is not a high bar for employee experience. *Inclusion, Inc* is driven by the knowledge that too many people aren't being given equal opportunities to demonstrate their talents. Underestimated individuals don't want to be tolerated—they want to be valued and appreciated on the same level as their peers.

DEI can be confusing for employers and employees alike. This book provides clarity so that employees can understand and recognize the facets of a truly inclusive workplace. It also provides businesses with an answer to *"What can we do that works?"* in the form of workplace design elements they can adopt immediately to become equity-centered, better serving employees, consumers, and society.

A Quick Guide to the Rest of This Book

This book has three goals, pursued in three parts.

The first, tackled in part 1, is to convince you that the trim-tab hypothesis is true. I want you to believe that shifting our perspective on DEI is important, that we need to leave old ways behind and focus on changing mechanics, not mindsets. This part will define who we're changing the workplace for, what will happen to them (and all of us) if we don't change course, and what it looks like to debias processes rather than people.

The second goal, addressed in part 2, is to show you how to implement the trim-tab approach by adjusting cultural levers throughout your organization.

You'll learn how to attract more qualified candidates, hire the best person for the role, get the most out of meetings by actually hearing from everyone, and conduct a pay gap audit that's meaningful enough to turn into a pay equity strategy. I'll share why you should scrap the yearly review and what you should do instead. You'll learn why mentorship isn't enough, but sponsorship is, and how to make difficult decisions around transparency and target-setting.

This section will show how policies such as paid leave and flexibility may seem inclusive on the surface, but there is a right and a wrong way to implement them. From recruiting to professional development to office aesthetics and governance strategy, this part will reveal the trim tabs that unlock both social and financial returns.

The third goal is to get a handle on DEI tomorrow. Part 3 reckons with the future but starts by looking at the past, specifically at lessons learned from the COVID-19 pandemic. This probably won't be the last society-wide crisis that employers face, and we can learn from businesses that managed to keep equity in focus, even in the midst of upheaval. Businesses that double down on equity in times of crisis come out of them stronger and continue to outperform the competition. An equitable emergency response plan is a more successful response plan.

Part 3 will also provide tools and principles to navigate how AI and machine learning will impact the workplace. I believe we'll be seeing more and more businesses stating that their DEI strategies are "data-driven." This doesn't mean that their DEI strategies are *data-smart*. Depending on how it is collected, analyzed, and interpreted, data can either drive transformative inclusion, or it can become a weapon of math destruction,[16] encoding human bias and scaling it across an organization. This section will give you a framework for asking the right questions in your engagement surveys and analyzing DEI data with an intersectional lens.

Finally, this part finishes with DEI principles to live by, including a focus on communication. Alongside the opportunity gaps in many organizations, I also see persistent communication gaps. Managers and executives who want to further their DEI strategies fear that they'll say the wrong thing. Human Resources leaders create effective policies, but employees never hear about them or don't understand the benefits because the message is not communicated clearly. This section covers common DEI communication mistakes and provides alternative scripts that you can rely on for difficult conversations.

≈

Before we move on to learning how to shift our DEI perspectives and embrace more equitable systems, we need to answer one critical question: What if we didn't?

CHAPTER 2

"But We've Always Done It This Way. . ."

I am biased against women in leadership.

Specifically, I associate men with leadership and career, and women with family.

At least, that's what the Harvard Implicit Association Test told me.[1] And, as the creators of the test recommend in their book, *The Blind Spot*, I took the test more than once. All six times that I took an iteration of the test, the result was the same: I harbor a strong unconscious bias against women in leadership roles.

If you asked me if I believe women belong in leadership roles, I would confidently answer yes. But, if forced to quickly pair masculine- and feminine-associated terms (man, woman, Mr., Ms.) with domains such as leadership, career, or family, my unconscious is firmly stuck in a biased rut.

Discovering this bias after taking the first test didn't make me any better at suppressing it in the retakes. My unconscious biases overrode my willpower, every single time.

Seated in our amygdala, our unconscious mind drives up to 95 percent of our decision-making.[2] If you've ever attended a training on unconscious bias, you've probably heard how our biases are interwoven with an unconscious recognition of patterns, a scheme whose purpose is to keep us safe from potential threats. This combination of sensory perception and unconscious interpretation signals to us how we should respond to our surroundings, including who we should regard as friend or foe.

This unconscious self-defense system keeps ticking away when we go to work, influencing who we associate with, who we think of as capable, and who we do—or don't—value.

Understanding how ever-present and influential our biases are is key to understanding why current approaches to DEI aren't working.

But the Bias—Is It Really That Bad?

In 2014, the United States Institute for Peace partnered with the Geena Davis Institute to release a study on gender in media. Part of the study involved observing people in large groups, and researchers witnessed a bizarre behavior: When women made up 17 percent of a group, men estimated that they actually made up 50 percent of the group. Once a crowd was 33 percent female, women were perceived as the majority.[3] The study's participants, however, did not overestimate the presence of men in large groups.

When typically underrepresented individuals are in spaces where we're not used to seeing them, we tend to overestimate their presence. A female minority, for example, can seem like a female majority in a space that is typically male-dominated.

Most of us don't have to estimate the number of people in groups at work, but our perceptions of others' behaviors can be influenced by what we're used to seeing and have come to expect. For example, while women have been stereotyped as talking more than men, multiple studies have found that they spend less time than men talking in meetings. Their comments are shorter, and they are interrupted more often. One study found that women needed to make up 60 to 80 percent of a group before they used as much speaking time, collectively, as men in the conversation. Another now-classic study recorded university faculty meetings and found that, with one exception, the men at the meetings spoke more often, and without exception, spoke longer.[4] The longest comment by a woman at all seven gatherings was shorter than the shortest comment by a man. In online discussions on professional topics, messages written by men have been found to be, on average, twice as long as those written by women.[5]

And despite this, our perceptions of women as "chatty" remain. As stated in a PBS summary of research on gender and language, "[In] seminars and debates, when women and men are deliberately given an equal amount of the highly valued talking time, there is often a perception that [women] are getting more than their fair share."[6]

Because a gender-balanced workforce is a fairly new phenomenon, female voices can be heard as more present than they actually are. Even when we believe we're comparing the talking time of women to that of men, we're unconsciously comparing the talking time of women *now* to the talking time of women *in the past*.

Our perceptions of the ways people behave are built on a baseline of the ways we *expect* them to behave, and these differences impact how we treat people. Anything exceeding our expectations or past experiences feels extreme, and we push back against it. These unconscious expectations—the norms our amygdala clings to—sabotage one of the common approaches to DEI that has gained momentum over the last few years: *leaning in*.

Lean In: The Self-Empowerment Paradox

In 2013, the term "lean in" became the rallying cry of (mostly white) women looking to climb the corporate ladder and smash the glass ceiling. Sheryl Sandberg popularized the self-empowerment slogan in her monumental bestseller, *Lean In: Women, Work, and the Will to Lead.*

Initially, I was one of her early devotees. When the book came out, I was feeling stuck, but still ambitious. I wanted to be taken seriously.

Her book seemed to provide answers. If there wasn't a seat for me at the table, I was going to bring a folding chair! If someone spoke over me in a meeting, I was going to insist on finishing my point. I was going to practice *The Shine Theory* and highlight the work of other women in the office.

Most daunting: I was going to renegotiate my salary.

I unearthed my copy of *Lean In* recently and discovered that I had highlighted the entire section that gives tactical advice on ways women can negotiate and still be seen as "likable" enough for their peers to keep wanting to work with them. At the time of my *Lean In* enthusiasm, my employer was about to be acquired by another company, giving me an opening to renegotiate my role. I was going to pitch myself for a new position, with a new title and a specific salary. I had memorized all of Sandberg's one-liners. I substituted "we" for "I," because a woman will still be seen as communal if she asserts, "We had a great year," as opposed to "I had a great year." I visualized the conversation, including how I would counter potential objections.

I remember being more nervous than I expected, but I stuck to my plan. I was polite but firm. I made the conversation about our common goals, and I concluded with a firm handshake. I left the meeting with the kind of adrenaline high I had only felt in athletic competitions. Whether or not I had persuaded, I had stuck to my guns, and my script.

I got the call: I would be getting a new title and a new salary. At the time, I felt a sense of success beyond myself. It felt like a mini-victory for women, a tiny step toward closing the pay gap.

Years later after I had left that role, I reconnected with a former co-worker from the same company. She had just moved on to a new employer and wanted to share something with me she had held on to for years: The salary I negotiated for myself that day was actually below the bottom of the range for that position at that company. I had leaned in to a starting salary below what they would have offered me, and they said nothing. The amount employers had paid me in the past influenced what I felt comfortable asking for in my negotiation, and this employer took advantage of my own biased baseline. I might have done more to help close the pay gap if I had said nothing at all. By leaning in, I had sold myself short.

Leaning In to a Double-Bind

I want underestimated individuals to feel as free as their peers to ask for what they deserve. But the consequences of treating *Lean In* as a DEI solution can do more harm than good. While women are often criticized for not negotiating more, their reticence has a rationale: Asking for more penalizes some groups in ways that it does not harm others.

In a series of studies conducted by the Harvard Kennedy School and the Harvard Law School, researchers found that when women do dare to negotiate for a pay raise, people in hiring and management roles like them less and are less likely to want to work with them. Male employees asking for the same raise do not suffer this penalty.[7] In these studies, managers were presented with demands from a job candidate, who was given a gender-neutral name. The studies found that managers had strong negative reactions to the demanding job candidate when referred to throughout as "she" but not when the candidate was referred to throughout as "he."

Beyond being viewed negatively, women often don't reap the same rewards as men when they do negotiate. A 2018 study questioned workers about their "asking" habits and compared the level of ask with the level of reward, by gender.[8] Their conclusion: "Women are asking for raises as much as men. They're just not getting them."[9]

Holding background factors constant, the data sets demonstrated that males and females ask equally often for promotions and raises, but women are less likely to get them. Over a lifetime of salary negotiations, this adds up, and the un-likeability risks women take each time compound.

Every time a woman negotiates, she runs the double risk of not getting what she asked for *and* being liked less by her peers for asking in the first place. While she may be passing up a raise if she doesn't ask, she may be putting herself in an even worse position if she does, especially if her negotiation is unsuccessful.

We're not used to women asking for pay raises or advocating for themselves, so when they do, it feels extreme. Once again, because of our biased baselines, we feel a sense of disruption to our unconscious expectations. What often gets misdiagnosed as a "confidence gap" when women don't negotiate may actually be an acute awareness of how advocating for oneself can be perceived and how that friction can harm one's career, rather than advance it.

This limit to leaning in is not specific to gender. Expectations we have of what people will do, how they will react, and where we expect to see them impact how we treat them. When these norms are disrupted, we perceive actions committed by one person differently than actions committed by another. This empowerment double-bind extends to workers of color, and Black employees most severely.

In a series of studies published in the *MIT Sloan Management Review,* participants were shown a number of resumes of white and Black job applicants, along with their headshots.[10] The participants were asked to evaluate each job seeker and rate the likelihood that the applicant would negotiate if offered the job. Controlling for outside factors, the participants identified Black Americans as less likely to negotiate than white Americans. In the second half of the study, the job seekers and their evaluators actually interacted. Black job seekers negotiated similar numbers of offers and counteroffers as their white counterparts, but their evaluators reported that the Black job seekers had negotiated *more* than white job seekers. Because evaluators *expected* Black job seekers to negotiate less, the evaluators had an exaggerated view of their behavior. Furthermore, the perception of having been "pushy" resulted in Black job seekers receiving *lower* starting salaries.

Women of color face the most stringent double-binds when attempting to lean in. While white women are stereotyped as communal, caring, deferential, and concerned about others, Black women are stereotyped as assertive, angry, and "having an attitude."[11] This means that while white women face a challenge of being seen as so communal that they can't lead, Black women walk an even thinner tightrope. They have to counter preconceived notions that they are aggressive and angry by being extra accommodating; however, they cannot seem so subservient that they can't be seen as strong, individual leaders. They have even less permission to assert themselves, and even thinner margins for negotiating.

Despite being the most educated group in America,[12] by percentage of their group population, and starting their careers with more ambition than white women and men,[13] Black women fill only 1.4 percent of C-suite roles, while comprising 7.4 percent of the population.[14] While walking the thinnest of tightropes, they still manage to ask for promotions at the same rate as men but are only 58 percent as likely to receive them.

If the research so clearly shows how bias is sabotaging these interactions, it seems that training to build awareness around our biases would be the obvious solution. Bias, unfortunately, can't be trained away.

The $8 Billion Training Trap

On February 11, 2018, former Starbucks CEO Howard Schultz was asked at a town hall meeting about the arrest of two Black men in a Philadelphia Starbucks the previous April. He stated, "As somebody who grew up in a very diverse background as a young boy. . .I didn't see color, and I honestly don't see color now."

In response to the arrest, Starbucks closed 8,000 stores for an afternoon and hosted its largest one-day corporate training on unconscious bias. Bryan Stevenson, the founder of the Equal Justice Initiative, took part as a leader. In a video at corporate headquarters, hip-hop musician and actor Common delivered an opening meditation, urging employees to participate with open minds. Starbucks didn't skimp. This was venti-sized diversity-and-inclusion star power.

And yet, almost a year later, Starbucks's chief executive couldn't understand why "I don't see color" is off the mark at best, and more likely, harmful. Starbucks is just one of many US companies that spend a total of $8 billion a year on diversity training, only to have it backfire.

As noted in chapter 1, one of the most pernicious aspects of bias is that learning about it doesn't make us any better at recognizing it in ourselves or stopping it from impacting our behavior. As I experienced through the Harvard Implicit Association Test, being faced with my own biases over and over didn't make me any better at countering them in the kinds of split-second decisions that make up most of our lives.

But why do these trainings backfire? Why are white men who are asked to attend diversity trainings actually less likely to hire and promote women and minorities?

This unintended consequence can be credited, in part, to a pesky phenomenon known as *moral licensing*.

Diversity Trainings: Issuing Moral Licenses

To better understand where trainings go wrong, let's look at a study examining a phenomenon that confused political pundits following the 2016 election: Obama voters who voted for Trump.

Daniel Effron, a psychologist at the London School of Business, pioneered a study focused on people who publicly self-identified as supporters of Barack Obama. He found that not only did voting for Obama fail to indicate that the voters would be racially open in the future or continue to vote for progressive legislation, it could indicate the opposite—*if those voters had a chance to let people know they voted for Obama.*[15]

In two studies that yielded the same results, participants were asked to decide between equally qualified white and Black candidates to fill a hypothetical role. The participants—most of whom were white or Asian, and all of whom supported Obama—were divided into two groups. One group was allowed to openly endorse Obama before being given the study scenario. The other group wasn't.

Those who could not express their support for Obama before making a hiring decision tended to play it safe, saying that either candidate would be equally suited for the job. Those who had been allowed to openly endorse Obama before making a hiring decision were more likely to pick the white candidate for the job.

Another test explored the behaviors of those who harbored prejudice toward Black people. Effron's team used the Modern Racism Scale, which gauges people's racial attitudes, to identify participants who voted for Obama despite harboring negative feelings about Black people. These participants were given a scenario in which local government money could be given to two private organizations. One organization served a Black community, the other, a white one.

The subjects—who again were mostly white or Asian Obama supporters but who *also* backed Kerry in the 2004 presidential election—were split into two groups. One group was only given an opportunity to openly endorse Kerry, while the other group was only given an opportunity to endorse Obama.

When participants with more negative attitudes toward Black people, according to the Modern Racism Scale, had the opportunity to say they supported Obama, they allotted more money to the white organization than those who could only endorse Kerry.

What Effron and his team observed was a classic case of moral licensing. When those who harbored prejudicial attitudes were able to acquire moral capital by endorsing Obama, they felt more comfortable acting on prejudices that favor white people. It's the equivalent of saying "I have a Black friend" before making a statement that favors white people, to absolve oneself of the consequences of saying something prejudiced. Those who harbor prejudices feel they have more permission when saying something racially questionable, because they believe they've already proven through a different action that they're racially open.

This psychological mechanism is present in many parts of our lives, in ways that have nothing to do with race, gender, or bias. Classic examples include eating a donut because we ran an extra mile on the treadmill, or feeling okay about buying from a morally questionable but convenient business because we went to church yesterday. We provide mental loopholes for ourselves that justify certain behaviors, even if it doesn't lessen their consequences. These examples only sabotage small goals in our own lives, but moral licensing can wreak havoc in the workplace, especially following diversity trainings.

These trainings can actually amplify our tendency to morally license poor behaviors that will disproportionately impact women, people of color, and other underestimated groups. The training becomes the "good deed" we do now, that unconsciously makes us feel freer to do something less virtuous later. As we've seen in the Obama voter studies, this impulse to morally license one's own biased behaviors is even stronger in more prejudiced people—typically, the exact audience that trainings are intended for. Trainings provide an "out" for those who need the trainings the most. Employees who already hold discriminatory views feel they've earned a sense of protection from being accused of being prejudiced by acquiring their "I attended a training" certificate. They treat their accumulation of moral capital as a visible shield for themselves, rather than the beginning of a journey to becoming less biased in their behaviors.

Beyond Moral Licensing

Trainings don't work for another much simpler reason: We don't like being told what to do. Even with great diplomacy, trainers often come across as trying to police attendees' thoughts and actions. When we feel coerced into a choice or behavior, we often do just the opposite, even when we wouldn't have in any other situation, just to prove that we are our own person.

In research from the University of Toronto, subjects of a study read a brochure critiquing prejudice against Black people.[16] When pressured to agree with it, participants actually strengthened their bias against Black people. When left to come to their own decisions about the reading, however, they were more inclined to agree with the critiques of prejudice.

Trainings that invite participants but allow participation to be fully voluntary have shown some promise. Those who voluntarily attend these trainings are more likely to promote Black men, Hispanic men, and Asian-American men and women. These findings don't necessarily speak to the role trainings play in countering bias, though. Participants who are willing to volunteer their time and energy to attend these trainings are probably already more comfortable with the concept of equity for underestimated groups, compared to their peers who choose not to attend.

Attending Trainings While Underestimated

The *Journal of Experimental Social Psychology* described white men's reactions to pro-diversity trainings and messaging as follows: "We found evidence that it not only makes white men believe that women and minorities are being treated fairly—whether that's true or not—it also makes them more likely to believe that they themselves are being treated unfairly."[17]

If white men saw that diversity messaging was present before applying for or interviewing for a job, "[these] messages signaled to these white men that they might be undervalued and discriminated against. These concerns interfered with their interview performance and caused their bodies to respond as if they were under threat. Importantly, diversity messages led to these effects regardless of these men's political ideology, attitudes toward minority groups, beliefs about the prevalence of discrimination against whites, or beliefs about the fairness of the world. This suggests just how widespread negative responses to diversity may be among white men: the responses exist even among those who endorse the tenets of diversity and inclusion."[18]

Underestimated employees aren't unaware of the reactions that their peers can have to diversity trainings and programming. They witness their co-workers becoming defensive or angry and worry that this friction will turn into retaliation.

Because trainers are aware of the defensiveness that white employees may feel, they often try to "tone down" the training content to avoid conflict. For many employees of color, this means having to sit through hearing their experiences being minimized or trivialized. The discrimination they've experienced becomes euphemized as "differences in perspectives," or they are encouraged to "find common ground" with those who have excluded them. Consequently, underestimated groups can leave trainings feeling even more discouraged and undervalued than before.

Finally, in reviewing responses that employees have provided to GEN's national workplace experience survey, we noted repeated versions of this experience: "Any time we have a training or company meeting about diversity, I am the only Black person in the room. Even if I don't raise my hand, at some point, someone will turn to me and ask me for my opinion—as a Black person—about diversity in our office. What am I supposed to say? I don't speak for all Black people. And I'm not gonna say what I really think."

The status of being "the only" suddenly becomes synonymous with being "the expert" or "the representative" in conversations about diversity. As this respondent stated, "I don't speak for all Black people." No race or gender is a monolith. The experiences of one underestimated individual do not necessarily reflect those of other underestimated individuals, and asking one to speak on behalf of a group is an unfair burden. Not only do individuals not want to misrepresent their peers, they do not want to put themselves at risk. Should the one Black person in the room be honest and risk making their white peers defensive and angry? Or, should they perform the emotional labor of comforting their peers with a watered-down version of their experiences as The Black Person in the Workplace?

Trainings create impossible choices for anyone who is "the only" in the room.

Finding Affinity: Employee Resource Groups

For those who are often "the only" in the room, employee resource groups or affinity groups can provide a sense of community and solidarity. While these communities can provide a safe space for people and opportunities for networking, they are also too often treated as a substitute for inclusive workplace cultures. Rather than acknowledge and support the specific role that affinity groups can play, employers often see them as an opportunity to "check" the DEI box and consider the "diversity issue" handled. Providing a siloed space for people to come together over shared identities does not counter the bias they'll continue to face throughout the organization.

These groups also don't guarantee safe spaces for all employees; while organizations may offer women's groups, or groups for people of color, this does not mean that women of color have been offered a safe space. They still face a great deal of risk sharing their experiences with either white women or men of color in spaces where they may once again be "the only."

While I believe companies should continue to support affinity groups, treating them as a DEI solution is flawed in the same way that encouraging employees to lean in or attend trainings is flawed: It puts the onus on employees to compensate for biased institutions, rather than on the employer to debias them.

≈

"But we've always done it this way. . ."

I chose this as the title of the chapter because it is the response I hear most often when clients are faced with the shortcomings of the DEI approaches they've been using for years. I understand the inertia that comes with abandoning these approaches. It feels like a risk. But as we'll see in the next chapter, clinging to these methods poses an even bigger risk to the survival of companies that don't evolve.

CHAPTER 3

Why Should We Care?

Three years ago, a high school student named Sanaika reached out to me to ask if she could volunteer for GEN. I confess that I was slow to answer, but she was persistent. She messaged me on LinkedIn, found me on social media, and sent multiple emails. She was going to make herself heard.

I had some reservations about taking on a high school student. I wasn't sure what I could hand over to her. She didn't even have her driver's license yet. What was our liability for a minor? But her messages were so thoughtful and persuasive that I agreed to a one-hour phone call.

Sanaika impressed. She was the head of her school's refugee alliance club; she volunteered playing music for senior citizens; she was partnering with her city's chamber of commerce to pilot transportation options for low-wage workers. She had her sights set on becoming an international human rights lawyer.

I was still hesitant. Then I asked her why she wanted to volunteer for GEN.

"My friends and I are all working really hard to go to college and do big things in the future," she started, "but I already see the girls being treated differently. They're not called on as often. They're called loud if they speak up. And some of us are going to keep working hard anyways, but we know what bias is, and I don't know what happens to all this hard work if we end up in businesses that are still biased. It's like all our hard work will be wasted."

She shared how she, herself, was already coming up against the stumbling blocks of bias. "Being an Indian and a woman, I feel like there's a lot of animosity toward me. It could be a major problem if everyone's thinking this way in the future, because these people are going to be CEOs of companies one day. If this is the same attitude they're going to show toward employees, I don't know how the world's going to progress."

Years later, I still see the moment I said "yes" to Sanaika as one of the best decisions I've made for GEN. Sanaika wasn't a charitable mentoring project. She furthered our organization's mission. She brought perspectives I hadn't considered. Her ability to see past herself to her community and anticipate the future—these were leadership skills. And we almost missed out.

If businesses in the future continue to miss out on Sanaika, the way we almost did, "How," as she asked, "is the world going to progress?"

The Future of Work

When I say that Sanaika is the future of work, I don't mean that in a figurative sense. Today in the US, the workforce is 47 percent female.[1] Forty-four percent of millennials, who make up the largest portion of the workforce, are non-white,[2] and the majority of the US population will be non-white before the year 2050.[3] Ten years from now, if you were to randomly select an employee, the odds are good that this workforce representative would look a lot like Sanaika.

Race and gender aren't the only facets of our workforce identity that are rapidly changing. Approximately one in six adults in America is considered to be neurodiverse,[4] meaning they experience different neurological functioning than the majority of the population. The age of the average employee is also shifting. Over the past 25 years, the percentage of workers aged 55+ has doubled, and 20 percent of the workforce is now 55 years of age or older.[5]

Employees are also facing more caretaking demands than previous generations. As longer lifespans have become the norm, more adult children of retirees find themselves "sandwiched" between caring for their own young adult children and their retired parents, who are now living into their late eighties and nineties. According to an AARP survey, 6 in 10 unpaid caregivers also hold paying jobs.[6]

Finally, a Gallup survey from 2021 found that more adult Americans are identifying as lesbian, gay, bisexual, or transgender with each passing year, and one in six adults in Generation Z identifies as LGBTQ.[7]

These shifts all impact how employees experience the workplace. DEI is now more than a "nice to have" or a compliance requirement to be minimally satisfied. Getting DEI right means getting access to the next generation of talent.

DEI: In Demand

Not only is today's workforce more diverse, they also care about inclusion more than previous generations. A 2020 hiring survey revealed that 83 percent of Gen Z candidates prioritize a company's commitment to diversity and inclusion when choosing where to work.[8] Ninety-four percent of millennials said they consider whether a business is an ethical employer before purchasing from them,[9] and multicultural consumers comprise almost 40 percent of the total US population. Non-white consumers are expected to comprise the majority of the US population by 2040.[10]

It's not surprising that investors are following consumers. In 2014, Google released its first workforce diversity report, pressuring other companies to do the same. As more and more businesses followed Google's lead and released their own reports, researchers had a chance to answer a long-debated question: Do investors actually care if a company is diverse?

Margaret Neale, an organizational psychology professor at Stanford's School of Business, studied shareholder reactions to nearly 60 diversity announcements made by publicly traded firms between 2014 and 2018. The study was largely comprised of firms from the financial and tech sectors, including companies such as JPMorgan, BlackRock, eBay, and Facebook. The researchers measured each firm's stock returns on the day of their diversity announcements and found that stock prices increased more when higher levels of diversity were reported. In the tech sector specifically, investor support was even more positive when diversity numbers were higher than Google's.

When companies delivered reports in subsequent years that did not show any increase in diversity numbers, stock prices did not rise.

"This goes beyond saying diversity is a good idea because it's ethical," Neale noted. "Shareholders are saying, 'If you're not as diverse as we want you to be, there are going to be economic consequences.'"[11]

Investors are demanding more than just diverse representation. They're pushing companies to eradicate inequitable policies. Nia Impact Capital is one of many investor funds leading the charge by challenging Tesla to end its use of mandatory arbitration. Forced arbitration came under fire when the #MeToo and Black Lives Matter movements exposed how it's often used as a tool to stifle harassment and discrimination complaints. The Nia fund brought a proposal to the floor of Tesla's annual shareholder meeting, asking the electric car maker to prepare a report on its use of employee arbitration.[12] When Tesla's board pushed back, several other institutional shareholders, including Calvert Research & Management, and proxy advisors Institutional Shareholder Services Inc. and Glass Lewis, stepped up to voice their support of the proposal.

Nia has also leveraged its assets to achieve progress elsewhere. In a celebrated decision, IBM accepted a Nia-led proposal to increase transparency around the company's workplace practices and report publicly on the effectiveness of its diversity, equity, and inclusion programs. The fund also succeeded in advocating for cybersecurity giant Fortinet to compile and release annual diversity reports.

Nia is just one example of the kinds of Environmental, Social, and Governance (ESG) funds that are pushing businesses to evolve. Investments in ESG funds doubled in 2020, accounting for 25 percent of US stock and bond mutual funds, a huge leap from the one percent share they held in 2014.[13] Younger investors appear to be driving this shift, and their accumulating wealth will continue to follow companies that go beyond talk to meaningful action.

This undeniable demand, unfortunately, hasn't translated into impact. Reviewing GEN's national survey data, only 22 percent of employees believe that their employer has publicly stated DEI as a priority *and* has a clear roadmap for getting there. A 2020 study surveying over 800 HR professionals demonstrated similar findings: 76 percent of companies have no diversity or inclusion goals.[14]

As the workforce has changed, most companies' approaches still haven't, and this comes at a great cost.

Invoicing Exclusion: The High Cost of Underestimating Employees

Exclusion carries an amorphous price tag. At best, we can itemize pieces of it. For example, the EEOC estimates it collects $120 million a year in relation to harassment charges, in pre-litigation processes alone. The average harassment claim settled outside of court will typically run an organization between $75,000 and $125,000,[15] and lawsuits resulting from age discrimination have cost companies collectively as much as $250 million.[16] These figures don't include the cases settled privately or the enduring costs of damaged reputations and tarnished brands.

Organizations also lose millions each year to diversity turnover. For example, in technology-related industries, women are twice as likely to leave as men, and Black and Latino workers are 3.5 times more likely to quit than their white or Asian colleagues.[17] Underestimated employees cite "culture" as their top reason for resigning, and businesses pay an annual $16 billion diversity attrition tab.

The full expenses of exclusion extend far beyond litigation and attrition, though. Our most costly mistakes are the ones we're convinced we're not making.

The Myth of Meritocracy

In its early days, tech was seen as a triumphant return to merit-based competition. Unlike their counterparts on Wall Street or in law firms, tech entrepreneurs didn't have to "know someone" to get ahead. A guy with a garage and enough entrepreneurial spirit and grit could bootstrap his own success. The "wild west" of Silicon Valley was rumored to be a new land of equal opportunity, where a competitive work ethic and superior code would determine who rose to the top.

Today on this supposedly level playing field, women represent only about 11 percent of developers.[18] The computer science departments at California Polytechnic and North Carolina State University wanted to understand why. Do women underperform their male peers that badly? Does the sector need to do a better job of marketing to women? Is it just a pipeline problem?

A deep dive into GitHub revealed some answers.[19] This 12-million-person open-source coding community allows members to make and respond to public requests for code for programming projects. This massive exchange provided the opportunity for researchers to observe how gender played a role in coding interactions. They found that code written by women was approved at a higher rate than code written by men. Women's coding acceptance rates dominated men's in the top ten programming languages.

There was one important catch: This trend only applied if women kept their gender a secret.

When female developers publicly displayed their gender, their code acceptance rate was lower than men's. While women may have been producing more competent code than men, their contributions were less likely to be accepted if their gender was known.

Even when we believe we've created objective digital meritocracies, bias left unchecked sabotages our access to excellence.

The Best Person for the Job

"I don't hire for diversity. I just hire the best person for the job."

I hear this "best person for the job" objection to diversity initiatives most often in fields that tend to think of themselves as meritocracies. The tech industry isn't alone in its perception of itself as meritocratic, but it does give us a good example of how this belief plays out.

In a (since deleted) article in *Forbes*, tech industry commentator Brian S. Hall declared, "If you aren't able to make it here [Silicon Valley], it's almost certainly not because of any bias." Anyone claiming bias, he argued, should blame their own "refusal to put in the hard work."[20]

It appears that bias may play a bigger role than Hall realized. A 2012 randomized, double-blind study found that when hiring managers in STEM fields were given application materials of a fictitious candidate randomly assigned a male or female name, both male and female hiring managers rated the male applicant as significantly more competent and hirable than the woman with identical application materials.[21] A similar 2014 study found that both men and women working in tech fields were twice as likely to hire a man for a job that required math, even when presented with female applicants who were equally qualified.[22]

The "pipeline problem" is a common excuse used to explain away the underrepresentation of tech workers of color. The numbers tell a different story. According to a *USA Today* study, Black and Hispanic computer science and computer engineering students graduate from top universities at three times the rate that top tech companies hire them.[23] Even when Black and Hispanic graduates each made up 9 percent of computer science degrees earned, the sector continued to hire only 2 percent Black and 3 percent Hispanic tech workers.

If they do manage to get hired, underestimated employees face promotion processes that are framed as meritocratic, but actually lead to biased outcomes. Many tech companies have jettisoned long-standing traditions of managers choosing who gets promoted. Instead, they've embraced a more crowd-sourced approach: Those who self-nominate and receive the most peer accolades are chosen to advance.

As we learned in the previous chapter, when women and minorities advocate for themselves, they can disrupt unconscious expectations of how they should behave, triggering negative reactions from their peers. The self-nominating phase of the tech promotions process puts these employees in a double bind. They can self-nominate and risk retaliation, or say nothing and risk being passed over for promotions.

The second stage of the promotion process—peer approval—triggers in-group favoritism, an implicit bias in which people are more likely to support others who remind them of themselves. In the largely white and male world of tech, this phenomenon scales to a widespread advantage for other white men.

The inherently biased dynamics of self-nomination and peer approval put underestimated groups at a disadvantage. Returning decision-making power to the masses may have been seen as promoting fairness and performance-based competition, but it has actually tilted the playing field in favor of bias, not merit.

Tech isn't the only industry suffering from this mismatch of meritocratic beliefs and favoritism-fueled outcomes. Across the US we treasure the idea that we are a meritocracy, and this belief that we reward people for their efforts and abilities actually keeps us from hiring the "best person for the job."

The Meritocracy Paradox

Pay-for-performance schemes are supposed to foster workplace meritocracies. To study how they actually play out in organizations, MIT's Sloan School of Management observed a 9,000-employee service sector company that had implemented a "merit-driven compensation system." This employer emphatically communicated to all their employees that they were implementing this program to ensure workers were rewarded equitably, based on their performance.

The study revealed counter-meritocratic outcomes: Women, ethnic minorities, and employees born outside the US received smaller increases in compensation for the same performance scores as those made by white men. These findings controlled for whether or not employees held similar jobs, worked in the same units, and had the same supervisors. Women, minorities, and those not born in the US had to "work harder and obtain higher performance scores than white men to receive similar salary increases."

Emilio J. Castilla, one of the study's lead researchers, wondered if telling employees that they worked in a company that rewards merit impacted employees' behaviors. In partnership with Indiana University Sociology Professor Stephen Bernard, he conducted a series of lab experiments that all led to the same outcome: When companies emphasized "meritocratic values" to employees as part of their core identity, managers were *more* likely to award larger "performance-based" bonuses to male employees than to equally performing female employees.

Much in the same way that attending a training could make employees feel they had gained moral capital, being told they worked for a meritocracy made them more likely to believe they were making merit-based decisions. They felt their decisions were impartial and correct, by proxy. Taking fairness for granted, though, actually allowed bias to dilute merit, rather than enhance it. Castilla and Bernard named this phenomenon the "Paradox of Meritocracy."

When businesses put processes in place, however, to ensure that they don't overlook valuable individuals, the benefits compound in a surprising way. Underestimated employees don't just add their own talents to the workplace—they amplify the talents of their co-workers. We can look to the 2002 Oakland Athletics for an example of how this plays out.

Baseball Biases and the Power of the Collective

In the Athletics' year of *Moneyball* fame, Billy Beane made a $44 million ball club competitive with the $125 million New York Yankees. The key to Beane's success? He saw the value in players that the market had traditionally undervalued, and he brought complementary players together to bring out one another's strengths.

For decades, baseball franchises had been relying on a narrow set of metrics—stolen bases, home run averages, and batting averages—for scouting valuable players. Beane decided to widen the scope of what could be considered valuable. He and his scouts searched for players who performed well against metrics that typically go unnoticed, such as on-base percentage and slugging percentage (the number of bases a player gains each time he's at bat). These methods of player evaluation flew in the face of conventional scouting wisdom, but Beane's strategy proved successful.

Having players with higher on-base percentages meant that when a home run hitter came to bat, the odds were greater that another player would already be on base. This meant that hitting a home run would knock in two runs instead of one. Players with high slugging percentages were more likely to be on second base, rather than first, increasing the odds that they would make it home if the next batter hit a single.

The underestimated strengths that these players brought to the team amplified the benefits of more traditionally valued players. If you evaluated the team as an average of the players' metrics, it didn't look good, but the players' complementary strengths reinforced each other, creating a team that was greater than the sum of its affordable parts.

Beane fielded a team with a diversity of skills that was as powerful, collectively, as teams that were spending three times as much on traditional all-star players. This once controversial approach has now become widespread; historically undervalued metrics, such as on-base percentage, are now accepted as statistically strong indicators of a team's overall offensive success. These undervalued talents just needed to be given a chance.

Any business leader would jump at the opportunity to unlock the same rewards as their competition at a third of the price. But does this method translate? Carnegie Mellon Organizational Psychology Professor Anita Williams Woolley wanted to find out.

From Baseball to Business

In her research, Woolley had seen that managers tended to think of team performance as the *average* of each individual member's performance. Just as baseball clubs had historically depended on a narrow definition of what "success" looked like, though, managers only seemed to recognize and select the same kinds of all-stars, over and over again. Traits such as extroversion or public speaking were easily recognized as desirable, while other traits, such as emotional intelligence or long-term thinking, tended to go unnoticed. This often led managers to build teams with strengths that were redundant, rather than complementary.

Woolley wanted to test how groups stacked with these traditionally recognized all-stars performed *as a collective*, compared to teams with more diverse skill sets.[24] Woolley brought teams into a lab and studied how they, as groups, tackled a series of tasks, such as playing checkers, solving logic puzzles, and debating the ethics of complicated moral problems. She gave each group a collective intelligence (CI) score based on how well they navigated these challenges. She also assessed each group's average intelligence (AI), meaning she averaged the individuals' scores across metrics traditionally considered to be indicators of success.

The groups that had the highest CI scores, meaning they performed the best on this series of tasks, were more diverse, had higher social sensitivity scores, and took steps to ensure that everyone in the group had a chance to contribute. The groups with the highest AI scores performed worse.

The same groups were then given a more complicated second round of tasks. Those groups with higher CI scores again outperformed groups with high AI scores in these more challenging scenarios.

Wooley concluded that when complementary intelligences were combined, they amplified one another, and outperformed teams with higher average scores in historically valued areas. While one team member may have had a technical understanding of a problem, another may have had unique experiences that revealed certain solutions wouldn't work in certain contexts, and a third may have had the social intelligence to make sure the two of them communicated their ideas clearly to each other. Alone, these forms of intelligence weren't as effective as when brought together. Just as players who got on base helped home run hitters score two runs instead of one, those with undervalued talents brought the intelligence of the collective to its full potential.

The power of a diverse collective has proven key to helping ball clubs and businesses multiply their impact. As a society, what are we missing out on by overlooking the undervalued? One Wall Street pacesetter believes that harnessing the power of the collective could have kept us from reliving the largest financial crash since the Great Depression.

Lehman. . .Siblings?

Sallie Krawcheck, the founder of the Ellevate Index Fund, has been called by many the "most powerful woman on Wall Street." She is also known for her widely public firing from Citigroup. In Krawcheck's assessment, her dismissal wasn't due to her gender, but to the problem of "groupthink," which she ascribes to the lack of diversity on Wall Street. Her firing came after she pushed Citi's then-CEO, Vikram Pandit, to reimburse Citi's clients who lost large sums on investments that Citi had marketed as low risk.

Her assessment: She was punished for speaking out against the majority opinion. Wall Street's lack of diversity, she argued, created a "false comfort of agreement" from pervasive groupthink.

"There is no doubt in my mind that was a cause," Krawcheck told *CBS MoneyWatch*. "I didn't see evil geniuses who perfectly foresaw the crisis, and I was at the table. They really believed what they were saying—that the risk was dispersed, that they didn't have much on their balance sheets."

Krawcheck became one of the first high-profile figures to speak out publicly about how different the economy of 2008 might have looked if, instead of the Lehman Brothers, we had had the Lehman Siblings at the helm. She believed that greater gender diversity, which tends to correlate with greater cognitive diversity, would have helped to avoid the groupthink that caused the bubble to burst.

In 2012, a research scientist named John Coates, who formerly ran a derivatives trading desk, wanted to follow up on this theory. He found that male traders were significantly influenced by something called the Winners Effect—when men are "winning," their testosterone levels spike, increasing their appetite for risk and willingness to take chances, even if the odds say not to. When they are losing, their testosterone levels are reduced and they become more risk-averse, even if the odds say they should bet.

Women, on the other hand, appear to be largely immune from this Winners Effect.

Coates wondered if greater gender diversity could help prevent booms and busts, and played it out in experimental market simulations. The answer to the hypothesis was a resounding "yes." Simulations with exclusively male or exclusively female traders revealed substantially larger speculative bubbles in all-male than in all-female markets. In some cases, all-female markets even produced negative bubbles with prices below fundamental value.

A follow-up experiment showed that evenly mixed gender markets fell somewhere in between, where healthy markets thrive. Balancing the genders and risk-taking tendencies of a group could help prevent another 2008.

Beyond Diversity to Inclusion

"I don't know how the world's going to progress."

When I think back to my first conversation with Sanaika, the challenge in those words still resonates.

Inclusion-minded businesses are rising to meet the challenge by showing us that progress is possible. An analysis of the S&P Composite 1500 found that companies that embrace gender-balanced leadership teams have been evaluated as more innovative, and the returns on their innovations outpace those of their less gender-balanced competitors. *Scientific American* has published research demonstrating that racial diversity delivers similar benefits.[25] Another study from North Carolina State University found that firms that have embraced pro-DEI policies are producing more products and registering more patents per year than firms that haven't implemented inclusion-minded practices.[26]

As some business leaders have experienced, though, a diverse workplace alone does not automatically yield these benefits. In his book, *Rebel Ideas: The Power of Diverse Thinking*, Matthew Syed notes that diversity can actually lead to greater conflict, friction, and stagnation.[27] Leaders are often disappointed when they put in the work to build diverse teams, wait for collective intelligence to "happen," and instead see groupthink or tokenism persist.

This doesn't mean that diversity isn't worth pursuing. It just means that diversity is the first step.

Billy Beane didn't recruit undervalued players and let them sit on the bench. Coates's experiment didn't include female traders but deny them access to high-value accounts. The businesses that benefit from diversity take steps to ensure that voices like Sanaika's aren't just in the room—they're included.

≈

These companies have gone beyond diversity to inclusion by embracing one key perspective shift: They've ditched outdated approaches to DEI, and instead, they've adjusted their *cultural levers*. In the next chapter, we'll start to explore the promise of this design-based approach.

CHAPTER 4

Shifting to a Systemic Perspective

Heart disease is the number-one cause of death for women in the United States. While men are more likely to be diagnosed with the condition, women account for more than half of the fatalities. Even though women are more likely to die from heart disease, doctors are less likely to recommend tests for them that would diagnose it.

This disconnect doesn't come from bad intentions. Doctors do not care less about women having heart attacks. The biases that leave women untreated aren't personal—they're systemic.

For centuries, heart disease was synonymous with chest pain. Only recently did the medical community confirm that chest pain is the way heart attacks commonly present *in men*. Symptoms are different for women. They often include discomfort in the neck, jaw, back, or arm, and nausea or feelings of indigestion. For decades these symptoms weren't recognized as a heart attack, and women were sent home with misdiagnoses of heartburn or stomach ulcers. These women didn't receive the care that would typically aid recovery and healing following a heart attack and in turn were more likely than men to die within a year.

This tragic gap in treatment is a failure of design—research design, specifically. In landmark studies on heart disease from the 1970s, only middle-aged men were the research subjects. The study most often cited for establishing a link between cholesterol and heart disease included 12,866 men and no women. The Harvard Physician's Health Study concluding that aspirin could reduce the risk of heart attacks included 22,071 men, and zero women.[1]

These studies are still widely referenced in textbooks in medical schools, which means that well-intended practitioners have been upholding standards of care tuned to male default settings. The criteria they've been taught to rely on don't accommodate anyone non-male. No matter how well trained or dedicated doctors are, they've been working with protocols that don't recognize half the population.

When Bernadine Healy became the first female head of the National Institutes of Health, she began to require that female subjects be included in
research studies. Since that time we've learned that heart attacks present differently in women, and gaps in diagnoses and treatment are starting to close.

This progress wasn't made by sending doctors to trainings or asking wom-
en to *lean in* harder to survive their heart attacks. Inequitable design was the
problem, so inclusive design was the solution. Once barriers to access were
removed for certain groups, their outcomes changed.

For businesses that haven't been able to diagnose their DEI deficiencies,
inclusive design—specifically, behavioral design—may also hold the cure.

Designing Some In, Others Out

Behavioral design is not new. It drives success in environmentalism, software
development, product packaging, and many other fields. As discussed in
chapter 1, hotels embraced the power of design by engineering key cards that
turn off the lights when guests leave the room, saving on energy costs. Governments have used behavioral design to increase tax compliance. For example, researchers in Poland found that telling taxpayers that others had paid
their taxes increased the likelihood that they would do the same. Reminders to pay taxes started to include updates on how many other citizens had
already paid, and compliance improved.[2] Behavioral design accommodates
the realities of the ways people perform and tailors environments and experiences to optimize results.

In workplaces, though, we're still asking employees to tailor their behavior to the environment. The promise of design hasn't caught on, but the legacy
of how the modern workplace was designed—and who designed it—remains.
As former deputy managing editor of the *Wall Street Journal* Joanne Lipman
notes, "The modern workplace was created after World War II in the image of
the military, a hierarchical model, and to this day, women make 1,000 adjustments every single day, all day long, to fit into a workplace that was created
by men for men."[3]

While Lipman's comment focuses on gender, noting who was and wasn't
in the decision-making room when the modern workplace was designed gives
us some insight into who was and wasn't accounted for. That proverbial room
did not include many people who weren't white, male, heterosexual, and
middle-aged. The lived experiences of employees of color, the neurodivergent, women, an aging workforce, LGBTQ employees, immigrants, and nontraditional caretakers simply weren't accounted for. These employees were
aberrations, not the default. They weren't designed in.

A workforce as diverse as today's is a fairly new phenomenon. We've never hit the pause button to ask who the workplace was designed for and if those default settings still make sense. Decades after World War II, employees are still making "1,000 adjustments every single day."

Size: Male, Style: White

When hospitals were overwhelmed with COVID patients in 2020, PPE was in high demand. Even the hospitals that could get access to PPE quickly realized that protecting their female healthcare workers was going to be a challenge. Most healthcare workers were women, but PPE was designed for men. As one National Health Service worker put it, "PPE is designed for a six-foot three-inch bloke built like a rugby player."[4]

Female healthcare workers worldwide were either kept from working when they were most needed, or they did so at risk to their lives. Some fastened masks to their jawline with duct tape, leaving facial rashes. Some attempted to pin up the sleeves of their fluid-repellent gowns, which were made for longer-limbed men.

PPE wasn't the first example of exclusive design keeping women from doing their jobs. In March 2019, Anne C. McClain and Christina Koch were on the verge of a historic mission: the first all-female spacewalk. The morning of March 26, McClain and Koch learned that they wouldn't be taking this small step for women. NASA had only one spacesuit available that would fit a medium-sized female frame. McLain would be replaced by her fellow astronaut, Nick Hague, for whom there were plenty of spacesuits at the ready.

McClain and Koch were two members of 2013's eight-person class of astronauts, who were selected from over 6,000 applicants. That year's class was half female. Women had leaned in and finally achieved gender parity, but NASA hadn't caught up. Legacy default settings meant that no matter how qualified women were, and how many other people they outperformed, there wasn't space for more than one.

In her groundbreaking work, *Invisible Women: Data Bias in a World Designed for Men*, Caroline Criado Perez writes, "Modern workplaces are riddled with these kinds of gaps, from doors that are too heavy for the average woman to open with ease, to glass stairs and lobby floors that mean anyone below can see up your skirt, to paving that's exactly the right size to catch your heels."

Bias is built into the ways that workplaces accommodate just one gender. Women workers sustain more work-related carpal tunnel and tendonitis injuries, attributed to a lack of ergonomic workspaces.[5] If you're a woman reading this and you've ever wondered why you're still wearing a sweatshirt to the office in August, it's because office temperatures are set to accommodate a 150-pound man in a business suit.[6]

Most design exclusions don't manifest in such blatantly physical form. They're more often baked into our policies and practices, institutionalized as standards of workplace culture.

In 2016, Chastity Jones applied to work as a customer service representative with CMS, an insurance claims processor. Ms. Jones wore short dreadlocks throughout the interview process and CMS hired her on the spot. After she was given a start date, she was asked by CMS human resources to cut her dreadlocks. When she refused, CMS rescinded its offer of employment, despite its own human resources manager confirming at the time that her dreadlocks weren't "messy."[7] They just weren't covered in CMS's definition of "professionalism."

These types of "professional standards" have long favored Eurocentric conventions, without explicitly discriminating on the basis of skin color. CMS's grooming policy showed an implicit preference for hairstyles that suit white hair texture better than Black hair texture. Without stating that they're less tolerant of Blackness, these standards raise the cost of being Black at work.

Advisory group Coqual reports that more than 35 percent of African Americans and Hispanics, as well as 45 percent of Asians, say they "need to compromise their authenticity" to conform to their company's standards of style or demeanor. Forty percent of African Americans—and a third of people of color overall—feel like outsiders in their corporate culture.[8] When the hoops people have to jump through every day remind them that they haven't been accounted for, they start to wonder if they should be there at all.

These are the easily identifiable forms of design exclusion—the low-hanging fruit. But what about the unconscious biases more subtly driving workplace inequities, the unintuitive ones most of us aren't even aware we have? Can we design our way out of biased resume reviews or flawed performance assessments?

Cultural Levers: Disrupting Bias

If a woman is asked to state her gender before filling out a job application or taking a skills-related test, she performs worse than if she were not asked. Stereotype threat is to blame. Social scientists have found that when people are reminded of certain aspects of their identity (such as gender) that are negatively associated with performance in certain areas (such as math), neural activity increases in the part of our brains responsible for processing negative information. As this activity increases, performance worsens.

These pathways are wired early in life and apply to many facets of our identities, including race. In experiments conducted by Stanford Psychology Professor Nalini Ambady and later replicated by UCLA Professor of Management Margaret Shih, Asian American children were given a math test. Some were reminded of their gender before taking the test, some were reminded of their race, and others were simply shown a picture of a landscape (the control). Girls who were reminded of their gender performed significantly worse than the control. Those who were reminded of their race, though, performed significantly better than the control.[9] These follow-up experiments found that internalized expectations cut both ways; long-standing stereotypes that Asians excel in math were triggered, increasing positive neural activity that can *improve* performance.

On job applications and skills tests, organizations often ask for demographic information before candidates complete the rest of the application. This valuable data helps companies understand if they're on track to meeting their DEI recruitment goals. Unfortunately, this step also triggers associations between aspects of identity and performance.

Simple solution: Just move the "gender" and "race" checkboxes to the end of the application. This is a *cultural lever*. It can be adjusted to design bias out and equity in.

This small adjustment harms no one, removes performance-inhibiting reminders of stereotypes, and ultimately helps to debias recruiting practices. Companies are closer to finding the "right person for the job" when applicants are able to fully represent their skills and talents, unhindered by internalized stereotypes.

These kinds of cultural levers can disrupt bias at every stage of the career life cycle, from hiring to promotions, and even the dreaded performance evaluation.

Fortune Magazine conducted a review of yearly performance evaluations across industries. They found that the "constructive criticism" that women received was often related less to job skills and performance than to personality traits. (You're aggressive. You're not warm enough. You're too timid.) These kinds of comments showed up in 71 of 94 yearly reviews received by women. In the 83 reviews of men, personality criticism showed up twice.[10]

The cultural lever: In businesses that conduct shorter but more frequent reviews—five-minute weekly evaluations focused on specific projects—the personality criticism vanishes, and the perceived performance gap between women and men is nearly nonexistent. Annual reviews rely on overall impressions, which are like petri dishes for bias, but short, frequent reviews engineer bias out.

These "fixes" don't actually rid individuals of their biases; instead, they address the reality that we have them and we can't train them away. Systemic changes take the onus off employees by debiasing processes rather than people. Instead of changing mindsets, cultural levers change mechanics.

At GEN, we partnered with the University of Washington to identify where else cultural levers were hiding that could optimize workplaces for equity. We found over 200.

Part 2 of this book, "Adjusting Cultural Levers," reveals how businesses can successfully institutionalize these fixes. Before we start adjusting levers, though, I'd like to answer an important question I receive quite often:

Do cultural levers really work?

Charting Paths of Least Resistance

Willpower is a hard thing to research. Lab experiments can oversimplify the human experience, samples tend to be small, and tasks that require great will-power from one individual may not require that much from another. Over the years social scientists have reached vastly different conclusions about this puzzling aspect of humanity. Researcher Roy Baumeister published find-ings indicating that willpower is a finite resource that can be depleted,[11] but later research has countered this, claiming that no "depletion effect" can be found.[12] Others claim that willpower boils down to self-belief: If you believe that you have enough willpower to complete a task, you will! If you don't believe it, you won't![13]

No matter what the elusive truths about willpower may be, we can employ a strategy that covers all the possibilities: Play it safe.

In *Willpower: Rediscovering the Greatest Human Strength*, Baumeister explores how people have hacked willpower to develop healthy habits and keep the New Year's resolutions that have notoriously high failure rates. One simple "hack" plays with the power of proximity. Every year, many resolution-makers commit to reading more, instead of watching TV. When they come home from work or class, they see the TV, see the remote, and attempt to sum-mon enough willpower to resist Netflix. Successful born-again readers have a trick: They proactively leave a book on the couch and hide the TV remote in a closet. Reading is now *the path of least resistance*.

This sounds too simple, but it has proven to work over and over again. In Baumeister's experiments, "Office workers ate a third less candy when it was kept inside of a drawer rather than on top of their desks." Baumeister also found the key to avoiding late-night snacking is "to brush your teeth early in the evening, while you're still full from dinner and before the late-night snacking temptation sets in. Although it won't physically prevent you from eating, brushing your teeth is such an ingrained pre-bedtime habit that it unconsciously cues you not to eat anymore."[14]

Cultural levers employ behavioral design techniques to reroute us away from our biases and toward objectivity, without us even having to think about it. Let's revisit the two cultural levers explored in this chapter. If "gender" and "race" checkboxes are left at the beginning of job skills tests, we're asking candidates to exert willpower to ignore the internalized stereotypes that are triggered and keep those thoughts at bay for the duration of their test. Adjusting a cultural lever by moving the checkbox to the end removes this willpower-intensive step, charting an unobstructed path to optimal performance.

Similarly, getting rid of yearly evaluations relieves managers of the effort needed to recall and accurately assess every assignment, project, and interaction they've had with reports. Frequent, short, focused evaluations make objectivity more *convenient*.

Cultural levers create paths of least resistance that lead us to less bias-prone behaviors, without relying on willpower. Embracing these behavioral designs decreases the cost of merit-based decision-making, and in turn, the human cost of working while underestimated.

Yes, some job applicants may be able to overcome stereotypes they've been taught about themselves. Some managers may be able to fairly assess employees based on their long-term memories of them. But why take the chance? Why not play it safe?

Check. Check. Check.

In his brilliant work, *The Checklist Manifesto*, Atul Gawande posits that the next big medical breakthrough is not a 3D-printed heart, or a stem-cell-grown organ. It's the checklist.

A world-renowned surgeon, professor at Harvard Medical School, and program director at the World Health Organization, Gawande breaks down the anatomies of decades' worth of operations gone wrong to arrive at the conclusion that checklists save lives. For doctors who spend four years in undergraduate studies, four years in medical school, and another three to seven years learning a specialty, this was a little hard to hear. No matter how elementary this solution seems, the results of implementing checklists are undeniable.

Peter Pronovost, a critical care specialist at Johns Hopkins Hospital, was the first to test Gawande's theory. He started by focusing only on reducing central line infection, a common cause of patient fatalities that occurs when bacteria or other germs enter the patient's central line and then enter into the bloodstream. ICUs in the US put five million lines into patients every year, and 4 percent of those lines become infected within 10 days. Depending on how sick the patient is to begin with, these infections are fatal between 5 and 28 percent of the time.[15]

On a sheet of plain paper, Pronovost listed the steps that could help avoid patient infection when putting in a central line: doctors must (1) wash their hands with soap; (2) clean the patient's skin with chlorhexidine antiseptic; (3) put sterile drapes over the entire patient; (4) wear a mask, hat, sterile gown, and gloves; and (5) put a sterile dressing over the insertion site.

Because these steps are "back to basics," it felt silly at first, but the critical care teams agreed to adhere to the approach. Nurses were tasked with observing doctors' actions and holding them accountable to the checklist. They found that doctors skipped at least one of the steps in more than a third of central line procedures.

Pronovost piloted the checklists for a year and watched the 10-day line-infection rate in his hospital fall from 11 percent to zero. He kept it going for another 15 months and during that time saw only 2 infections. The checklist was estimated to have prevented 43 infections and 8 deaths, and saved the hospital $2 million in related costs.

Johns Hopkins expanded the checklist approach to other units in the hospital. The proportion of patients not receiving the recommended care dropped from 70 percent to 4 percent, the occurrences of pneumonia fell by a quarter, and the likelihood of a patient enduring untreated pain fell from 41 percent to 3 percent.

Gawande believes these checklists work because, regardless of the physician's specialty or the particular patient case, the problem that all healthcare workers have to solve for is complexity. "Clinicians," Gawande notes, "now have at their disposal some 6,000 drugs and 4,000 medical and surgical procedures, each with different requirements, risks, and considerations. It is a lot to get right."

Building inclusive work environments can also be "a lot to get right."

Out from Under the Overwhelm

As an inclusion researcher, one of the biggest challenges I face is keeping up with how quickly language around DEI keeps changing. Terms I'm using in this book may no longer be relevant in a year.

The term "people of color," for example, was widely used for years, but it was criticized for failing to capture that not all people of color have similar experiences or face the same barriers. To address this, some started to use the term *BIPOC* instead, and it widely replaced the term "people of color" by the end of 2020. In 2021, the term BIPOC faced criticism for leaving out Latin Americans and Asian/Pacific Islander Americans, and some feel that the "I" in BIPOC is not specific enough and that individual tribes should be named. The debate over how to balance inclusion and specificity means that a simple Google search on "What does BIPOC mean?" will return over 20 pages of relevant links on navigating the use of this single term.

In an attempt to create shared understanding around DEI-related vocabulary, experts have created online glossaries of "commonly used" terms. Several of these glossaries include over 200 words each. A search on how to correctly use each of these terms will generate approximately the same amount of online resources as researching the term "BIPOC" does.

DEI information overwhelm is real—and this is *just* looking at language.

In my experience, building inclusive workplaces has required the most interdisciplinary, cross-functional combination of soft skills and technical knowledge of any field I've consulted in or studied. DEI does not just live in HR. Here's a quick rundown of the knowledge disciplines I often have to call on to support businesses in crafting their DEI strategies:

- Vendor and supply chain management. (Hospitals didn't manufacture the PPE that their female employees couldn't wear, but someone did! How does inclusion get factored into vendor choice?)
- Legal. (Just launching an employee survey involves liability. At what point do companies need to engage their general counsel to ensure they're covered while still getting the employee information they need to learn where their gaps are?)
- Advanced statistical analysis. (If I'm advising companies to take an intersectional approach to their employee data, how do they assess small sample sizes with any confidence?)
- Marketing. (What do you do when your company's language around DEI has "caught up" but your target audience's language hasn't?)
- Change management. (How does a change in policy get communicated, and what are the impacts going to be on processes downstream?)
- FMLA, compensation laws, employee discrimination laws, and state-by-state exceptions. (There are five states in which you currently can't ask candidates what their salary expectations are in an interview. I've worked with employers in all five of these states who had been asking this and didn't know they weren't compliant.)
- The differences in processes for amending bylaws, depending on how an organization is structured. (If no board member is facing an expiring term, how does a board expand to become more diverse?)
- The terms being used for DEI in countries where multinational organizations have divisions. (In the UK, for example, *EDI* is used instead of *DEI*, and *BAME* has been used instead of *BIPOC*, but is now being replaced by *Minority Ethnic Group*.)
- Conflict resolution and tactical empathy. (The moments in which people realize they've either benefited from or been held back by systems tend to be emotional.)
- Inclusive accommodations and architecture. (What should a gender-neutral bathroom include? What size refrigerator is appropriate for a

nursing room? How large should a quiet space be, and in what direction should it face to accommodate employees who take prayer breaks during Ramadan?)

- An ongoing awareness of current events, to ensure that employers are accommodating the mental health needs of employees who may have experienced a crisis close to home. (Many Indian American workers were personally impacted by the COVID surge in their home country in May 2021 but did not feel that their employer addressed this.)

This list is not exhaustive, and most of these topics don't even have to do with the theoretical "core" of DEI knowledge: what diversity means beyond race and gender, how you know you've reached equity, and what it looks like to go beyond diversity to inclusion.

DEI is an art of managing extreme complexity. Similar to the procedures Gawande observed, each "case" may be different, vocabulary is ever-changing, and unintended consequences persist. Cultural levers can get us out from under the overwhelm. Like Gawande's checklists, they pinpoint the exact steps we need to take to ensure that we don't miss crucial moments, we don't let personal feelings influence our judgment, and we empower employees at all levels to uphold a higher standard.

In the hospitals that employed the checklist method, administration had authorized nurses to stop doctors if they saw them skipping a step on the list. While nurses previously had to walk a line between ensuring that their supervisors adhered to standards and offending them, the new rules empowered them: Everyone was expected to speak up to uphold the rules.

Cultural levers relieve the burden in other workplaces as well. While it's risky for an entry-level employee to call out a manager's biased behavior, it's a lot less risky to point to a set of agreed-upon standards and ask, "Have we moved the checkboxes to the end of the application? Have we checked all the steps?"

Make DEI Boring Again

This may all seem very boring. A checklist? Processes? Is DEI really that dull? We're used to associating DEI with discrimination scandals, marketing campaigns, or yearly office parties celebrating Women's Month or Black History Month. It can feel odd to solve for it in a way that feels more like project management or accounting. Fortunately, the "how" doesn't have to be exciting, because the results are.

I keep a printout of an email pinned to the wall above my desk. It's from an employee of a company that GEN certified:

Sara, I don't think I'm exactly the person you do your work for, but I wanted to write and say thank you. I'm a white, straight dude, in my thirties, but I never felt like I "belonged" here. I'm not that loud or extroverted, but I've tried to act like a "bro" to fit in. I don't have to anymore. People who are just quieter or communicate differently are more included now, and I don't have to pretend to be someone I'm not. So, thanks.

—Trevor

I remembered Trevor. He encouraged his underestimated co-workers to take seats in front of him. Over the course of multiday workshops, he had some of the most insightful, detailed feedback, but only delivered it in written form, after group discussions were over.

In the process of getting certified, his employer had adjusted cultural levers to give more airtime to employees with Trevor's communication style (more on this in chapter 12). Now his company is hearing ideas from him they've never heard before, and he's helped them launch a whole new product line.

The outcomes of adjusting cultural levers don't always look like the poster version of DEI initiatives. They look like innovation, like picking the right person for the job, and surfacing unheard ideas. Adjusting cultural levers opens up a new sense of possibility that goes beyond any one -ism.

≈

As we'll see in the final chapter of this section, Trevor *is* actually who we do this work for. He, and his underestimated co-workers, meet every day at an intersection.

CHAPTER 5

Inclusion at the Intersections

A colleague of mine named Diya was being interviewed about a net-work she had founded that supports women of color.[1] "Why is it im-portant for women of color to have a community just for themselves?" the interviewer asked. "Are your experiences that different?"

In response, she shared an incident that had happened while picking up her mother from the airport. Diya had met her mother at baggage claim to help with her luggage. As they were crossing the garage to Diya's car, a white woman tapped her on the shoulder, stopped them, and asked what their daily rate was. Diya and her mom stared back, not sure what she was asking.

"For cleaning. Do you do house cleaning?"

Diya asked the woman what made her think they cleaned houses. The woman stammered and walked away.

It wasn't the first time this had happened to her.

Diya doesn't experience life only as a woman *or* only as an Indian. She lives at the intersection of those two identities. *In addition* to facing the bar-riers of her gender and the barriers of her race, she faces barriers that only surface when these two intersect. As a white woman, I will never be mistaken for a house cleaner. I'm fairly sure Indian men are not often mistaken for house cleaners, either.

Frameless

Intersectionality has made its linguistic way out of academia and into the mainstream. When Columbia Law School Professor Kimberlé Crenshaw coined the term 30 years ago, it was within an obscure legal context. Now, her TED Talk on intersectionality has over four million views,[2] and Hollywood stars are dropping the word in red carpet interviews.

As noted in chapter 4, understanding language around DEI can be overwhelming. This book is designed to provide a guide for anyone, regardless of their level of DEI knowledge, but "intersectionality" is a concept that is important to understand before we start adjusting cultural levers in part 2.

Over the decades, the definition of *intersectionality* has evolved. In broad terms, it describes how class, race, age, gender, sexual orientation, and other aspects of identity "intersect" with one another or overlap. In her TED Talk, Kimberlé Crenshaw lays out a more impact-focused definition: "If you're standing in the path of multiple forms of exclusion, you're likely to get hit by both."

To illustrate this point, Crenshaw presents us with the case of Emma DeGraffenreid, an African American woman who had applied for a job with an auto manufacturer but was not hired. She believed her application was rejected because she was a Black woman. A judge had dismissed her claim of race and gender discrimination based on the employer's argument that they did hire African Americans, and they did hire women.

The judge was not willing to acknowledge the nuanced but pivotal points of Emma's argument: The African Americans who were hired, usually for industrial and maintenance jobs, were all men. The women who were hired, usually for secretarial or front-office work, were all white. The overlap of these unwritten rules meant that Emma was faced with twice the discrimination and none of the opportunities. She could not fit the role typically given to African Americans because of her gender, and she could not fit the role typically given to women because of her race.

The antidiscrimination policies that did exist at the time would not protect African American women, because their experiences were not the same as those of white women or African American men. There was no frame of protection for someone like Emma.

Most workplaces continue to have no frame for including women of color and other individuals living at intersections, including introverts like Trevor, whom we met in chapter 4. Unless these individuals are intentionally included, they will be unintentionally ignored.

Minorities in the Margins

On March 24, 2021, my inbox filled with emails announcing that it was, once again, Women's Equal Pay Day. I receive several versions of this email every year, marking the date through which women had to work to make as much as men in the previous year. This subject line, though, wasn't quite accurate.

Asian American and Pacific Islander Women's Equal Pay Day would have been March 9; African American Women's Equal Pay Day would have been August 3; Native American Women's Equal Pay Day would have been September 8; and Latina Equal Pay Day would have been October 2.

Overall, women employed full-time, year-round in the US are paid 82 cents for every dollar paid to white, non-Hispanic men.[3] Black women? Sixty-three cents for every dollar. (Chapter 10 includes a more in-depth look at what these numbers mean, and at different definitions of the "pay gap.") We're able to track the gaps between these specific groups because organizations like the Economic Policy Institute look at the intersection of race and gender. Most employers, though, do not.

When I work with employers to conduct a pay gap audit, their compensation specialists usually come to me with their pay data aggregated in two separate categories: by gender and by race. They're siloed. This means that when I'm looking for gaps, all I can see is the difference between what women make and men make, and the difference between what white employees make and employees of color make. I have no way to compare, from looking at the data, the earnings of women of color to those of white women.

A company I recently worked with proudly turned over their compensation data with an analysis concluding that they had reached pay equity. With proper controls applied, accounting for variables such as education, job difficulty, and tenure, they stated that they were compensating men and women, and white employees and employees of color, with similar pay for similar work. We took the individual employee data, did our own regression analyses, and as long as the categories stayed separate, we came to the same conclusion. It was only when we looked at the intersections that the gaps appeared. Eight out of the ten women of color were making at least 25 percent below what white women made in similar roles, and 17 percent below what men of color were making in similar roles.

Companies that ignore intersections in their data can go for years thinking that they have reached pay parity, when they have not. This hurts both employees and employers. As chapter 10 explores in depth, pay gaps that are not caught early widen over time and cost more to remediate when they are finally discovered.

Pay, though, is just one part of the workplace experience. Employees who experience multiple forms of exclusion are pushed farther into the margins over the course of their careers. Looking at GEN's survey data, Black women are the least likely to report that they have someone at work they can confide in, and most likely to report feeling isolated. Asian women are the most likely to report being asked frequently to help with office "housework" such as making coffee, party planning, or other tasks outside their core job functions. Men of color are most likely to report retaliation or stigmatization when requesting time off for mental health reasons.

These gaps are the symptoms of a DEI mindset that assumes inclusion will trickle down from the "majority minority" to those at the intersections. While inclusion doesn't trickle down, exclusion does.

The Costs of Trickle-Down Exclusion

For years, Google had attempted to address the outsized turnover of women in their workplace. They provided more training and mentorship opportunities, started affinity groups, and publicly recognized the senior Google women who had moved up the ladder, but their attrition numbers didn't budge. Finally, they took another look at their data and aggregated it by one critical factor: parenthood status. They realized they were not losing women—they were losing mothers. Specifically, they were losing new mothers. In response, they tried extending the amount of time off that new mothers could take under their paid leave policy. The rate at which new mothers left dropped by 50 percent, and they are now no more likely to leave than their peers.[4] The cost of extending leave came nowhere close to the cost of replacing and retraining the talent they had been losing.

Intersectional aggregation doesn't just tell us *who* is falling through the cracks, it can often tell us *why*.

In the public survey that GEN uses to determine national benchmarks around employee experience, we ask respondents if they have had access to a range of experiences or opportunities in their workplace. For example: "Has your manager asked you about your career development goals in the last 12 months?"

If I aggregate the responses we've received to this question by race and gender, the results look like this:

Percentage of employees who replied "yes" by group	
Women	52%
Men	73%
White employees	68%
Employees of color	60%

This is how most companies sort their survey data (if they include race at all).

Nowhere in that aggregation can we see the following:

Percentage of employees who replied "yes" by group	
Women of color	44%
Mothers	46%
Fathers	75%
Employees over age 55	50%
Employees who state they have a disability	28%

If this same data represented an employer's workforce, and they did not aggregate beyond race and gender, they would not know that their managers were less likely to ask mothers about their career goals than fathers, or that employees over the age of 55 were less likely to get asked as well. Not only would these employees be missing out on potentially pivotal conversations, but employers would be missing out on insights that could improve employee retention and engagement.

At this point you may be asking, how granular should we get? Is the "women of color" category specific enough, or should we subdivide the category by race? Should Asian include a separate category for Southeast Asian? Should age be divided into every ten years? Five years?

And what about employees like Trevor, the introvert? As a straight, white male who does not have any caretaking responsibilities and considers himself neurotypical, Trevor is probably not going to check any of the boxes that represent underestimated groups. How do we account for employees who are not going to show up in any demographic grouping, but have often-overlooked and valuable contributions to offer?

Is it really possible to capture everyone?

Beyond Thin-Slicing

Thin-slicing indefinitely is not the point. For many organizations, aggregating data beyond gender just isn't possible. Even for large organizations, at some point there is a limit.

If your organization is not large enough to aggregate your data by intersections of groups, or even by more than gender, there are still solutions, which stem from one underlying principle:

Majority rule is not always the best rule.

When I was working with a Seattle-based tech company, one of the directors came to me with a challenge. Every six months employees got to vote, floor-by-floor, on how a discretionary "Fun Fund" should be spent. The short survey that collected votes offered several Fun Fund options: an Xbox for the floor, lunch delivery for a week, an early end to the workday, a ping-pong table, etc. The director told me that every time, without fail, all the guys got what they wanted, usually something game-oriented: a gaming console, ping-pong table, or set of games.

Men made up about 70 percent of the employees on the floor, and the results of the Fun Fund survey cut almost exactly along gender lines. Women voted for lunch delivery or time off, but several attempted to be "good sports" and join the guys in their gaming. They were told they weren't welcome because they hadn't voted for the games in the first place, so the games didn't "belong" to them. "I'm literally having to kneel down next to these guys' desks and ask them to share their games with the girls," complained the director. "As long as they're the majority here, nobody else is ever going to get what they want."

When "majority rules" is the policy, a homogeneous majority that makes up 70 percent of the office doesn't get what they want 70 percent of the time—they'll get what they want 100 percent of the time. When this approach is applied to policies with a more significant impact than the Fun Fund, it creates a culture that over-indexes on what the majority wants. Employers who are trying to attract and retain underrepresented groups will not do so by building a workplace that caters to, and therefore attracts, one overrepresented group, again and again.

While there is no thin-slicing rule of thumb that can guarantee an inclusive workplace, there are guidelines that can integrate intersectionality into your systems. As you kick off implementing cultural levers in part 2, these overarching principles can sustain intersectionality when designing, implementing, and evaluating new workplace policies and mechanics.

Designing Policy: Gathering Intersectional Perspectives

Often, organizations collect input from employees before writing a new policy or procedure. In theory, this is a great practice. The key to addressing more than one group's needs is analyzing this feedback through an intersectional lens. If you're a large company, look at the intersection of groups in your data. What are women of color saying? What are men of color saying? What are mothers saying? People in different age groups? Those who are legacy employees versus those who are still ramping up? Your categories should be large enough, though, that no individual is identified by the group label; if you only have one woman of color in your organization, don't have a "women of color" group.

If your organization is too small to look at these intersections, the following guidelines can help to ensure that all voices are accounted for.

Rotate into 2nd and 3rd choices. If a policy or opportunity you're creating receives input on a recurring basis, like the Fun Fund example, rotate which choice gets to "win" each time. Either let second place be the winner on an alternating basis, or, after the first round of voting, send the survey only to those who did not win the first time.

Weight by relevance. If employees are providing input on policy decisions, weight the answers of those who will actually be impacted by the policy. One employer I worked with was trying to determine if they should implement a keep-in-touch policy for employees who went on parental leave, to help them still feel included. Over half of the employees who provided input on this policy were not even considering using parental leave in the future, but their input overshadowed those who would have been affected. The employer was going to take all feedback into account equally, but weighting the responses of the relevant parties led to a policy that worked better for those who took leave, without disrupting their peers.

Provide space for open-ended responses. Trevor the introvert's way of thinking through problems and presenting feedback runs counter to his workplace culture. He likes to consider all possibilities quietly before weighing in, and he often highlights the work of others ahead of his own. When given opportunities that honor how he performs, though, Trevor—and his employer—can flourish.

Employee feedback surveys tend to be multiple choice. While this may be efficient, it also limits the answer choices to the realm of possibilities in the survey creator's mind. Ideas like Trevor's may not have ever gotten enough attention to make it into the options that appear on an employee survey. The creator of the survey simply may not have heard from those who think differently, are introverted, or come from underestimated backgrounds. Open-ended questions provide an opportunity for these groups to give feedback, in their own words, that would not have been represented in the answer choices.

Open-ended questions also allow people to provide input that they wouldn't feel comfortable volunteering otherwise. Veterans of color, for example, report feeling less comfortable speaking up about barriers they face—especially around race—than white veterans or other employees of color. Dr. Lamise Shawahin, a former Veterans Affairs psychologist, explains that the military champions the ideal of colorblindness, which can erase the idea of race-based experiences by emphasizing sameness: "This idea—'we're all green'—and these types of slogans, they instill the notion that racial differences are not important in the military."[5] This learned ethic of prioritizing the group's needs over one's own can persist when veterans return to an office setting. Open-ended questions offer an active invitation for feedback and the anonymity some may need to feel safe, without visibly "stepping out of line."

Who's in the room? Finally, when collaborating on policy design, pause, look around, and ask, "Who's in the room?" Are those who are actually going to be directly impacted by this policy represented? Who's overrepresented? Similar to weighting survey answers from relevant parties, this step ensures that the people you're attempting to include have their voices represented. If you don't want to single out individuals to provide their feedback, allowing space for anonymous comments on a questionnaire can provide the opportunity to capture all voices in the metaphorical room.

Implementing Policy

Designing policy with an intersectional lens is the first step toward equal treatment. Even if employees may have equal opportunities as written in company policy, accessibility to them can still be unequal. The following guidelines ensure that policies are implemented so that all employees have equal access to resources and opportunities.

Model the behavior yourself. This is especially important for those in leadership positions. You may create policies that do not apply to you personally, but you can make it easier for those who would benefit from the policy to feel comfortable taking advantage of it.

Let's say your company has decided to embrace the use of pronouns in email signatures, but the choice to do so is optional. You may never have experienced someone misgendering you, so you may not bother putting pronouns in your email signature. The fact that you personally have nothing to gain from this policy means you can have even more of an impact by embracing it. This opportunity was created for those who have been misgendered or feel they easily could be. They are the ones who are going to benefit, but they are also the ones who must take on the risk. If only those who "need" this policy are the ones taking advantage of it, it makes them stand out. Being one of the few to embrace pronouns in their signatures can feel like waving a giant flag that says, "Look at this choice I'm making!" It draws almost as much attention as correcting someone who has misgendered them in conversation.

If, however, it is common practice, or at least not a glaring exception, for people to include their pronouns in their email signatures, the person who would benefit feels less like an obvious outlier. Adding the pronoun comes at little risk for most and lessens the risk for those living at intersections.

Ask, "What are the criteria? What is driving our decision-making?" If there's one policy principle I repeat most often, it would be, "When criteria aren't present, bias will fill the void." This bias may not even have anything to do with an individual's demographic characteristics. Interviewers, for example, are more likely to hire someone they interview in the morning than in the afternoon (provided it's not right before lunch hour). This does not mean that your organization must ban afternoon interviews, but having criteria front and center makes it easier to assess candidates clearly, even when we're battling fatigue or undercover biases. Reviewing GEN's data, we find that organizations with clear criteria for evaluating candidates for promotions have greater percentages of leadership roles filled by women of color, parents, and others who live at intersections.

In the same way that the willpower hacks discussed in the previous chapter prepare the path of least resistance, it is easier to evaluate someone accurately with a checklist in hand. The harder we have to work, the more decision fatigue we take on, and the more vulnerable we become to defaulting to bias-ridden assessments. Preemptively reminding ourselves of what makes someone fit for a role lessens our chance of missing out on a good candidate.

Communicate "why" and communicate universally. Often I work with HR teams who have put admirable time and effort into crafting inclusive policies, but when I survey their employees, many of them do not know that the policies exist. What appear to be opportunity gaps are often communication gaps in disguise.

In one architecture company I surveyed, I noted that only half of their employees knew there was a nursing room located on the third floor. When I aggregated the data, I did not find that women knew and men didn't. Instead, certain business units knew, and others didn't. The difference? Business units with female managers knew there was a nursing room, while business units with male managers did not. For female managers, this policy may have been front-of-mind, while a nursing room may not have stuck in the minds of male managers.

Formalizing the ways that a policy is communicated can override the unconscious motivations that make some more likely to share out a policy than others.

In addition, make sure to state *why* you've created a policy. The benefits of some of the cultural levers we will recommend adjusting in part 2 are not always obvious. For example, employees may not understand why you're moving the gender checkbox to the end of the application. Communicating *why* fulfills two purposes: It increases buy-in by showing there is an evidence-backed reason behind the change, making it feel less arbitrary to employees. It also signals to underestimated employees that their employer is genuine in their commitment to inclusion. Broadcasting that you are taking an impact-driven approach to inclusion demonstrates that your strategy will lead to meaningful change.

Evaluating Policy Impact

You've designed your policies, you've implemented them, and time has passed. How do you know if they're working and what success looks like? These next steps can help you measure impact at the intersections.

Who's showing up? After policies are implemented, take note of who is or isn't taking advantage of them. If an opportunity, such as networking events with senior leaders, was meant for all employees, but you are seeing only homogeneous attendance, provide an opportunity for employees to state anonymously what would make them more likely to attend. One employer

I worked with took this step and discovered that some employees were not attending networking events because there were no kosher or halal options. Once they communicated this need to caterers, those employees felt more welcome and attended events, where they found mentors!

Evaluate Indicators "Upstream." Many organizations measure end results, or lag indicators, such as the percentage of people in leadership who are women or people of color. These indicators do not help to identify processes upstream that would lead to different outcomes. Measuring lead indicators—the processes that drive success on lag indicators—will drive inclusive success. An example of a lead indicator would be the survey question I shared earlier: "Has your manager asked you about your career development goals in the last 12 months?" If employers do not ask this question but look only at who has been promoted into leadership and see that women of color are not represented, they will not have any insight into the cause. They may misdiagnose the problem as a professional development issue, provide more training, and wonder why the gaps persist. Tracking indicators upstream lets you address the root causes of gaps, rather than just guessing at them.

(Re)gather intersectional perspectives. Finally, the rules about how you collect data, from the "Designing Policy" section of this chapter, also apply to how you *evaluate* policies. When gathering and analyzing feedback, make sure that you're looking at intersections as much as possible, and making use of open-ended questions when it's not.

≈

You know now why common approaches to DEI haven't worked, and why we need to change. You've gotten a preview of what it looks like to design equity in, and bias out, without missing individuals who live at the intersections.

It's time to start adjusting cultural levers.

It's time to hire the right person for the job.

Summary of Part 1

Chapter 1: Beyond Good Intentions

Some strides have been made toward workplace equality over the last 50 years, but over the last two decades, progress has stalled.

Common approaches to DEI have fallen short. Business leaders end up overwhelmed, trainings don't work or backfire, and statements of solidarity are called into question. Good intentions aren't enough.

The good news? When it comes to DEI, we've been doing it all wrong. The difference between businesses that break the DEI inertia and those who stay stuck is defined by one key perspective shift: Equity isn't personal. It's systemic.

Chapter 2: "But We've Always Done It This Way. . ."

Our unconscious mind drives up to 95 percent of our decision-making. It's where our biases are stored.

These biases often sabotage the most common approaches to DEI. When underestimated groups attempt to *lean in*, for example, they're treated differently than their peers. Because our perceptions of the ways people behave are built on a baseline of the ways we *expect* them to behave, we react negatively when those unconscious norms are disrupted.

We can't train our way out of these responses, and trainings often backfire. The more prejudiced people already are, the more likely they are to use the fact that they've attended a training to license less virtuous behavior later. This phenomenon is known as *moral licensing*.

Trainings also pose risk for underestimated individuals, who are sometimes treated as representative experts on their demographic's experiences.

Affinity groups can provide a sense of community, but too often they are treated as a substitute for inclusive workplace cultures. Providing a siloed space for shared identities does not counter organizational bias.

Chapter 3: Why Should We Care?

The workforce and consumers are rapidly diversifying. Employees and consumers care more about inclusion than previous generations, and investors are demanding diverse representation and equitable workplace policies.

As the demand for DEI has evolved, though, most companies' approaches haven't. This comes at a tremendous cost, keeping us from hiring the best person for the job or accurately assessing performance. Even when we believe we've created meritocracies, bias left unchecked sabotages our access to excellence.

When businesses do figure out how to include underestimated individuals, the strengths of the entire team are amplified. Teams with more diverse skill sets outperform teams stacked with traditional all-stars, strengthened by the benefits of collective intelligence.

A diverse workplace alone does not automatically yield these benefits. Companies must ditch outdated approaches to DEI and embrace mechanics that push them beyond diversity to inclusion.

Chapter 4: Shifting to a Systemic Perspective

Underestimated groups have been working in businesses that were never designed with them in mind. Physical workspaces accommodate men's bodies, dress codes default to Eurocentric standards of professionalism, and policies institutionalize workplace cultures that favor certain groups.

If exclusive design is the problem, inclusive design is the answer. A behavioral design approach to DEI means hitting the "pause" button to ask who the workplace was designed for, asking if these default settings still make sense, and making adjustments to optimize for inclusion.

We call these adjustments "cultural levers." They can be adjusted to design bias out and equity in. They harm no one, remove barriers to merit-based decision making, and accommodate the realities of how people perform by tailoring environments to optimize results.

These "fixes" do not actually rid individuals of their biases; instead, they address the reality that we have them and can't train them away. Systemic changes take the onus off employees by debiasing processes, rather than people. Instead of changing mindsets, cultural levers change mechanics.

Chapter 5: Inclusion at the Intersections

The term "intersectionality" describes how class, race, age, gender, sexual orientation, and other aspects of identity "intersect" with one another or overlap. If you're standing at the intersection of two forms of exclusion, you're likely to be hit by both. If employers don't take an intersectional approach to DEI, they'll overlook hidden gaps that only widen over years.

When possible, try to gather intersectional perspectives. When you can't aggregate your data by intersections of identities, there are some underlying principles you can adhere to.

When gathering feedback:

- To avoid accommodating a homogeneous majority 100 percent of the time, rotate into second and third choices, and weight the answers of those who will be most impacted by policies.
- Provide space for open-ended responses.
- Ask, Who's in the room? Are those directly impacted by policy represented?

When implementing policy:

- Model the behavior yourself, especially if you are in a leadership position.
- Ask what criteria are driving your decision-making. When criteria aren't present, bias fills the void.
- Communicate why you're implementing a policy, and communicate universally.

When evaluating policy:

- Note who's showing up and who isn't. If participation is homogeneous, provide an opportunity for employees to state anonymously what would make them more likely to participate.
- Evaluate KPIs "upstream." Evaluating indicators upstream that lead to different outcomes downstream will drive inclusive success.

It's time for part 2, "Adjusting Cultural Levers."

PART 2

Adjusting Cultural Levers

CHAPTER 6

Help Wanted—
Inclusive Recruiting

Today, my colleague Aaron is a principal at an accounting firm, but he can recall, still with a wince, when he applied for a role as an accounting specialist at a content streaming company. He had made it through the original resume review, a phone interview, and two rounds of in-person interviews. The only task standing between him and a potential offer was a personality test. He figured this was a formality, an exercise that wouldn't strongly influence the hiring team's decision.

He was given 30 minutes from his login time to finish the test. He imagined the first questions were supposed to be the softballs:

Do you believe you get along well with others?

Are you someone that other people trust?

There were two answer choices: *Yes* or *No*.

The "right" answers seemed obvious, but even these "easy" questions were hard for someone with an analytical mind and a strong moral code. "Who would say 'no' to either question?" Aaron wondered. "Is that the real test—assessing how honest I am? I may not have *always* gotten along with everyone. By 'get along well with others' are they actually asking if I'm afraid of conflict?"

The second half of the test got trickier:

Do you work better by yourself or in a team?

Aaron started to question if the test was assessing whether he was a good fit for the role or a good fit for the company. Someone who likes working alone could be a good fit for an accountant role, but anyone in the company would still need to work with others as part of a team. He wished there was an "All of the above" option.

Is it hard for you to stay cheerful when dealing with difficult people?

"If I admit that dealing with difficult people does not, in fact, put me in a great mood, would that be a red flag?" Aaron wondered. "Does it put anyone in a good mood?"

Aaron spent so much time contemplating how to navigate the test that by the end, he was hurriedly checking boxes, just attempting to finish.

He was not hired.

Typically, Aaron was a good test taker and had finished at the top of his class in his accounting program. Previous employers had been sorry to see him go. Some of the strengths that had made him successful, such as his attention to detail and his integrity, may have sabotaged him in this test.

Tests like the one Aaron took are now used in 60 to 70 percent of candidate evaluations.[1] Many businesses use these outsourced tests, typically created by workforce management companies, to deal with an overwhelming number of applicants. The Society for Human Resource Management (SHRM) found that "dealing with a high volume of applicants" was one of the top five concerns for employers at the beginning of 2021.[2] The number-one concern, though, was attracting top talent.

When millions of Americans are looking for jobs and companies are overwhelmed by applicants, how can it be so hard to find good hires? And how can companies distinguish between candidates who have learned how to perform well on tests, or in interviews, and those who will actually perform well on the job?

Debiasing the Job Description

Until 2015, the software development company Buffer referred to their coders as "hackers" on their website and in job descriptions.

"I think the original reason why we liked that word was because hackers are just people who get things to work well and fast," explained Buffer CTO Sunil Sadasivan.[3] "A 'hacker' doesn't necessarily need a computer science degree or a lot of experience or need to be excellent in mind games, puzzles, etc."

As the company started to grow and accelerate their hiring, they noticed that they were receiving few applications from female candidates. Sadasivan was concerned. He knew this meant that there was an entire pool of talent they were not accessing. He met with several directors of engineering fellowships for women for advice on getting more women to apply. He learned that the word "hacker" may have been playing a role. Angie Chang, the vice president of a leading engineering school for women, noted that the term probably did not appeal to male and female audiences equally. It also lacked clarity. Female coders may not see an ad for a hacker and intuitively associate it with a role for a coder, as they may not perceive their own coding skills as synonymous with hacking.

After considering a range of more neutral terms, such as *engineer*, *builder*, *programmer*, and *architect*, the hiring team went with "developer" as the term that sounded cleanest, clearest, and the most inclusive.

Buffer watched their number of female applicants skyrocket by 500 percent.

When I ask employers why they believe their workforce isn't more diverse, one of the responses I hear most often is that only white men apply. These businesses try to make their Careers web page look more diversity-friendly, they visit affinity groups' events at college campuses, and they ask their underrepresented employees to be ambassadors.

It would cost a lot less, and be more effective, to revisit their job descriptions.

Help Wanted: Highly Qualified Job Ads

Unconscious bias in job descriptions can drive strong applicants away from even considering an opportunity. In a hiring market where finding talent is the top concern, employers cannot afford to alienate candidates unconsciously.

Adjusting some key cultural levers can improve who is seeing your job openings and who actually applies. Both increase the odds that you will hire the best person for the job. These tweaks start with the language you use.

Striking a Gender Balance

A study published in the *Journal of Personality and Social Psychology* showed job descriptions with a range of gender-coded terms to men and women and recorded their reactions.[4] They found that women viewed job advertisements with masculine-coded language (indexing high in words such as *aggressive*, *dominant*, and *headstrong*) as less appealing and felt that they belonged less in those occupations. Men found feminine-coded job descriptions (indexing high in words such as *compassionate*, *sensitive*, and *community*) to be slightly less appealing, but this feeling did not influence whether or not they felt they belonged in those roles.

Textio, a language analysis platform, took these studies one step further. They found that the proportion of gender-coded words in a job description is a highly accurate predictor of which gender will be hired into that role. Without intending to, hiring managers can embed into job descriptions subtle cues of who belongs and who does not. Often this language isn't as obvious as words like "hacker" or "rock star" in the job titles. Typically, it's encoded into the body of the advertisement. Is the job description asking for "the ambition to compete as part of a domineering firm" or for someone who "collaborates well in a team environment and can develop lasting client relationships"? Both may be true, but one of these summaries is more likely to attract female applicants.

To provide some specificity, I've included the following lists of masculine-coded and feminine-coded terms. You can use these lists to evaluate the overall gender coding of your job advertisement. The terms are reduced to stems, to cover variants; for example, the stem "analy-" covers "analysis," "analyze," and "analytical."

Gendered wording in job advertisements[5]

Masculine-Coded Words		Feminine-Coded Words	
active-	greedy-	agree-	kind-
adventurous-	head-strong-	affectionate-	kinship-
aggress-	headstrong-	child-	loyal-
ambitio-	hierarch-	cheer-	modesty-
analy-	hostil-	collab-	nag-
assert-	impulsive-	commit-	nurtur-
athlet-	independen-	communal-	pleasant-
autonom-	individual-	compassion-	polite-
battle-	intellect-	connect-	quiet-
boast-	lead-	considerate-	respon-
challeng-	logic-	cooperat-	sensitiv-
champion-	objective-	co-operat-	submissive-
compet-	opinion-	depend-	support-
confident-	outspoken-	emotiona-	sympath-
courag-	persist-	empath-	tender-
decid-	principle-	feel-	together-
decision-	reckless-	flatterable-	trust-
decisive-	self-confiden-	gentle-	understand-
defend-	self-relian-	honest-	warm-
determin-	self-sufficien-	interpersonal-	whin-
domina-	selfconfiden-	interdependen-	enthusias-
dominant-	selfrelian-	interpersona-	inclusive-
driven-	selfsufficien-	inter-personal-	yield-
fearless-	stubborn-	inter-dependen-	share-
fight-	superior-	inter-persona-	sharin-
force-	unreasonab-		

The lists are not exhaustive, but they can provide a quick check on how far your description may have swung in either direction. The point is not to ban any of these words, but to raise awareness of ways in which you may have used language that would appeal to one group over others.

Gender-Neutral Job Titles

It's easy to accidentally imply gender in a job title. Trades like electrical contracting and plumbing have historically used male-default job titles, such as "journeyman." More and more licensing and certification agencies have shifted, though, to more gender-neutral language and now use "journeyperson" instead. Since most candidates' first impressions come from the title, it can have a significant impact on whether or not they apply. Even if the rest of the job description feels gender-neutral, women will be more likely to read the description if they have been included in the title.

Racial Bias in Commonly Used Phrases

Some words and phrases can also embed racial bias into your job descriptions. Often, hiring managers are not aware that these terms have racially biased connotations or origins. Some commonly used phrases, like those below, may discourage candidates of color from applying to your company. Tools such as Ongig's text analyzer can be used to provide a more comprehensive scan of your job descriptions to identify exclusionary phrases.[6]

- The word "blacklist" or "blacklisting" is often used in cybersecurity job descriptions. It describes the process of identifying known malicious or suspicious entities that should not be permitted access to a system or network. Companies have started to replace the term "blacklist" with words like "reject list" or "block list" instead, to avoid associating Black people with exclusion.
- Employers may use the terms "brown bag session" or "brown bag lunch" to describe the kinds of learning sessions they offer. The "Brown Paper Bag Test," though, has a history related to racism and colorism.[7] Some employers are now opting for more sensitive language, such as "lunch and learns."
- Similarly, "cakewalk" is a racially biased phrase that has been found in job descriptions. If something is referred to as a "cakewalk," it is considered to be an easy task. Historically, though, the cakewalk was a pre–Civil War dance originally performed by slaves on plantation grounds. While non-Black applicants may not be aware of this, Black candidates are more likely to be familiar with the history of this term and feel uncomfortable applying.

- Engineers at Amazon added the term "oriental" to a list of banned words in an internal Wiki they use to remove racist terms from their communications.[8] This term, which has racially biased undertones, is still often used by multinational companies to describe office locations or market segments in Asian regions.

- Some jobs may require English fluency, but being fluent in a language does not mean one has to be native to that country. Job descriptions that use "English fluency level: native," "native English speaker," or "English native speaker" exclude people who speak English as a second language. The phrases "fluent in English" or "proficient in English" are less biased options.

Axing Affinity Bias

Affinity bias describes our tendency to gravitate toward others who remind us of ourselves. In the context of job descriptions, the "top school" requirement is often seen as a type of affinity bias called *elite bias*. Companies that require candidates to have a degree from an "Ivy League university" or a "top engineering school" exclude applicants who did not attend elite institutions.

Google used to favor applications from candidates who attended Stanford, Harvard, and MIT. They learned from their people data, though, that those who did not attend elite schools performed as well as, or outperformed, their Ivy League–sourced employees and nixed this preference from their recruitment process.[9]

Instead of asking candidates to have a degree from an elite university, requiring a degree in a specific field is more inclusive. Assessing candidates for specific skills can bring you closer to hiring a good fit for the role.

Require Only Actual Requirements

For the role you are trying to fill, do you actually need someone with five years of leadership *experience*, or do you need someone with leadership *skills*? Women and people of color are more likely to have been passed over for promotions into management positions in the past, even if they demonstrated the skills needed to perform as managers. By requiring a certain number of years in a position with "manager" in the title, you can miss out on excellent candidates whose leadership potential has been overlooked in the past. Instead, advertise for competencies. Do you need someone who

- Can make difficult decisions?
- Is customer-focused?
- Can maintain a long-term strategic vision?

Identifying the real skills needed for success in certain roles will bring you closer to finding a good fit than relying on a title that may have meant different things at different organizations. The interviewing section in the next chapter will explore how to ask behavioral questions that give candidates a chance to demonstrate these kinds of competencies.

Listing only must-have's as requirements also addresses the oft-cited statistic that women tend not to apply for roles unless they meet 100 percent of the requirements, whereas men apply if they meet 60 percent.[10] Listing every possible qualification as a requirement lessens the chances that women will apply. It may also lead to the underqualified application overwhelm that SHRM noted employers are facing by attracting a high number of male applicants who do not actually meet the requirements.

Expand—and State—Your Definition of Transferable Skills

A CTO of a cybersecurity company—I will call him Sharad—makes a habit of hiring people who have little-to-no experience in cybersecurity, but who demonstrate excellence in other skills that he knows would make them top employees. His team includes former EMTs, hospice directors, an operations manager from a cruise line, and a kindergarten teacher. They are all able to stay calm in times of crisis, solve complicated problems, and triage priorities effectively. His team has the lowest turnover and highest peer-performance ratings in his organization.

These prize employees would not have even applied if Sharad hadn't included these key lines in his job advertisements: "Background in cybersecurity not needed. Anyone with experience managing crises welcome— Teachers, emergency workers, etc., highly encouraged to apply!"

Even though Sharad does not identify diversity as a top hiring goal, his method of hiring has implicitly attracted more underestimated individuals, and his team is the most diverse in his organization.

LinkedIn made a move in 2021 that recognized the power of nontraditional transferable skills. Starting in April, users could select "Stay-At-Home Parent" from a list of job titles. In addition to explaining gaps in employment, the presence of these terms as job titles contextualized the skills needed to parent within a professional resume. Stay-at-home parents excel at handling crises, multitasking, and managing time. A first-of-its-kind study from WerkLabs quantified the impact that mothers have in the workplace. The study found that the presence of moms in the workplace, particularly in managerial and C-suite positions, created a more positive employee experience, heightened productivity, and led to an increase in retention outcomes.[11]

To signal to parents that you value their transferable skills, follow Sharad's lead by noting in your job description that you encourage caretakers or those with gaps in their resume to apply. This signals that applicants won't be wasting their time with an employer who won't take them seriously. Also, use these new features on LinkedIn to expand your own search for qualified candidates.

Tell Us a Little Bit About Yourself

One of the reasons we launched the GEN Certification was to recognize companies that were doing the right thing but didn't have the marketing resources to publicize it. They often had to compete for talent against companies with seemingly little DEI strategy but robust equity and inclusion PR budgets.

If your company is the former, the job description is your low-budget, high-impact opportunity.

In chapter 15, you'll learn how to write a comprehensive equity strategy. For now, if your organization is taking specific steps to create an equity-centered work environment, note it in your job description, not just on the Careers web page.

If you offer flexible or remote work arrangements, announce it! If you offer paid leave, announce it! If you conduct pay gap audits, announce it!

Not only will this demonstrate your commitment by showing that you go beyond a general statement of solidarity, the extra bullets in your job description will actually draw more underestimated applicants. Studies by labor economist Claudia Goldin found that when employers included more information about their flexibility policies and compensation structures, underestimated groups were more likely to apply.[12] The extra information minimized ambiguity, which was attractive to those who tended to be more risk-averse or appreciate transparency.

An important note: If your company has not yet taken steps to implement policies or practices that make your workplace more inclusive, stay away from statements about your commitment to DEI. When not paired with evidence of action, these statements often backfire. Studies by Textio found that companies who declare themselves "Equal Opportunity Employers" or "Affirmative Action Employers" without sharing specific actions they take perform worse than job descriptions that don't include any kind of EEO statement.[13]

Who Is Seeing You?

You've written the job description. Now, how are you getting it in front of diverse audiences, and how do you get the candidates to apply?

Show Them Who Else Is Applying

More specifically, show them how many people have applied.

Tufts University economist Laura Gee discovered this cultural lever when studying job applicant behavior on LinkedIn. Not only did posting the number of people who had started an application garner more total applicants, traditionally underrepresented applicants were far more likely to apply. While overall applications increased by up to 3.6 percent, the percentage of women who applied increased by 10 percent.[14] Those who had less overall experience were also more likely to apply to postings that shared the applicant numbers.

This finding surprised those who typically think of women as competition- and risk-averse. The risk aversion typically associated with underestimated groups may have played a key role, though. As noted in the earlier part of this chapter on writing the job description, more information is associated with less ambiguity, and therefore, less risk. Seeing that other people applied for a job could have made it seem "worthy" of applying for. Underestimated groups are less likely to have leisure time, and women of color, in particular, report the least amounts of free time.[15] These groups may feel that it is a better use of their limited spare time to apply to jobs that appear to have been "vetted" by other applicants.

This tactic also appeals to the specific ways in which certain groups feel comfortable competing. While men are typically stereotyped as being more competitive than women, some research suggests this only holds true in public settings. In private, from behind the comfort of a screen, or in teams with few men, women are perfectly fine with competing, sometimes more so than their male counterparts.[16] Because competitiveness is not seen as an attractive trait in women, though, they are more likely to compete in private, without an audience. Sharing how many applicants they are up against may appeal to these competitive instincts.

Where Are You Advertising?

When employers tell me they advertise to diverse audiences, I ask them where they're advertising, and most of them respond, "LinkedIn." While 29 percent of white online adults use LinkedIn, only 18 percent of Latinx online adults do.[17] They are more likely to use other professional sites, such as Indeed or Monster, and Latinx applicants are 2.5 times more likely to use newspapers in their job search, compared to the general population.[18]

In addition, even though the gender balance of LinkedIn users is getting closer to even (women at 49 percent and men at 51 percent, as of 2021), their profiles are still treated differently. Recruiters are more likely to click on male candidates' profiles and applications, even when female and male profiles show equal qualifications.[19]

The more pernicious danger of posting only on LinkedIn is rooted in "homophily"—a tendency to build networks of people similar to ourselves. As noted by researchers Khanam, Srivastava, and Mago, "Homophily is a well-established phenomenon that has been observed to occur frequently in social networks."[20]

This means that when companies are advertising on LinkedIn, they are advertising to the networks they already have, which tend to look like the networks already inside the company. If your company is largely white and male, and you are advertising through a network that resembles and therefore connects with that demographic, you are over-indexing on that group. In addition, the LinkedIn users who have more influence—typically executives—are algorithmically positioned to have their posts promoted more often, seen by more people (who look like them), and have people in their network reshare (to other people who look like them). These influential users are most often white and male, their networks are more likely to be white and male, and the members of those networks are more likely to share to other users who are white and male. The impact of homophily, online, grows exponentially.

To counter this phenomenon and ensure that you are reaching a diverse pool of candidates, intentionally promote your job openings where underestimated individuals are more likely to see them. The following communities, for example, provide channels to promote employment notices to underestimated groups:

- *BlackJobs.com*. A leading online job board for diversity hiring. The online community promotes job openings to over 300,000 African American job seekers, over half of whom are women.
- *Code Fellows*. Focuses on educating the next generation of underrepresented software developers. Job postings can be shared with their alumni.
- *Women in Digital*. Online and in-person community of women in the digital space.

Also, searching for job boards for underrepresented individuals specifically within your industry can foster the greatest gains. Applicants of color in the outdoor industry, for example, are more likely to apply for jobs at REI through the online platform Malakye than they are on REI's own website. Just like marketing to any other customer, recruiting diverse audiences means meeting them where they are.

Go In Blind

While we like to think we're above certain biases, our perceptions of candidates' qualifications are influenced by their race, gender, age, and even the pronounceability of their names.

- A study conducted by *HR Daily Advisor* found that, when reviewing a pool of resumes with identical qualifications, hiring managers were more likely to call back the applicants with male names. When asked why they preferred those applicants, hiring managers cited their level of education, even though all resumes had the same number of years of relevant education.[21]

- On average, ethnic minorities must complete 50 percent more applications than candidates in the majority to be invited for a job interview.[22]

- Individuals with common, easy-to-pronounce names have an easier time getting hired, and are seen as more trustworthy.[23] To try to overcome these biases, immigrants often Americanize their names. Those who change to the most popular American names, such as John or William, enjoy gains in occupation-based earnings of at least 14 percent.[24]

The obvious response to these biases would seem to be blind resume reviews, a process in which identifying information is removed before reviewing candidates' resumes or applications. These details could include their names, any demographic information they entered as part of the application fields, and links to personal profiles, such as on LinkedIn.

Blind reviews are the low-hanging fruit of debiasing the hiring process, but currently, 72 percent of respondents to GEN's online survey state that their employer does not conduct them.

Your organization can conduct blind resume reviews while still collecting the demographic information essential to understanding who your recruiting strategies are reaching. The following workflow can help your organization implement a blind resume/application review process:

1. Decide which identifying factors you want to remove. The list below identifies possible options for removing identifying information. Some of these are table stakes (name), while others may not be realistic for your organization (name of college) to remove.

   - Name.

   - Ethnic background and gender (if these are fields that applicants fill in when they apply).

   - Exact dates that the applicant worked for previous employers. (Instead, redact dates and substitute the number of years worked in the role. While the total years of experience will still hint at an applicant's age, ageism plays less of a role when hiring managers aren't staring at exact dates.)

   - Names of the college(s) or university(ies) attended. (This prevents affinity/elitism bias from playing a role, and as noted earlier, elite schools do not always correlate with higher performance.)

- Any other obvious indicators of gender or race. (Volunteer groups, Greek organizations, and clubs, for example, can include demographics in the organization's name. This can be easily replaced with "volunteer group" or "civic group.")

2. An administrative professional who is not in a decision-making role should assign a number to each application, then redact the identifying information you have chosen to keep hidden. Those elements can be tracked by number separately, on a spreadsheet. If you do not use an online portal or web form and instead ask applicants to send cover letters and resumes by email, ask them in the application to attach the files as Word documents, so that the name and any additional information can easily be removed.

3. The administrative professional can track the demographic data of your applicant pool. Once you have met your candidate diversity targets, move on to resume review.

4. After resumes have been reviewed and top applicants have been selected for interviews, re-match names (and contact information) with application numbers so the applicants can be contacted.

Many organizations with the technical resources have automated this process, and others have outsourced it to their recruiting agencies. If you work with an outside recruiter, ask if they conduct blind reviews.

≈

Recruiting a diverse set of candidates means designing bias out of how they find—and evaluate—you. Hiring the right person from this set of applicants means debiasing how *you* see *them*. As we learn in the next chapter, one of the most common methods for evaluating the right person for the job can also be the most flawed.

CHAPTER 7

The Best Person for the Job—Merit-Based Hiring

U nstructured interviews are hiring managers' favorite hiring tool. They're also the worst predictor of on-the-job performance.

In studies published in the *Journal of Industrial and Organizational Psychology*, over 200 HR executives were asked to give their perceptions of the effectiveness of a range of hiring tools, such as aptitude and skills tests, unstructured interviews, personality tests, and assessments of cognitive strengths.

They considered the traditional unstructured interview to be the most effective.[1] In reality, every single other method predicted on-the-job performance more accurately.

Even when confronted with this information, HR professionals and hiring managers commonly refuse to believe that they themselves lack the judgment needed to assess a candidate well from an interview.

The study states, "HR professionals agreed, by a factor of more than 3 to 1, that using tests was an effective way to evaluate a candidate's suitability and that tests that assess specific traits are effective for hiring employees. At the same time, however, these professionals agreed, by more than 3 to 1 that you can learn more from an informal discussion with job candidates and that you can 'read between the lines' to detect whether someone is a suitable hire." Researchers found their test subjects' belief in their own intuitive powers to be absolute.

In another study, researchers found that hiring managers placed more emphasis on competencies assessed in interviews than on competencies measured by tests.[2] For example, if they assessed extraversion through an interview and mental ability through a pen-and-paper test, they were more likely to stress the role of extraversion in the role they were hiring for. If they tested for mental ability in an interview, and extraversion in a test, though, they believed that mental ability was actually more important to the role.

Despite evidence from dozens of studies that unstructured interviews are poor indicators of job performance, it appears that hiring managers won't be doing away with them any time soon. As long as interviews are here to stay, there are cultural levers that we can adjust to assess candidates more accurately.

Debiasing the Interviewing and Scoring Process

When conducting in-depth interviews for research, one of the sacred but socially awkward cardinal rules I've had to learn to abide by is "Same questions. Same order."

Why is this interviewing oath so important?

Same Questions

The gender gap in venture capital funding isn't news to many founders. As of 2017, approximately 2 percent of VC funding went to female entrepreneurs,[3] despite 38 percent of businesses in the US being owned by women.[4] While in-group nepotism often gets the blame, another subtler culprit impacts how little funding women receive: the questions that funders ask them.

In a study published in 2018, researchers observed funding interviews and other types of Q&A interactions at TechCrunch Disrupt, an annual startup funding competition.[5] They started to notice patterns in the types of questions venture capitalists posed to male versus female entrepreneurs.

Male founders were asked about achievements, ideals, hopes, and growth. Women were asked about security, responsibility, safety, and recovery.

VCs asked men questions that were promotion-oriented, focused on their *potential to win*. They asked women questions that were prevention-oriented, focused on *not losing*.

No matter how qualified the entrepreneurs were, the questions they were asked positioned them to answer with what psychologists refer to as different *regulatory focuses*. The American Psychological Association uses this term to describe how people can be fundamentally promotion-oriented or prevention-oriented when making decisions.[6] Being promotion-oriented focuses an individual on accomplishments, aspirations, and wishes. A prevention orientation focuses on safety, security, duties, and obligations. In the context of interviews, interviewees are stuck responding within the regulatory framework where the interviewer's attention is focused: Questions about prevention got answers about prevention. Questions about growth got answers about growth. This perpetuated a cycle in which the founders were associated with domains of either losses or gains, no matter how well they responded.

The difference in question orientation ultimately influenced funding. As the researchers noted in a summary article they published in the *Harvard Business Review*:

> *Examining comparable companies, we observed that entrepreneurs who fielded mostly prevention questions went on to raise an average of $2.3 million in aggregate funds for their startups through 2017— about seven times less than the $16.8 million raised on average by entrepreneurs who were asked mostly promotion questions. In fact, for every additional prevention question asked of an entrepreneur, the startup raised a staggering $3.8 million less, on average. Controlling for factors that may influence funding outcomes. . .we discovered that the prevalence of prevention questions completely explained the relationship between entrepreneur gender and startup funding.*[7]

This tendency to ask women and men different questions extends to job interviews, as well. A study conducted by Resume.io that included over 2,000 participants found that women are asked more questions requiring them to "prove themselves."[8] Specifically, women are more likely than men to be asked the following questions:

"Why should we hire you?"

"Why do you want this job?"

"Why didn't you like your last job?"

"What is your greatest weakness?"

"Describe a time you failed and how you handled it."

Men were asked the last two questions least often, if at all. Instead, they were asked more "brain teaser" questions, such as "How many gas stations are there in America?" or "How many lightbulbs are there in this building?"

While the questions women were asked were not necessarily "bad," they were more concerned with proving one's worth. By not asking men the same questions, interviewers were treating them as more capable. While women's answers were required to be defensive to fit the context of the questions, men's answers could show off their creativity and problem-solving skills.

Same Order

In a study pioneered by Solomon Asch in 1946, he asked participants to quickly read the following descriptions of Person A and Person B:[9]

> Person A: intelligent-industrious-impulsive-critical-stubborn-envious.
> Person B: envious-stubborn-critical-impulsive-industrious-intelligent.

Participants described Person A as "an able person who possesses certain shortcomings which do not, however, overshadow his merits." Person B, though, "impresses the majority as a 'problem', whose abilities are hampered by his serious difficulties. Further, some of the qualities (impulsiveness, criticalness) are interpreted in a positive way under Condition A, while they take on, under Condition B, a negative color."

You may have discovered already that the descriptions contain identical traits, listed in a different order.

Information that participants are exposed to first produces what is called a "halo effect"—a propensity to let an initial impression or feeling inform overall judgment. This bias was first studied by Edward Thorndike, who found that military officers who were ranked higher for physical qualities, such as physique and voice, later received higher evaluations for intelligence and leadership skills, despite their peers' superior aptitude in these areas.

Some interview questions are inherently more fun to ask and answer than others. "How did you hear about our company?" is at worst going to elicit a neutral response from an interviewee. It can set a different tone at the beginning of an interview than "Why are you leaving your current job?" When candidates are given different sets of opportunities to form a first impression, it can affect how they are perceived for the rest of the interview.

Prepping for the Interview

Now that you know how important it is to ask candidates the same questions in the same order, how do you decide what questions to ask? And how do you set yourself up well to evaluate the answers?

Developing Competency-Based Hiring Questions

Competencies identify the desired or required skills and behaviors needed to perform a job successfully. Clearly defining competencies ahead of an interview focuses interviewers on the skills they're evaluating, rather than on whether or not they "like" a candidate. Competencies can identify required soft skills—for example, "attention to detail" or "fostering communication"—as well as technical skills needed for success in specialized roles. Competency-based interviewing relies on behavioral interview questions to assess candidates accurately.

To craft these behavioral interview questions, first decide what core competencies you're going to focus on. Ideally, try to keep your list to no more than five. Technical competencies can often be assessed through other tools, such as computerized tests, so if you're trying to narrow down a long list to five critical competencies to focus on in your interview, it often makes more sense to pick the soft skills.

To develop behavioral interview questions, focus on behavioral indicators of the competency. For example, let's say you're hiring for an account executive role, and you have decided that client focus is a critical competency to assess in your interview process. The following two behavioral indicators could drive your interview questions:

Behavioral Indicator #1: Shows clients that their perspectives are valued.

Behavioral Indicator #2: Enhances client service delivery system and processes.

The STAR framework can be helpful for structuring interview questions around these behavioral indicators:

- The **S**ituation or **T**ask in which the candidate was involved,
- The **A**ction that the candidate took to complete the task or address the situation, and
- The **R**esult of the candidate's action.

Here are examples of how the STAR framework could be used to create interview questions for the two behavioral indicators:

Behavioral Indicator #1: Shows clients that their perspectives are valued.

- Question: Provide an example of a time you sought feedback from clients or partners.
- Probes: Why and how did you seek the feedback? What feedback did the client or partner provide? How did you use their feedback?

Behavioral Indicator #2: Enhances client service delivery system and processes.

- Question: Tell us about a time when you took steps to improve the service being provided to a client.
- Probes: What service was being provided? How did you go about improving it? How did the client respond?

Deciding Wording, Order, and Weighting

Decide on the exact wording and order in which you are going to ask these questions and write them in a document that every member of your selection committee uses. Make sure that your document includes room for scoring the candidates' answers to questions, from 1 (unsatisfactory) to 5 (excellent). Leave room for taking notes, as well.

Finally, once you have decided what questions you're asking and the order in which you're asking them, decide what each question is "worth." How relevant is the core competency, compared to the other core competencies, in performing well in this position? Note the weightings for each question before starting interviews. This keeps interviewers from overvaluing one answer that resonated with them at the expense of other areas of focus that may be more important.

Scheduling the Interview

When scheduling the interview, make sure to reserve an extra 20 minutes on each interviewer's calendar to complete their individual scoring of each candidate immediately after the interview concludes. The more time that passes, the more bias may impact the memory of the interviewer.

In addition, when scheduling interviews, try to schedule them for approximately the same time of day. For example, don't conduct interviews with two candidates in the morning and two in the late afternoon. Interviewers have demonstrated more negative feelings toward candidates they interview toward the end of the day, giving morning interviewees an advantage.[10]

Finally, when emailing candidates to confirm their interview, it can be helpful to give them advance notice that you use a structured interview process that can feel awkward, but is intended to make the assessment as unbiased and fair as possible. Here is a sample statement:

> At COMPANY NAME, we've incorporated best practices into our hiring process that help minimize the impact of unconscious bias. One of these practices is a standardized interviewing process. I wanted to let you know this before you come in for your interview. Part of this process involves asking all questions of all candidates in exactly the same order, so even if you've already answered a question earlier in our conversation that we had planned to ask later, we will still be asking you that question to ensure fairness of process. I know that can feel a little uncomfortable, so I wanted to let you know that we're just following a process to ensure everyone gets the same treatment.

During the Interview

After greeting your candidate, make a statement similar to the one in the email confirmation above to remind them that you will be using a standardized interview process and ask them if they have any questions about the process. In addition, let them know that as part of this process, you will be taking time after *each of their responses* to make careful notes before moving on to the next question. Let them know that this is meant to aid you in accurately reflecting on their answers.

Listen fully to the candidate's response to each question and then take notes, pausing to record your immediate reflections on the candidate's response before moving on to the next question.

In the 20 minutes immediately following the interview, assign a numerical rating on your evaluation form for each answer the candidate gave. It is extremely important to note your ratings immediately following the interview to reduce the likelihood that bias will influence your memory over time.

If you are conducting interviews in a committee or panel, it is also important that you **not** share or discuss your notes with one another immediately following the interviews. As the next section explains, doing so could activate the HiPPO effect.

After the Interview

After completing this process for all candidates, write final notes and compare your own scoring of each candidate **on your own** before reuniting with the rest of the selection committee to discuss. Each member of the selection committee should write down their top candidate before meeting, to ensure they are bringing their own perspective to the final discussion.

Countering HiPPO

Scoring and selecting a top candidate privately sidesteps an authority bias commonly known as the "HiPPO effect"—a tendency to conform to the Highest Paid Person's Opinion (HiPPO) in the room. While this bias doesn't necessarily cater to the highest paid individual, it speaks to the tendency of groups to defer to the authority figure in the room when a difficult decision must be made. While trusting experts and authority figures can sometimes serve us well, junior members of a team can often provide perspectives on the more tactical factors that drive success in an organization. A study from the Rotterdam School of Management found that projects led by senior leaders failed more often than projects led by junior managers.[11] The junior managers had the benefit of being more in touch with customers and day-to-day priorities. These valuable insights can also help to identify the best person for the job, but they can only surface if the HiPPO effect is actively countered.

Evaluating the Candidates

By the time you meet to discuss the candidates, your evaluation process should be fairly straightforward. You have assigned numerical scores to all, and hypothetically, the candidate with the highest score should get the job.

But what if it's not that simple? What if someone is the highest scorer simply because other members of the panel rated some candidates with extremely low scores? What if someone on the panel dislikes the candidate who was the top scorer? While whether or not someone "likes" a candidate is generally a sentiment steeped in bias, there is still room for conversation when committee members disagree.

If you end up debating the merits of candidates, compare them directly to one another, rather than discussing each candidate separately. Experiments conducted by Bohnet, van Geen, and Bazerman found that when job applicants were explicitly compared to one another, selection committees were more likely to choose a candidate based on performance, rather than subjective judgment.[12] In these experiments, when evaluators looked at candidate profiles individually, men were more likely to be hired for math tasks and women for verbal tasks, including both male and female candidates who had performed below par. When evaluators were comparing candidates, though, they overcame these stereotypical assessments. Comparative evaluation focused attention on individual performance, enabling evaluators to choose the top performer for the role.

Testing, Testing

So, what about personality tests like the one that Aaron agonized through in the previous chapter? Do these assessments ever make sense to use, and what about other tests, such as skills tests? In addition to behavioral interview questions, predictive tests can be helpful, when they've been vetted for bias and are used appropriately. The following tests have been reviewed by GEN and can provide a range of predictive assessments:

- *PI Behavioral Assessment.* This EFPA-certified assessment identified 17 "reference profiles" from millions of assessments to create a behavioral map for different types of people.[13] You can think of these as easy-to-reference groupings of the characteristics of people who have similar drives, suited for certain professions.

- *PI Cognitive Assessment.* Cognitive ability is the number-one predictor of job performance.[14] The timed PI Cognitive Assessment measures a person's general mental ability and capacity for critical thinking.
- *eSkill Talent Assessments.* An inventory of 800 modular, subject-based, and job-based standardized tests covers the more technical skills that you want to assess but do not have room to ask about in your interview.

If you do ask someone to take a behavioral assessment, it is important to evaluate the answers in combination with the rest of the application. Behavioral or personality assessments are considered to be less effective than cognitive assessments at predicting on-the-job performance. Personality tests can help employees gain insights into themselves, enhance team building, and inform managers on the best ways to communicate with certain employees. Rather than relying solely on personality tests to filter out candidates, though, consider them as a tool to inform how best to work with them if you hire them.

If you are going to ask candidates to take an assessment, here are some levers you can adjust to level the playing field:

- Do not ask multiple candidates to take the test in a room together at the same time. As noted earlier in this chapter, women are less likely to compete in public environments. This dynamic is activated even during test-taking. A review of SAT scores found that women's scores increased when they took the test in less crowded rooms. Even though test-takers were obviously aware that thousands of people were taking the test on the same day, physically being in a room full of other test-takers served as a reminder of the competition embedded in getting into college.[15] If group tests are necessary, attempt to make the groups as homogeneous as possible, if there are multiple test-taking sessions. Studies published in *Psychological Science* found that when women were put in groups of three and asked to complete a difficult math test, the women performed worse in the presence of men.[16]
- Allow candidates to adjust the temperature in the room. The male-default office temperatures noted in chapter 4 have a real impact on performance. Peer review studies found that women perform better on math and verbal tasks when the temperature is adjusted above the typical office setting.[17]
- Do not penalize test-takers for guessing, and be sure to state this at the beginning of the test. In 2012, the United States College Board removed the quarter-point penalty for wrong answers on SATs, and they watched the gap in scores between demographics shrink. For decades, the test had penalized test-takers for wrong answers, but not for skipping

questions. Skipping a question simply meant that you didn't accumulate points toward your overall score. Those who were more risk-averse, typically underestimated groups, guessed less often and gained fewer points toward their overall score. An analysis of SAT test scores found that women's tendency to skip more questions explained up to 40 percent of the gender gap in performance. Decreasing the risk around guessing creates a more level testing experience for all.

$\approx$

By adjusting levers in recruiting, interviewing, and testing, you've attracted a diverse set of candidates and hired the right people. Now, how do you make sure they stay?

CHAPTER 8

It's Who You Know— Protégés and Professional Development

I n 2018, 46 percent of male managers said they were uncomfortable mentoring, socializing, or meeting one-on-one with female colleagues.

In 2019, that number rose to 60 percent.[1]

A survey released by LeanIn.org and SurveyMonkey in 2019 found that senior-level male managers were nine times more hesitant to take work trips with junior women than they were with junior men. The previous year, they were only twice as hesitant to travel with women, compared to men.[2]

Multiple studies released in 2019 and 2020 came to the same conclusion: Men were less likely to mentor women than they were before the #MeToo movement. GEN's survey results showed a similar trend related to race following the rise of the Black Lives Matter movement. White respondents to GEN's survey were less likely to state they had a mentee who was a person of color than they were before 2020.

This is a pernicious problem.

In 2020, about 86 percent of Fortune 500 CEOs and over 70 percent of senior executives were white men. When underestimated individuals find the majority of white men hesitate to meet with them, they lose access to one of the most influential keys to advancement: time with senior leaders.

The Seniority Gap

Even in organizations where men and women report equal access to mentors, men's mentors are far more likely to be in senior roles. Reviewing GEN's survey results, men were twice as likely as women to state that they had been offered an opportunity to shadow someone in a senior position. Employees of color were 60 percent less likely than white employees to have had one-on-ones with a senior leader, and women of color were 70 percent less likely than white men to have been sponsored by someone in a leadership role. When Black women did have sponsors, only about a third of them reported that those sponsors were white men.[3]

Different Mentors, Different Impact

Research from Catalyst compared the advancement timelines and pay trajectories of men who have had mentors to men who have not, and women who have had mentors to women who have not.[4] While mentors have an impact on career advancement for employees of all backgrounds, men benefit much more.

Equal percentages of men and women in the study had been offered mentorship, but the results were nowhere near equal. Both mentored men and women were more likely than their non-mentored peers of the same gender to have advanced into mid-level manager roles or above. Men who had mentors, though, were 93 percent more likely than non-mentored men to be placed into higher-level roles, while mentored women were only 56 percent more likely to be placed in those roles than non-mentored women.

Having a mentor led to greater compensation benefits for men as well. Men who had a mentor were paid, on average, $6,726 more than men without a mentor. Women with a mentor were only paid $661 more than women without.

Even after taking into account the number of years of experience, region of employment, job level of the mentee, and industry, the imbalance persisted. Men benefited from mentorship more than women.

The main difference between the mentoring experiences of the genders? The seniority of the mentor.

Men's mentors were far more likely to be CEOs or executives at the senior level. This held true regardless of the job level of the mentee. A male project manager, for example, was more likely than a female project manager to get access to a senior leader.

Catalyst also tracked how these mentoring relationships were formed. Almost 70 percent of mentors were found informally, meaning that mentees had to find mentors on their own. Only 17 percent of mentoring relation-ships were arranged through a formal matching process. These figures echo my experience with most organizations I've worked with. When I ask how mentorship is initiated, I'm almost always told, "Mentorship is widely avail-able to anyone who wants it here. They just have to ask around, and they'll eventually find someone who will say yes."

When left to this kind of random selection, mentors are most likely to accept mentees who remind them of themselves. A report released by the Center for Talent Innovation found that 71 percent of executives they sur-veyed picked protégés who matched their own demographic background.[5] This built on past research they had conducted, in which they found that 58 percent of women and 54 percent of men admitted to choosing a mentee who "made them feel comfortable."[6] Given that leadership roles are largely held by men, this means that male mentees are more likely to pair up with leaders than female mentees are. White women are also likely to mentor other white women.

If underestimated individuals were intentionally paired with advanced leaders, would their pay and advancement match that of their peers? Cases in which women were matched with senior mentors suggest that it would help.

Catalyst continued to track their research participants and found that women who had mentors in senior roles advanced as quickly as men with senior-level mentors. Those women also saw their compensation increase faster than women with more junior mentors.

Access to leaders has a similar impact for employees of color. When inten-tionally paired with a sponsor in a leadership role, they reported 65 percent higher job satisfaction than non-sponsored employees of color.[7] Having male sponsors has an especially significant impact on the careers of women of color. The Working Mother Research Institute tracked multicultural women over the course of 24 months and found that those who had access to male leaders as allies were more likely to have been promoted, received a pay increase, been publicly recognized for an achievement, and been offered an opportunity to join a leadership program.[8]

Closing the mentorship seniority gap could catalyze career advance-ment and pay equality for employees of all backgrounds. It starts with inten-tional matching.

Matching with Meaning

We already know that when mentees are left to find their own mentors, white men get more access to senior leaders. This dynamic doesn't impact only mentees; it affects female leaders and leaders of color, as well. Because there are typically few of them, they often find themselves inundated with requests to be the mentors for all underestimated individuals. The one woman leader becomes the mentor for all women; the leader of color becomes the sponsor for all people of color. This can lead to burnout for leaders who already carry the pressure of being "the only" at their level but feel that they can't turn down these requests.

A mentorship matching program can evenly distribute access to senior leaders and protect underrepresented leaders from unsustainable demands on their time. It can also increase the likelihood that mentorship will evolve into sponsorship. Successful mentorship matching programs incorporate the following key elements.

An inventory of potential mentors and mentees. The mentees' information should include their goals for mentorship, skills they would like to develop, and the attributes they are seeking in a mentor. The potential mentors' information should outline their areas of expertise, as well as the amount of time they are willing to commit to a mentorship relationship. It is perfectly acceptable for a mentor to be a generalist without specific areas of expertise. Tracking expert skills is helpful for times when a mentee is seeking a specialist, but it is more important for a mentor to learn about their mentees' career goals and help them navigate their way to resources and development opportunities.

Matching mentees to more than one mentor. Use the inventory to match mentees with at least two mentors. Giving mentees a second choice protects them in case the first match is not someone they are comfortable spending one-on-one time with.

Early KPI tracking. In addition to the inventory and matching information above, include data that will be useful for tracking the access to, and impact of, mentorship over time. For both mentees and mentors, include demographic information (gender and race, if available), as well as their job levels and the amount of time they have been with your organization. This will allow you to run "seniority audits" to ensure certain groups aren't getting less access to senior leaders.

Meeting: Quality over Quantity

The time demands on senior leaders can be intense. A mentoring relationship can sound like a lot to take on, but it doesn't have to mean weekly, or even monthly, meetings. I often advise executives with full calendars to commit to quarterly meetings, with one caveat: Structure your time together for maximum impact.

If you are a first-time mentor, here are some tips for structuring your meetings to optimize your time together so the quality of your meetings can make up for quantity of time.

This meeting is not like other meetings. Do not focus on status updates or the day-to-day tasks of your mentee's job. This is the time for establishing a sense of understanding around your mentee's holistic career goals, or defining those goals if your mentee is not sure yet. This meeting should be about long-term purpose and potential.

This is the time for feedback. Your mentees would not have asked for mentoring if they didn't think they could use some advice. This is the time to identify blind spots or opportunities for improvement, provide constructive feedback, or point them to resources. Your mentees will appreciate you taking the time to identify opportunities for growth that they probably were not aware of.

What should we talk about? Even though your mentee sought out this opportunity, he or she may not know how to get the conversation going. If you don't already have a relationship with your mentee, here are some questions to help establish rapport:

- How did you end up in your current role?
- What do you look forward to each day?
- What's something you've done lately that you feel proud of?
- What drives you? What motivates you to come to work each day?

Now that the conversation is flowing, you can get more goal oriented. For example:

- What work are you doing here that you feel is most in line with your long-term goals?
- Whom do you really admire? Why?
- What are your superpowers? What powers would you like to develop?
- What do you want to do in your next job?
- Do you feel challenged at work? Are you learning new things?
- What area of the company would you like to learn more about?
- What skills would you like to develop right now?
- Who in the company would you like to learn from? What do you want to learn?
- What additional training or education would you like?
- Are there any roles in the company you'd like to learn more about?

Feedback can help employees become more self-aware and focused on specifics. Here are some questions to drive a feedback-oriented discussion:

- How do you prefer to receive feedback?
- Do you feel you're getting enough feedback? Why/why not?

- What's a recent situation you wish you had handled differently? What would you change?
- What do you think are key skills for your role? How would you rate yourself on them?
- What's an area of your work that you want to improve?
- What aspect of your job would you like more help or coaching on?

These next questions can move both of you toward deciding on action items that will make progress toward your mentee's goals:

- What's one thing we could do today to help you with your long-term goals?
- Could you see yourself making progress on more of your goals here? What would need to change to do so?
- What skills would you like to work on most right now?
- Are there any events or training you'd like to attend to help you grow your skills?

Before the end of your meeting, be sure to ask, "What do you think we can both do for next time based on the things we talked about?" Bullet point the answers each of you has for this question and add specific dates. Ask your mentee to email the list to you as soon as possible after your meeting so that you're both clear on action items.

Whether or not you use these exact guidelines or questions, the following three core elements have proven to produce the greatest benefit for underestimated mentees:

- *Onboarding/orientation meeting.* Mentees and mentors should have an initial meeting to decide on the terms of their relationship, including how frequently they meet and for how long.
- *Goals.* Overall goals, intermediary milestones, and a timeline for reaching the goals should be established in the first two meetings.
- *Feedback system.* Mentee and mentor may meet in person or by teleconference, but each meeting should be followed by written feedback from both mentor and mentee, including a summary of the meeting and agreed-upon next steps.

Mentoring After #MeToo

As noted earlier in this chapter, men are now more reluctant to mentor women than they were before the #MeToo movement. This reticence seems to be driven by a fear that women will misinterpret cordial interactions as sexual advances or that women will fabricate false harassment claims. The statistics around reporting prove these fears to be unfounded.

Disentangling hype from facts and data, actual formal complaints are exceedingly rare. The University of Massachusetts analyzed data from the EEOC and determined that, of the five million employees who are harassed each year, 99.8 percent of them never file formal complaints. Those who do often face severe retribution, with 68 percent of harassment complaints citing instances of employer retaliation and 64 percent citing incidents of job loss. Even in cases in which the plaintiffs continue to pursue their charges and are successful, the benefits are minimal. Only 23 percent receive some form of monetary compensation, the median award is $10,000, and fewer than one percent of awards exceed $100,000.

The risks of reporting still outweigh the benefits so severely that women who have not experienced harassment are far more likely to view the experience of filing a complaint as a hardship rather than an opportunity. The *Minnesota Law Review* estimates that the number of false reports, in comparison to the number of actual sexual assaults, is close to .005 percent. The odds are far greater of a man sexually harassing another man than they are of having a false claim filed against him by a woman. If the relatively few cases that have been filed by women are enough to scare men into avoiding meetings with women, the much more pervasive instances of men harassing other men should be enough to keep them from ever meeting with each other as well.

Mentoring Outside Your Circle

If you choose to mentor someone of a different gender or who comes from a different background than your own, first, congratulations. You are contributing to a culture of equity! But you may be wondering if there are aspects of your relationship that you need to navigate differently.

Be transparent and visible. Even if you understand that false harassment claims are nearly nonexistent, you may still have concerns about the perception your meetings could create. You can put questions to rest by being vocal and transparent about whom you are mentoring. Schedule mentorship meetings on your public calendar and meet in public places during work hours, not in a bar or over dinner.

The matching process can help with this visibility by incorporating public announcements of the mentor-mentee pairs as they are formed. This proactively addresses why employees who typically do not work together are having one-on-one meetings, and it encourages others to apply for mentorship, as well.

Be consistent, but acknowledge difference. Use the same structure for mentees of all backgrounds, and be consistent in the questions you ask and the help you offer. The sample questions from earlier in this chapter can help you to focus your conversation.

If you are mentoring someone of a different background, make it clear that you realize their experiences are likely different from your own and that their paths to advancement may also differ. Invite your mentees to share their experiences and whether they feel they have had to make changes to fit in. At the same time, let them know you would understand if they are not comfortable sharing. Mentors can learn from these conversations about the unique challenges that certain groups face and shape their advice or perspective, given this different baseline.

As chapter 2 outlined, some approaches that work for you may not work for someone of a different background. For example, advising your mentee to simply "ask for a raise" or speak up more during meetings ignores the risks of leaning in. Being sensitive to these risks may make you feel limited in support of your mentee, but you actually have the potential to make a bigger impact with an underestimated mentee than with anyone else.

Your mentees may not be able to ask for a raise or feel that they can assert themselves without consequences, but perhaps you can.

From Mentorship to Sponsorship

Mentorship and sponsorship are often used interchangeably, but they require different levels of commitment, advocacy, and connection. While mentorship asks you to be a guide to your mentee, pointing them to resources and reflecting lessons learned from your own experience, sponsorship requires a little more risk. It asks you to tie your reputation to someone else. Sponsoring someone means verbally advocating on their behalf, connecting them to others in your network, and volunteering their name for visible "reach" assignments.

Mentors help mentees develop a career vision for themselves, work through decisions about ways to advance their careers, and share the unwritten rules for success. Sponsors have protégés and champion their visibility, often using their own networks to connect them to high-profile assignments and people, actively involving them in experiences that enable advancement.

Sponsorship is key to getting past many of the consequences that underestimated individuals face when they *lean in*. Mentees from underestimated backgrounds may be seen as pushy or aggressive when advocating for themselves, but you can help overcome these barriers of bias by advocating on their behalf. Women, especially, have a pivotal role to play.

While women who advocate for themselves face consequences for disrupting gender norms, advocating for others has the opposite effect. Standing up for their peers, especially other women, aligns with gendered expectations of women as caring and communal-minded.[9] If you are a woman in a position of power, advocating on behalf of another woman will not receive the same backlash as advocating for yourself, and will protect women—especially women of color—from the risks of leaning in.[10]

Sponsees aren't the only ones who benefit from sponsorship; sponsors reap dividends, as well. Research from Coqual shows that sponsors become more effective leaders by having an easily accessed bench of talent that can expand their knowledge of their consumer base, pick up assignments they don't have time for, and enhance their awareness of new potential market segments.[11] Coqual's survey results show that sponsors are more likely than non-sponsors to deliver on "mission impossible" projects. Advocating for rising employees enhances how sponsors are perceived by those above them, elevating their own careers along with their sponsees'.

Choosing a Sponsee

Choosing a sponsee tends to be a more selective process than choosing a mentee. As a sponsor, you will be directly volunteering your contacts and hard-earned resources, and your reputation may be influenced by your relationship with your sponsee.

Often, potential sponsors tell me that they are interested in sponsoring someone from a different background, but they don't want to feel forced into advocating on behalf of someone they don't know. How do you brag about the accomplishments of someone you've never worked with?

It is possible to sponsor underestimated individuals in your organization even if you have not had a consistent relationship with them before. To facilitate this, widely communicate your plans to become a sponsor and allow candidates to apply informally. The following text is an example of an email announcing that you are openly inviting people to "apply" for sponsorship:

> *I am going to be making a conscious effort this year to go beyond being a mentor to being a sponsor. If you would like to be considered for sponsorship, please answer the following questions:*
>
> *Do you have a vision for your career? If so, please describe it.*
>
> *How have you demonstrated that you're capable of a leadership role or assignment?*
>
> *If I were going to advocate for you, what would I share about you with others?*

These questions provide insight into the leadership potential of people you may have never met, and they help you to imagine advocating on their behalf.

Finally, adding a statement that you are choosing to become a sponsor because you understand the impact it can have on underestimated individuals sends a powerful signal to those applicants that they will be taken seriously.

Just One

GEN survey data shows that men are 21 percent more likely than women to have been asked about their career goals in the last 12 months. If you don't have time to sponsor or mentor but still want to further the professional development of underestimated employees, asking this one question in a one-time, 15-minute check-in can serve two important functions:

1. Puts people on your radar for promotions or visible assignments whom you may not have thought of otherwise. As previously noted, we tend to associate with people who remind us of ourselves. The people we associate with most will be front-of-mind when opportunities for advancement surface. Connecting with those outside your immediate circle takes intentional effort, but it allows individuals to make their way into your mental roster of promotion candidates.

2. Provides a fast-tracked way to find out what kinds of professional development opportunities people are looking for, and connect them. You may know someone who would be a great fit as a mentor or sponsor, or you may be able to point to trainings or classes that you know are available.

Simply asking underestimated employees about their career goals makes it more likely that they will get access to the professional development opportunities they need.

Different Inboxes, Different Opportunities

"Bring Your Whole Self to Work"
 "Work–Life Balance: Find It. Keep It!"
 "Accessing Your Authenticity in the Office"

These are the subject lines that crowd my—and many women's—inboxes. The emails are usually promoting workshops or training opportunities, many of which are hosted by employers.

Men's inboxes look different, full of promotions for project management seminars, Salesforce certifications, and coding classes.

In GEN's survey, we ask respondents if they have been offered the opportunity to participate in either of the following:

- Training focused on building technical skills.
- Training focused on building business-critical skills.

For each of these options, men were at least 68 percent more likely than women to say "yes." We thought this could be because men were more likely to be working in technical or business-critical roles. So, we aggregated the data by job type.

Still, within groups of employees who performed technical roles, men were 47 percent more likely than women to say "yes," and in business-critical roles, they were 51 percent more likely.

We asked a follow-up question. For those respondents who said they had been offered these opportunities, we asked if they chose to participate, and if they found the experience valuable. Women were more likely to say "yes" to both.

Despite being more likely to take part in and value the experience, women are less likely to be invited to opportunities to grow their technical and business-critical skills. In principle, these opportunities may be open for all to take part, but men are more likely to come to mind when these programs are promoted.

Chapter 5 discussed the importance of communicating policies universally. This is just as important for professional development. If you are about to forward an announcement about a class or workshop to the perfect employee who you knew would be interested, use that as an opportunity to send it to all the employees in your department instead.

As a sponsor, check back in with your sponsees to see if they got the email. This "nudge" can be the boost that encourages them to enroll. After they have completed the course or training, ask if they would be willing to share their experience with others through a short presentation or summary in your company newsletter. This kind of peer-to-peer communication can be a powerful motivator. For example, one financial company I worked with was trying to recover the reputation of their sales workshops. They had dismissed a trainer who had marginalized women in the classes, and they had made an effort to acknowledge how the program had failed women in the past. It was only after a woman who had taken the revamped courses shared her positive experience and invited other women to talk to her about the workshop that they finally saw their female enrollment increase.

Networking That Works

In addition to inviting employees to classes and trainings, make sure they are included in your networking events as well. That inclusion starts with the planning phase.

Respectful scheduling. I have been invited three separate times to give a company talk on inclusion during Yom Kippur, the holiest day of the Jewish year. I awkwardly had to explain that as a Jew myself, that day would not work for me, and that their Jewish employees may not feel included in the scheduling of the inclusion event. Google Calendar now has a free Diversity Calendar import that can help planners avoid these kinds of mistakes. If you do not use Google Calendar, DiversityResources.com also has an excellent diversity calendar.

Inclusive hours. Try to schedule networking events during the workday. Often, networking events are hosted after hours, which means they disproportionately exclude parents, which tends to disproportionately exclude mothers, who still take on the majority of childcare duties in heterosexual working couples.

Inclusive food choices. Does your event offer halal options? Kosher options? To ensure that everyone feels comfortable joining in, distribute a quick survey before the event explicitly stating that you want to respect cultural considerations around food. Leave open-ended comment boxes so that people can note their preferences anonymously.

Sober socializing. When I worked in finance, I often felt stuck in a networking double-bind. I received a lot of advice at the time to be "one of the guys." I was encouraged to play golf, drink whiskey, and eat steak if I wanted to be included. So, when the company hosted work parties or networking events, I made a point of always having a beverage in hand, just for appearances. I would rely on old bartender tricks (drink a little, replace with soda, repeat) to look like I was keeping up with the men. The choice to drink only a little was less out of concern for my safety than for my reputation. I didn't want to appear drunk or say something inappropriate. Despite being advised to drink with the guys, I was concerned about how I would be perceived. Turns out, my fears were not unfounded.

Research conducted by the Worcester Polytechnic Institute found that women who are seen drinking are perceived as more intoxicated than they are, and their character gets called into question, which can damage their professional reputation.[12] In the study, participants were shown pictures of women standing at a bar holding a beer and women standing at a bar holding a water bottle. Similar pictures were shown of men holding beer or water. Participants were asked to rate the barflies' level of intoxication from 1 to 7. The women in the photos were not doing anything to make them seem more intoxicated than the men, but the women with a beer were assessed to be more inebriated than the men. The women holding beer were also more likely to be described as "lacking restraint" and "behaving like an animal," but these descriptions did not appear for beer-holding men.

Women who attend work functions with alcohol have to navigate competing risks. They can abstain but be seen as not playing along or taking part. Or, they can "drink with the guys" and risk their reputation. Dry events take the risk assessment out of networking events.

Required attendance from senior leaders. I often hear accounts of senior leaders treating company networking events as rare chances to get "focus time." Many underestimated individuals see these events as their chance to connect with someone on the leadership team. Often they show up to the event and see only the people they work with every day. For networking events to add value, members of the senior team must be present.

What Gets Measured Matters

How do you know if any of this is working? If your networking events appeal to everyone? If everyone is hearing about educational opportunities?

Chapter 5 discussed the importance of measuring indicators upstream that impact outcomes downstream. In addition to tracking the seniority and demographics of your mentors and mentees, be sure to include KPIs for other professional development opportunities. Each time you hold a networking event or class, try to track who is attending and who is not. If your events appear homogeneous, distribute a survey asking what would make employees more likely to attend in the future. On an individual level, how homogeneous are your one-on-one conferees or mentees? Does everyone look the same? Are you diversifying in terms of gender but not race?

≈

These KPIs can help you fine-tune how you measure your own DEI performance, and that of your organization. But what about your employees' performance?

That's next.

CHAPTER 9

Exceed Expectations— The Performance Evaluation

I n 2020, teachers had to "embrace creativity." I was lecturing in a graduate school program, and each week, I tried to think of new ways to force personality through a digital rectangle to maintain some sense of personal connection with my students. Many of them were out of their home country for the first time, quarantined and isolated, or navigating living arrangements with several roommates. When the George Floyd protests erupted in the middle of the term, I had students asking to be excused from class because they were sick from tear gas seeping in around their apartment windows. Some wanted to schedule meetings to process their feelings.

Educators were called on to balance competing forces. As their teacher, I felt like it was my responsibility to make sure they were learning, but I also wanted to be realistic about what they were up against. Grading them as if they weren't surviving a civic crisis, during a pandemic, did not seem fair.

I went a little easier on grades but made sure to be thorough in my feedback so that students still would have enough guidance to improve. I fit in as many one-on-ones as possible, some in late evening hours and on weekends. I sent emails throughout the term acknowledging the hardships they were all facing and encouraging them to reach out if they needed to miss classes or turn assignments in late.

There were two other members of my teaching team—both men. We were all teaching sessions of the same survey course at different times, and we would meet once a week to compare notes and problem-solve. I asked how they were managing all the extra one-on-one meetings and requests for accommodations. They hadn't received many requests, and they each had, on average, an extra meeting a week. My inbox was filled with appeals to turn assignments in late or reconsider grades I had given. I was taking at least 10 one-on-one meetings a week, outside of office hours.

Six weeks into the quarter, students had a chance to give midterm feedback on the instructor and the course. I received some kind, positive reviews, but I also received feedback that I was not being "lenient" enough, was not available enough, and, as one student put it, "could be more understanding." I was a little baffled. Maybe this was just par for the course. Maybe I could do more.

I checked in with my teaching team. They had not received similar comments. I asked what they were doing that I could emulate. One of them said he flat-out refused to take meetings outside office hours, would never take a meeting on a weekend, and was not allowing students to turn in assignments late, unless they were sick. The other said he simply hadn't received these kinds of requests. Both were grading their students harder than I was.

Neither of them had sent communications acknowledging what their students were coping with. They asked if they could use mine as a template and sent slightly altered versions to their own students. One of their students replied, copying the dean to say how much it meant to receive a caring email like this from an instructor.

A week later I met with the dean and asked for her insight on how I could adapt my teaching based on my students' feedback. She half-laughed and confided that she used to get the same feedback. "It's not enough to be their instructor," she said. "You're also expected to be their mom." She shared that, compared to her male colleagues, she had always endured more pushback on her grading, requests to extend deadlines, and expectations that she would listen to her students' personal problems. "In a time of crisis, everyone wants to be taken care of," she added. "You fit the profile more than your male peers. They'll want more from you."

The university decided that student evaluations would only be used for "development" purposes during the 2020–2021 academic year. In any other year, these reviews would have counted against me. The practice is not unusual. In universities across the US, student evaluations affect whether or not an instructor receives a raise, is hired to teach the next term, or is awarded tenure. Student evaluations can make or break academic careers.

For women, and people of color, evaluations often break careers.

Rate My Professor

RateMyProfessor.com, a popular site used by students to rate their professors anonymously, now boasts over 15 million reviews of professors at US, Canadian, and UK colleges and universities. Benjamin M. Schmidt, a professor of history at Northeastern University and a faculty member in the NULab for Texts, Maps, and Networks, created an online tool that allows users to enter a word, such as "smart" or "cold" and immediately see how often it is used in ratings of male instructors versus female instructors, in 25 leading disciplines.[1]

I entered "smart," "warm," "cold," and "genius." Figures 9.1 through 9.4 show the results. These four graphs display the occurrence of the words "smart," "warm," "cold," and "genius" in teacher evaluations across a range of disciplines. The words "smart" and "genius" appear more frequently in men's evaluations across all disciplines, and the words "warm" and "cold" appear more frequently in women's evaluations across all disciplines. (Disciplines on the y-axis are ordered by frequency of occurrence of search term.)

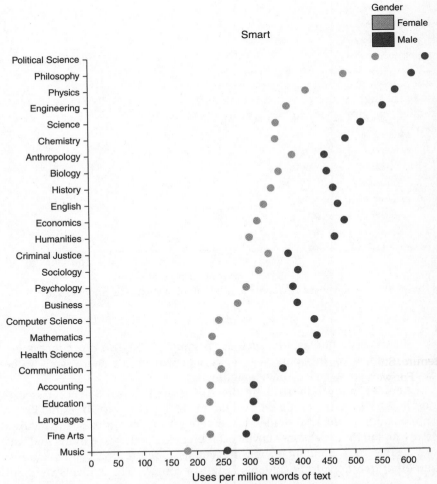

FIGURE 9.1 Occurrences of words in ratings of female vs. male professors, by discipline

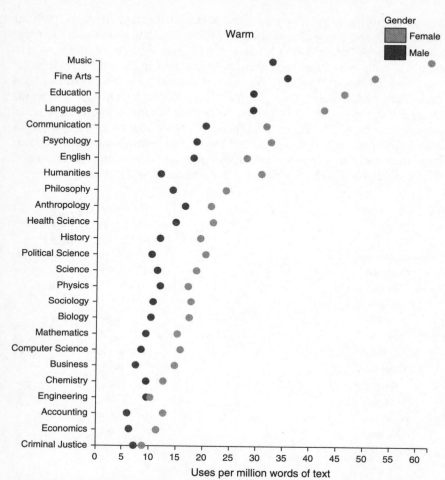

FIGURE 9.2   Occurrences of words in ratings of female vs. male professors, by discipline

Words related to fashion, such as "frumpy" or "stylish" are much more likely to show up in women's reviews, and women are more likely to be described as bossy, strict, and demanding.[2]

Another study published by the American Political Science Association in 2019 examined Student Evaluations of Teaching (SET) results for 14 online courses, which were identical except for the identities of the instructors, who taught the classes via videoconferencing tools.[3] One individual was responsible for responding to inquiries, emails, requests for accommodations, and other questions from students for all 14 courses. The students were not

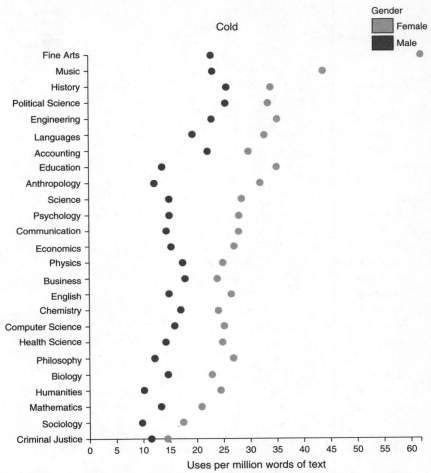

FIGURE 9.3   Occurrences of words in ratings of female vs. male professors, by discipline

aware that they were addressing a proxy rather than the instructor. The proxy responded to students across all 14 courses with the same promptness and standard of leniency.

Even with all course elements held constant—content, assignments, schedules, and communications via the proxy—women and faculty of color received lower SET scores than white men, both in assessments of the instructors and the curriculum materials. Despite correspondence with students all being driven by the same individual, only female instructors received criticism regarding their communications and correspondence.

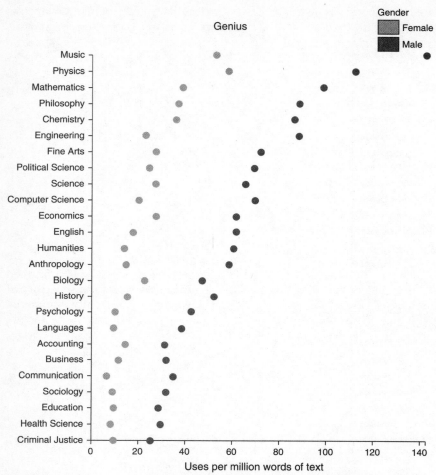

FIGURE 9.4   Occurrences of words in ratings of female vs. male professors, by discipline

A meta-analysis of hundreds of summaries of SETs found that students' evaluations were significantly influenced by how closely teachers' behaviors aligned with expected stereotypes.[4] Female instructors were rated poorly if they exhibited behaviors incongruent with gender norms. Regardless of their effectiveness as educators, female instructors were rated higher when they were assessed as communal-minded, sensitive, nurturing, available, and encouraging. Male instructors were rated higher when they displayed a more agentic nature: authoritative, assertive, independent, confident. The traits expected of men were also traits more closely associated with pedagogy. Even when women excelled in areas correlated with successful pedagogy, students rated them poorly as instructors and were less likely to recommend their class to others, if the instructors were not perceived as adhering to gender norms.

Unfortunately, students' perception of teachers' effectiveness bore little correlation to actual effectiveness. In another study that used final exams as a measure of student learning, those students who had female instructors performed better in the final exam than those who had male instructors, for the same course at different times.[5] Despite this, students rated their female instructors as less effective.

Gender and race aren't the only factors that influence SETs. Another study asked students the same basic questions found on most SETs, but also threw in one unusual question: Students were asked to rate how physically attractive their instructors were, on a scale of "not hot" to "hot." Not only were "hot" professors more likely to receive high ratings in most categories, it was nearly impossible for them to be rated poorly. Out of 100 professors with an overall rating of 4.9/5, 85 of them were professors rated as "hot." Out of 100 professors with a rating of 2.1 or below, only 2 of them were "hot" professors. The "hotness" effect was equally present for all genders.

Despite hundreds of studies on student evaluations that have confirmed the presence of bias in SETs, they still significantly impact the trajectory of instructors' careers. As stated in a Cambridge analysis of faculty evaluation, "Although the importance of SETs varies among institutions, they often are used as an indicator of teaching effectiveness, for hiring and tenure decisions, and in considerations of raises and promotions. . .likely because they constitute a low-cost metric of performance that automatically aggregates and interprets responses."[6] The biased impact of SETs on instructors' careers has been so severe that a meta-analysis published by Cambridge University Press concluded that using SETs is a "discriminatory hiring and personnel practice."[7]

I don't blame students for the impact their evaluations have on instructors' career trajectories. As part 1 explored in-depth, we all have bias, and consciously recognizing and disrupting it is extremely difficult. Students are responsible for their learning, not for ensuring their instructors are assessed fairly. That responsibility belongs to institutions. The good news is that key cultural levers can be adjusted to protect both professors and students.

Beyond the Ivory Tower

Even though universities are fundamentally dedicated to advancing knowledge and educating the next workforce, this mission can be sabotaged when bias infiltrates performance evaluations. Teachers who could have mentored students into brilliant careers are sidelined. Research dollars are allocated for reasons that may have nothing to do with the recipients' research capabilities.

Individuals evaluated as "high performers" may rise to positions of leadership, making decisions that affect their colleagues and students, simply because they were favored by biased systems of assessment. Slanted performance evaluations damage more than individual reputations. Their effects ripple out, disrupting universities' commitment to merit, evidence, and critical thinking.

The standard corporate performance evaluation poses similar domino-effect risks to other employers as well. As we explored in chapter 4, women's yearly performance reviews are far more likely to include "constructive criticism" related less to job skills and performance than to personality traits. (You're aggressive. You're not warm enough. You're too timid.) For women of color, this effect is compounded, as they are more likely to be perceived as "angry," even when their behavior mirrors that of their peers.

You may also remember that in businesses that conduct shorter but more frequent reviews—five-minute weekly evaluations focused on specific projects—the personality criticism vanishes, and the perceived performance gap between women and men is nearly nonexistent.

This cultural lever is the first of several that can be adjusted to assess and reward performance accurately.

What Gets Measured Matters

In addition to focusing on personality, women's performance evaluations tend to focus more on skills that are not as promotable, even if the distribution of their responsibilities is similar to that of their male counterparts. Men are more likely to receive longer performance reviews focused on the technical aspects of their jobs; women's reviews tend to be shorter and concerned with the communications aspects of their roles. For example, a meta-analysis of reviews of medical faculty found that reviews of female instructors were more likely to refer to teaching instead of research, even when they conducted as much research as their male colleagues.[8] Their reviews also tended to be shorter and were more likely to raise doubt (faint praise, hedges, unexplained negative comments).

The feedback women receive is also more likely to be vague, lacking specific directives for improvement or clear connection to business outcomes. A review of performance evaluations across three large high-tech companies and a professional services firm found that even when women received positive feedback, it came in the form of a general "You're doing a good job!" or "You had a great year!"[9] These comments failed to highlight the specific skills that were valued or the impact the employee made on business outcomes. Negative criticism tended to focus on communication, even for technical roles, and lacked specific recommendations for career development. Comments such as

"Her approach can be off-putting" were common in women's reviews and were not paired with suggestions of ways to improve.

The feedback men received tended to be more detailed, focused on technical skills, and paired with constructive suggestions for improvement, such as "You need to deepen your domain knowledge in the X space—once you have that understanding, you will be able to contribute to the design decisions that impact the customer."

Without specific feedback on the skills they need to develop, women won't know where to focus. Without a documented record of contributing to business accomplishments, they are also at a disadvantage when pitching for promotions. These missed opportunities can lead to women being sidelined into support functions, which typically do not advance into leadership roles, becoming dissatisfied, and leaving the employer. To salvage the value that performance evaluations could have, we must design in constraints.

Closing the "Open Box"

The "open box" on performance reviews usually presents as a comment field, prefaced by a generic question that can apply to every employee in the company: "How did this employee succeed?" or "How did this employee not meet expectations?"

The question is convenient, in that it can apply to everyone. It is also ambiguous. Managers have to reinvent what success looks like for each employee, and what expectations their employees are supposed to meet. Researchers from INSEAD and Stanford compared the results of two different kinds of performance evaluations to understand how this ambiguity plays out.[10]

In reviews featuring the unstructured "open box," reviewers redefined merit or success depending on the gender of the employee being reviewed. They did not necessarily view men and women as having different strengths, but they redefined the criteria for success in comparable roles based on the skills stereotypically associated with the employee's gender. Stereotypes about women's capabilities meant that reviewers were less likely to focus on technical accomplishments or contributions to business outcomes. Their achievements were also more likely to be credited to "teamwork" rather than "leadership."

In an alternative experiment, Stanford's VMware lab asked managers to commit to a set of criteria before the review to see what role constraints could play in closing this gap. When managers committed to and consistently applied criteria to their evaluations of employees, the performance gap between genders disappeared almost entirely. While the "top performers" categories had previously been mostly male, when managers used checklists, women and men were proportionately represented in the top, middle, and lower performance categories.[11] Over 90 percent of managers reported that the process helped them be more consistent in the ways they evaluated their reports. Employees of all backgrounds were more likely to receive constructive feedback.

With no clear guidelines for evaluation, bias fills the void. With structured criteria, though, managers can see beyond gender, race, and other stereotypes when assessing performance.

But not all criteria are created equal.

What Are the Criteria for Criteria?

Measuring performance is difficult. Some fields have developed longstanding definitions of success intended to make it easier. Professors, for example, are encouraged to work toward one crowning metric: the "h-index". This composite assessment is meant to measure both the impact and the productivity of scholars by counting the number of publications for which an author has been cited by other authors. For example, an h-index of 17 means that the scientist has published at least 17 papers that have each been cited at least 17 times.[12] An h-index score above 40 is considered difficult to achieve, while interviewing for tenure with a single-digit h-index score is pretty much a lost cause. This metric is so widely used and understood that Google Scholar can give academics up-to-the-minute calculations of their h-index scores, on-demand.

Most fields and professions, though, lack the equivalent of an h-index. In businesses where many employees are knowledge workers, finding this kind of clarity is difficult. Knowledge workers want to prove that they are contributing to business outcomes, but units of delivery are less tangible, and they are rarely the output of a sole individual. In an attempt to measure performance and productivity, many business leaders revert to an era of easily measurable production: the industrial age. While knowledge workers don't stand at an assembly line and can't point to a number of widgets produced per hour, they can sit at their computers, send and answer emails, respond to instant messages immediately, and roam open office spaces, "checking in" with everyone, appearing busy. Businesses that have adopted these behaviors as measures of performance are relying on what Georgetown University professor Cal Newport calls "busyness as proxy for productivity."

In his book, *Deep Work*, Newport argues that the criteria that comprise this proxy are actually antithetical to the kind of work most knowledge workers are hired to do. Their work requires deep focus, but if "emails per hour" is a criterion that is measured, employees will work toward that metric. Even if someone was hired to perform analysis that requires deep concentration, if busyness is rewarded, the focus-destroying behaviors that go along with it will take priority.

Investing the time to develop meaningful criteria is crucial to optimizing performance. When employees know how their performance is measured, they will align their behavior to that version of success. When criteria are not carefully rendered, businesses see poor organizational performance, even with confusingly high individual performance. When developed with care, however, criteria bring these two tracks into alignment.

The process of thinking through criteria is just as important as the process of abiding by them. Here are some guidelines for developing performance evaluation rubrics with meaningful metrics.

Quantify competencies. In chapters 6 and 7 we discussed how competency-based hiring will increase your odds of selecting the best candidate for the job. Focusing on those same competencies can also help you evaluate how well an employee is performing in a role. Performance evaluations, though, should go a step further by quantifying the level of maturity employees have achieved in these competencies. This level of evaluation documents progress over time and identifies readiness for promotions. For example, in the hiring chapter, we used "client focus" as a sample competency. For performance evaluations, you could establish five levels of maturity for this competency, as follows:[13]

- Level 1—Responds to immediate client needs in a timely, helpful, professional manner. Meets service standard.

- Level 2—Maintains client contact by keeping client up-to-date. Follows up with client to ensure their needs have been met. Addresses client concerns in order of urgency.

- Level 3—Provides value beyond clients' immediate needs. Anticipates clients' needs and concerns. Enhances client delivery processes.

- Level 4—Provides seasoned advice by proactively bringing possible issues to client's attention, in their best interest. Advocates on behalf of client. Assists with decision-making.

- Level 5—Ensures continued service excellence by evaluating future opportunities and threats to meeting clients' needs. Evaluates the client service model to identify opportunities for improvement. Highlights how business strategy can better align with meeting clients' needs.

Document examples. When evaluating your employee's level of maturity, note specific examples. The STAR method used for hiring can be used to assess maturity levels as well. Include the Situation or Task in which the employee was involved, the Action that the employee took to complete the task or address the situation, and the Result of the employee's action. This structure requires evaluators to focus on the kind of evidence that guards against bias. In addition, your employee's growth is documented, which plays a critical role in underestimated individuals being considered for promotions.

Tie performance to progress toward individual goals. Evaluating performance as progress toward preset goals turns reviews into tools for development, which can lead to more meaningful feedback, and in turn, advancement. Goals can be competency-based or not, but they should be measurable. If competency-based, for example, employees could set a goal to reach a certain level of maturity within a year. Other goals could focus on finishing a course, aspiring to meet with reports a certain number of times a quarter, or coming in under budget on 90 percent of projects. Each evaluation or check-in could measure if they are 10 percent of the way to the goal, 20 percent of the way, and so on. Checking in on goals frequently also aligns with the best practice we discussed earlier of conducting rolling, shorter reviews, instead of a single yearly evaluation.

Tie performance to business outcomes. Your rubric should also include a list of strategic organizational goals, with space to note how employees contributed to them. While this is an "open box" approach, it introduces constraints to ensure that *all* employees have a chance to document how they have contributed to *all* business outcomes. This way, women are not evaluated only on communication outcomes, and men on technical outcomes. This "open box" also provides enough space to recognize contributions that may not fit within competencies or individual goal-setting. Listing business outcomes keeps them in employees' line of sight, reminding them of organizational goals they are working toward.

Include everything, even office "housework." When delivering talks, there's an example I always know will get a knowing laugh or nod from the women in the audience: The Office Birthday Party. Even though I have terrible handwriting, decorating skills, and taste in birthday cake, I've been asked to join the Party Planning Committee in every office where I've worked. Office housework is not just limited to party planning. It encompasses a range of tasks that are necessary but offer no career advancement reward, such as refilling the coffee filters, arranging the conference room for the client meeting, or making templates look "pretty" even if that task has nothing to do with one's job. Women, and especially women of color, are asked to take on these tasks more often.[14] This work didn't disappear when workers went remote during COVID. It simply morphed into finding a time when people could meet remotely, sending links to birthday ecards for everyone to sign, and picking up the mail for the staff. When women resist, they're often told it's a chance to be a "team player." This kind of time-intensive, low-prestige work does not have the same benefits, however, as pitching in on a challenging project or working extra hours for a visible client. One set of work leads to promotions, while the other does not.

When this kind of work is tracked and rewarded, though, men pick up more of it. Knowing that this work is part of all employees' evaluations motivates co-workers to distribute the tasks evenly. In addition, the time that individuals put into this type of work is finally accounted for, explaining why some employees may not have been as available for other opportunities.

Pre- and Post-Evaluation

What you do before and after the evaluation can make or break the success of your carefully selected criteria. Take these steps to get the most out of your performance evaluation rubric.

Share the criteria ahead of time. Too often, I hear that the performance evaluation is the first time employees learn how they are to be assessed. Managers should schedule separate meetings for discussing criteria and business outcomes, and for goal-setting. This also puts employees' goals on their managers' radar, so they can keep an eye out for opportunities that can help the employees succeed.

Managers should not see employees' self-evaluations before evaluating them. In a study examining self-perceptions of effectiveness, men show a tendency to rank themselves as more effective than they are, and women tend to rank themselves as less effective than they are.[15] This is especially true in areas in which men are expected to have expertise. If managers read employees' self-evaluations before writing their own, they risk being influenced by their employees' biased self-perceptions. As chapter 10 will explore in-depth, the role that self-evaluations play in decisions regarding pay or performance bonuses has been a significant factor in perpetuating the wage gap. This next chapter will propose some alternatives.

Ban personality words. If there is one word I would ban from performance evaluations, it would be "aggressive." In the same Stanford VMware studies that compared structured and unstructured evaluations, 76 percent of references to being "too aggressive" were in evaluations of women.[16] Communicating to managers that performance evaluations are not an opportunity to assess personality helps keep the focus on competencies, progress toward goals, and contributions to business outcomes. Ahead of evaluations, distribute a list of words such as "cold," "warm," "aggressive," and "likeable" that will not be accepted in performance reviews. If employees do exhibit problematic behaviors or have communications weaknesses, those can be addressed in a separate conversation.

Audit evaluations. Compare the results of performance appraisals by gender, race, and the intersection of the two. Is one group consistently rated higher than others? Do groups appear proportionately represented in each tier of performance? Do evaluations of certain individuals focus more on one set of skills than others with similar roles?

In addition, consider auditing evaluations for "performance support bias"—a bias in which overconfidence in certain groups' abilities gives them more access to opportunities. These opportunities in turn allow them to outperform their peers, reinforcing the original belief that they outperform others. A study conducted by Wharton School professor Janice Fanning Madden provides a clear example.[17] The gender pay gap in US stockbrokerage firms is 12 cents larger on the dollar than the average pay gap in the US. For the past 15 years, on average, female stockbrokers made less than 66 cents on the dollar, compared to male stockbrokers. Madden wanted to find out why.

Compensation for stockbrokers largely depends on the commissions earned on their sales. The obvious explanation that women were getting paid less seemed to be that men were outperforming them. Madden found a different reason. Because managers assumed that men were better at selling, they gave them transfer accounts that already had a profitable track record to start with, avoiding "risking" these accounts on women. Women were assigned inferior accounts, or given new accounts instead of transfers. The superior selling opportunities that men had access to led to gendered differences in performance-based pay. When given accounts with equivalent sales histories, women produced sales equal to those of their male counterparts.

When reviewing performance evaluations, check for this kind of bias. If account-based employees seem to be underperforming, take a look at the way accounts were originally assigned to them. Were they transfer accounts with robust sales histories, or were they new accounts that were just starting to grow?

≈

Performance evaluations and pay go hand-in-hand. As the next chapter explores, so do hiring and pay. And job descriptions and pay. And promotions and pay. Closing the pay gap doesn't just lead to pay equity—it leads to equity of opportunity for all employees.

But first, what is the pay gap, anyway?

CHAPTER 10

The Physiology of Pay

The compensation specialist at a company I was working with came to me one day with a thumb drive of pay data from the last 10 years. He was exasperated.

"Sara," he said, "every year we run a pay gap audit, and we find gaps. We increase salaries, and years later the gaps are back. I don't know what I'm doing wrong. What am I not seeing here? How is this possible?"

He wanted me to review his spreadsheets and find a bug, an error in their pay analysis algorithms. I removed the thumb drive from my USB port, closed my laptop, and asked him a few questions:

"Do you use referrals for hiring?"

"Do you invite candidates to negotiate their offer?"

"How do you use self-evaluations?"

He was flustered and annoyed. "Why are you asking me this? We're talking about pay."

I, also, was talking about pay.

I understood his confusion, and I explained that the data in these spreadsheets were just symptoms. To stop them from recurring, we had to find out what was causing them. Left untreated, these gaps would open back up, and they could cause other problems, like attrition, low morale, and low productivity. The salary increases were just short-term Band-Aids, and the spreadsheets didn't capture the cause or the full impact of pay inequities.

The pay data was only the anatomy. We needed to understand the physiology.

Pay Does Not Exist in a Vacuum

When I tell people that my work focuses on workplace equity, they often say, "Oh, like closing the pay gap?" I'm never quite sure how to respond. DEI encompasses so much more than pay, and, at the same time, those "other" agents of equity I focus on inevitably impact pay. Even when it doesn't appear that I'm working on closing the pay gap, I frequently am.

Organizations seeking to close their own pay gap for the long term must start with the underlying policies that interact with pay. In this chapter we will define pay equity and explore how to conduct a pay gap audit, what to do when you find gaps, and how much transparency is enough. If other cultural levers are not adjusted first, though, these steps will not matter. Closing opportunity gaps in hiring, evaluations, and promotions is key to sustaining equal pay. The following policies and processes may not seem compensation-related, but they have an inevitable indirect impact on pay equity.

The Referral

Referrals can feel like a foolproof way to build your talent pipeline. Your current employees know what it takes to succeed in your organization's culture, and odds are good that you trust their judgment. Relying on referrals, though, can hurt your efforts to build a diverse workforce and progress toward pay equity.

The compensation analytics company Payscale surveyed 53,000 workers to understand the impact of referrals on hiring and pay.[1] Their research shows that, holding other factors constant, white men are more likely to be hired from referrals than white women, women of color, and men of color. While white men make up 34 percent of the labor force, they make up 40 percent of referrals. In addition, men are more likely to experience a salary bump from being referred, compared to referral-based hires of other backgrounds. Payscale's analysis shows that white men who receive a business-contact-based referral experience an $8,200 salary increase, while women experience only a $3,700 salary increase. Men who receive referrals from their extended network (connections of immediate connections) also experience a $3,200 increase, while referrals from extended networks have no impact on women's pay.

The referral gap is two-fold: Men are more likely to receive the kinds of referrals that lead to pay increases, and the increases themselves are likely to be larger than those women receive, even when they are referred in. This doesn't mean that you have to do away with employee referrals entirely. The following steps can optimize your candidate referral systems to limit pay inequities.

Use standardized hiring and pay rubrics to avoid giving special treatment to referrals. Make referrals go through the same steps that every other hire goes through. The standardized hiring practices from chapters 6 and 7 should help counter the biases that favor candidates who "know someone," to ensure the most qualified candidate is the one who gets hired, but they must be applied consistently. If other candidates are required to have multiple rounds of interviews and a skills test, referrals should as well. Just as interviews should have structured guidelines, your pay decisions also should be driven by standardized criteria. I present the key elements of a pay rubric later in this chapter, but regardless of the exact pay criteria you choose, the rubric should be applied consistently to all new hires.

Consider an "extra" bonus for diversity referrals. Referral bonuses are already a widely used practice. The technology sector leads the pack, with 58 percent of employers in the industry saying they offer referral bonuses.[2] Some companies are countering the inequities that can result from this practice by adding extra bonuses for referrals that help them meet their DEI goals. Intel, for example, doubles the referral bonus employees get if they refer in a hire from an underrepresented background.[3] Incentives such as referral bonuses can be the push that gets employees to think consciously of qualified candidates from diverse backgrounds who would make great hires.

Audit. Audit. Audit. Chapter 5 explored the importance of evaluating KPIs "upstream" to better understand metrics downstream. Collecting data around referrals is one of these "upstream" opportunities. When hiring, make sure to note in a database whether the hire was a referral, how much they were offered, how much they actually signed for, whether they were given a sign-on bonus, and their demographics. This way, you can analyze your data on new hires to understand if referrals—or referrals of certain backgrounds—are getting special treatment. Analyzing this data can help you catch opportunity gaps before you are forced to discover them later as pay gaps.

The Offer

Following her very public Silicon Valley discrimination lawsuit in 2015, Ellen Pao gained further notice in her role as Reddit's interim CEO by introducing a controversial new policy: She banned salary negotiations. Citing the social risks that women and people of color face when they try to negotiate, Pao believed that banning negotiations could play a role in closing the pay gap. "As part of our recruiting process we don't negotiate with candidates," Pao stated. "We come up with an offer that we think is fair. If you want more equity, we'll let you swap a little bit of your cash salary for equity, but we aren't going to reward people who are better negotiators with more compensation."

We've learned that unstructured interviews can reward the person who is the best at interviewing, but not necessarily the best for the role. Similarly, open negotiations reward great negotiators who may not actually be more deserving of higher wages than their peers. A study from UC Berkeley found that negotiators tend to believe women are more easily deceived and therefore *try* to deceive them more often than men, because they think they will get away with it.[4] In addition to the social risks that women face when negotiating, they also have to try to judge whether their negotiator is being honest with them.

If you aren't ready to take the Ellen Pao route and abolish negotiations, you can still take other steps to debias the offer-and-negotiation process.

State the salary range. Candidates who are negotiating a job offer typically ask for a 10 to 20 percent increase over their previous salary.[5] Given that men have traditionally been paid more for similar roles, they enter negotiations from higher ground. Women and people of color would have to ask for a particularly large increase over their previous pay to negotiate from the same starting point. Sharing a salary range that the employer is willing to pay helps level this negotiating field. Studies published in the *Journal of Personality and Social Psychology* show that women are more successful negotiators, and the gender wage gap narrows when job applicants are clearly informed about the pay range for a position, benefits, and other conditions that are negotiable.[6]

Proactively offer every candidate the chance to negotiate. Because women and people of color face social risks by negotiating on behalf of themselves, they are less likely to initiate the conversation on their own. Women are as likely as men to negotiate, though, *if offered the chance.*[7] That chance, unfortunately, is offered to men more often. Studies published in *Industrial Relations: A Journal of Economy and Society* found that 49 percent of men and 35 percent of women in their sample were offered the opportunity to negotiate their pay during a job offer. The study also found that when employers do not explicitly share that wages are negotiable, men are more likely than women to take a chance on negotiating. When employers do proactively offer that wages are negotiable, though, the gap in willingness to negotiate disappears and is even slightly reversed. While men negotiate and succeed more often when "rules" around wages are ambiguous, women ask and succeed more often when opportunities and wage boundaries are made clear. When underestimated individuals don't have to violate norms by initiating a negotiation on their own behalf, they face less risk.

Don't ask for previous salaries or salary expectations. By mid-2021, 21 states had implemented Salary History Bans (SHB) that prohibit employers from asking candidates for their salary history. Emerging research on the states and territories that have already had SHBs in effect for several years suggests that they have played a significant role in closing earnings gaps between genders and racial demographics. Boston University's School of Law studied the impact of SHBs in 12 states and concluded that they closed gaps for women by 6.2 percent and African Americans by 5.9 percent.[8] Without this ban, the inequity that starts with a candidate's first job can carry over from one job offer to the next. A candidate's salary history may have nothing to do with actual skills or value. Instead it could be a result of a variety of other factors—discrimination, reduced hours from taking time off for caretaking, or from having worked in an industry that was female-dominated, and therefore underpaid because it was considered "women's work."[9] Initial offers affect employees' future earnings, including raises, bonuses, and retirement contributions. If your organization is not currently in one of these 21 states, you can catalyze progress toward closing the pay gap—and the long-term wealth gap—by banning questions about salary history from your offer process.

Separate Self-Evaluations from Pay (and Promotion) Decisions

Hiring has gotten a lot of the spotlight in the pay gap discussion, but policies that impact employees after they have been hired can play an even more significant role in expanding the pay gap. As discussed in the previous chapter, underestimated individuals tend to be more modest in their self-evaluations than their white male peers. In his book, *How to Be Good at Performance Appraisals*, Dick Grote asserts that self-evaluations are actually the least accurate measure of employee performance: "Study after study consistently demonstrated that individuals are notoriously inaccurate in assessing their own performance, and the poorer the performer, the higher (and more inaccurate) the self-appraisal."[10] The consulting firm Lominger Limited, Inc., published a study that echoed this. They found that the correlation between self-ratings and actual performance was .00.[11]

When these self-evaluations land in the hands of a manager who is making pay raise decisions, these inaccuracies easily turn into pay inequities. If a manager has $10,000 in pay increases to allocate, and she receives a self-evaluation from Bob saying he's exceeded expectations and deserves a $7,000 raise, and another self-evaluation from Mary that's more reserved and that asks for less, these biased self-perceptions will have consequences. Even if these employees performed equally, or Mary outperformed Bob, the manager has no reason not to give Bob a larger raise. The employees' internalized biases may influence their manager's perceptions of them, or the manager may simply not have the energy to put up the fight against Bob. When self-evaluations are allowed to influence pay decisions, managers end up rewarding aggrandized self-perceptions, rather than actual performance. Self-assessments can be effective tools for development and tracking accomplishments, but they should not influence pay or promotion decisions.

Defining the Pay Gap: Equity vs. Equality

By the time the US Women's National Soccer Team (WNT) faced off against Thailand in the 2019 World Cup, their fight off the field had garnered as much attention as their championship match. Their campaign for equal pay had even become a talking point during the presidential primary campaigns:

"The USWNT is #1 in the world and contributes higher revenue for @USSoccer than the men's team, but they're still paid a fraction of what the men earn. Women deserve equal pay for equal (or better!) work in offices, factories, AND on the soccer field," tweeted Senator Elizabeth Warren.

Senator Kirsten Gillibrand tweeted, "Here's an idea: If you win 13–0, the most goals for a single game in World Cup history, you should be paid at least equally to the men's team."

The WNT would go on to earn their fourth World Cup that year. The US men's team failed to qualify for the World Cup, again, and continued to be paid more than the women, again.

The class action suit that followed became a microcosm of the discussions that ensue every time a "pay gap" is discussed. What about performance? How much revenue does each party bring in? Do other forms of support, like field maintenance, count as compensation?

As the WNT's case played out, it became clear that what they were fighting for was pay *equity*, defined as equal pay for equal work. Defining equal work was tricky. They had to choose controls. For their argument, they chose the following.

Revenue Generated: Sponsorship revenue for the US Soccer Federation jumped 25 percent between fiscal year 2015 and 2016, when the women won the 2015 World Cup. Sponsorships are difficult to trace back directly to a single team, though, since they are sold as a bundle for all soccer games. Ironically, the publicity that the women's fight for equal pay created drove record-breaking merchandise revenue. Nike Chief Executive Mark Parker noted that the WNT's jersey became the number-one-selling soccer jersey, men's or women's, ever sold on Nike.com. Finally, the women's games brought in more revenue than the men's games in every year since the women won the 2015 World Cup.

Effort: The WNT typically played more games per year than the men's team, and in 2018, they played almost double the number of games.

Performance: The total prize money for the 2019 Women's World Cup was $30 million, and the winners walked away with about $4 million. For the 2018 Men's World Cup, the total pool was $400 million, and the champions walked away with just over $38 million, more than all the women's teams combined. Men's teams actually earned $3,000 more for a *loss* in a World Cup *qualifying* game than the women's team that won the World Cup.

Not All Analyses Are Created Equal

In 2020 I sat on the advisory council that helped create the Fair Pay Workplace certification and directed the auditing process for the council's first class of certified businesses. A dozen of us, including compensation experts, corporate HR presidents, and former EEOC chairs, spent months debating what the rules should be for conducting a pay gap audit the "right" way.

Not all methods of pay analysis are created equal. Most of them follow the same general format: Categorize employees into different professional groupings by role, implement controls that would explain differences in pay, and run regression analyses to compare the pay of different demographic groups. Within that high-level methodology, though, the advisory council found that there was still a lot of room to draw different conclusions about the same set of data. We finally agreed on a set of best practices that assess pay equity accurately and intersectionally. These guidelines are summarized below, along with the red flags that would give us pause when evaluating an organization.

Step #1: Choosing Groupings

The first step in comparing "apples to apples" is grouping employees by similar roles. For example, employers may group all engineers together, all administrative professionals together, and all creative services professionals together. Employees should be grouped together who conduct comparable work, and each of these groups should be analyzed separately to understand if employees within them are being paid similarly.

- *Red Flag*: Employees grouped together who do not share a similar function. Pay analyses cannot measure equal pay for equal work by comparing, for example, administrative assistants' pay to engineers' pay.
- *Red Flag*: Grouping by job code, level, or job family, without explicit grouping criteria for each category. Without any clear schema for organizing work this way, Level 1 could simply be all employees in the bottom pay quartile, Level 2 could be in the second pay quartile, and so on. When comparing these employees to one another, it will appear that employees within each group are paid similarly, but that doesn't mean that pay is being compared among employees who conduct similar work.

Step #2: Choosing Controls

Within groupings, the effort, risk, or education needed for a given role may affect how individuals within that group are paid. Controls can be understood as the factors that explain why employees in the same grouping may be paid different amounts. (Statisticians often refer to this as "variance explained.") To be effective, controls should be

- *Job-related and objective.* Relevant to skill, effort, risk, or accountability. For example, controls could include educational degree completed, years of experience, level of risk, hard-to-fill status, or level of accountability.

- *Neutral.* Not related to gender, race, age, or other demographic characteristic.

The chosen controls act as quantifiable measures that are applied to regression tests to assess whether protected classes (such as women or people of color) account for pay differences.

- *Red Flag*: Using "age" as a proxy for experience. Employers may not know how many years of relevant experience their employees have, which leads them to use age as a proxy. As with any proxy, though, it often does not work. For example, in industries and roles where switching careers is common, age is not representative of years of experience.

- *Red Flag:* Level (or grade). Similar to using "level" or "grade" as a grouping, using them as controls within groups can lead to inaccuracies. Because different managers might use different factors to define level, implementing this control evenly can be difficult. Instead, control for the factors that should determine level, such as tenure, education, or managerial status.

- *Red Flag*: Multicollinearity. This statistical term is code for controlling for the same factor multiple times, in seemingly different ways, for example, choosing both "tenure in months" and "tenure in years" as controls, or both "managerial status" and "has reports." Choosing redundant or overlapping controls inaccurately amplifies the impact that a single control can have on your regression analysis. The role that this factor plays in explaining gaps can become overemphasized and make gaps appear smaller than they are.

- *Red Flag*: Using performance evaluations as a control. As discussed in the previous chapter and this chapter, self-evaluations and performance evaluations from managers can carry significant bias. Unless you have implemented the measures discussed in these chapters to minimize this bias and have audited your evaluations for bias, rethink how you are using performance evaluations to decide pay.

Step #3: Identifying and Analyzing the Gap— Regression Analysis

For many of us, regression analysis may be a distant high school memory. To avoid turning this book into a statistics manual, this section assumes that you have someone in-house who can load your employee compensation data, group the data by the criteria you have chosen, apply the controls, and filter the data by "protected categories" (PC), such as gender, race, and the intersection of the two. After that, you should get graphs that look roughly like figures 10.1 through 10.3. These three models show the actual compensation of employees, and their predicted compensation. One chart models this information by gender, another by race, and another by the intersection of the two.

In addition to the traditional questions your compensation expert will ask—Is the data skewed? Can the outliers be explained?—the following guidelines will help drive an equity-centered analysis.

Choose an accurate measure of central tendency. In 2019, Starbucks released a report stating that they had achieved total pay equity. They voluntarily disclosed a set of statistics showing zero pay discrepancy between men and women, and no gaps along racial lines, either. While many praised the Seattle-based coffee giant for their pay equity achievement, data scientists were holding their applause. A close look at Starbucks's report found that they used the median to define average pay. When Starbucks disclosed their pay data to the UK, they were required to reveal both the median and the mean. When the mean defined average pay, Starbucks showed a 5 percent pay disparity between men and women.

As you may remember from middle school math, the median is the middle value that separates the data in half, with lower values on one end and higher values on the other. When Starbucks used the median to say they have no pay gap, they were actually saying that the man who makes the middle amount of all men is paid the same as the woman who makes the middle amount of all women. In any large service-based or retail company, this argument is not convincing.

Using the median to calculate averages isn't always "wrong." This measure of central tendency is often used to control for outliers that can significantly skew an average.

If you're analyzing pay data for the purpose of identifying gaps, though, the median is not the most accurate measure, especially for a company like Starbucks. The majority of their 300,000 employees work in coffee shops, and their wages are standardized. When the comparatively few corporate employees are lumped together with the coffee shop employees who make similar wages, and the median is the measure of central tendency, any gaps between corporate employees disappear. They just become part of the group on the other side of the coffee-house-wage median. The median treats corporate employees like outliers and gives no sense of what the distribution of pay actually looks like at the corporate level.

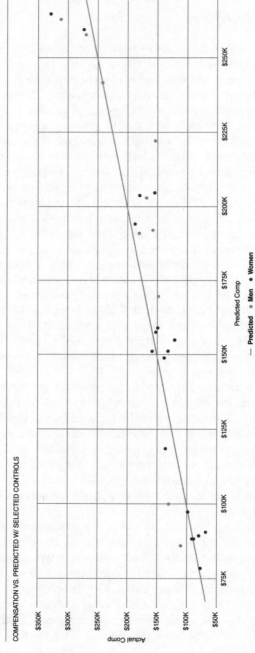

FIGURE 10.1 Comparing predicted and actual compensation, by gender

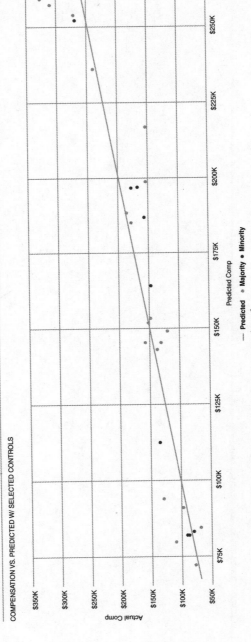

White vs. Non-White Human Resources

COMPENSATION VS. PREDICTED W/ SELECTED CONTROLS

FIGURE 10.2   Comparing predicted and actual compensation, by race

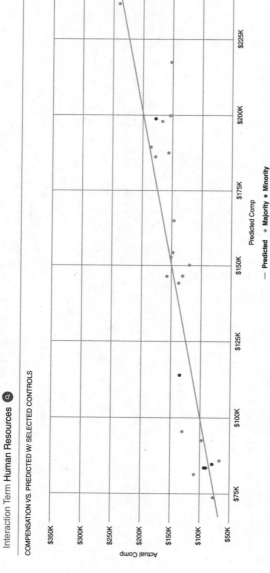

FIGURE 10.3 Comparing predicted and actual compensation, by intersection of race and gender

While the mean would not have perfectly captured this difference, it would have been more accurate.

Analyze your data with an intersectional lens. As chapter 6 covered, siloing your race data and siloing your gender data can hide gaps that exist for women of color. When analyzing your pay data, make sure to look at the intersection of gender and race, as well as any other intersections you have enough data to explore. Large companies should also be able to analyze their data by age and caretaker status, to search for any ageism or stigmatization of parents in pay decisions.

Measure total compensation. If your organization pays employees commissions, bonuses, or other rewards on top of their base salary, include that in your compensation analysis. As noted in the previous chapter, in performance-based or commissions-based businesses, gaps between what women earn and what men earn can often be attributed to factors that have nothing to do with performance, such as a biased allocation of accounts. If this type of compensation is not included in pay gap analyses, you won't be able to uncover these below-the-surface gaps.

You Found a Gap—Now What?

In 2015, Salesforce CEO Marc Benioff provided a master class in equity-centered leadership. As Benioff shares in his book *Trailblazer*, two of his top female executives, Cindy Robbins and Leyla Seka, brought to his attention that Salesforce, they believed, had a gender pay gap.[12] At first, Benioff was defensive and skeptical. "Back in 2015, I knew we still had a long way to go on this issue, but I was utterly convinced that Salesforce belonged to the tiny minority of tech companies that truly valued gender equality. I simply did not believe that pay disparities could be pervasive. 'Impossible,' I told them. 'That's not right. That's not how we operate.' Cindy leveled her gaze. Then, in the measured tone she'd used to talk me out of wrongheaded positions in the past, she explained that she'd invited Leyla to join her at this meeting because they had both independently arrived at the same concern."

Benioff approved a pay audit for all 17,000 Salesforce employees.

When the audit concluded, not only did Benioff accept the findings that there was a pay gap impacting 6 percent of their employees, he publicly announced that Salesforce had a pay gap, would be spending the $3 million needed to remedy it, and would continue to monitor their pay going forward.

One year after conducting their first audit, they acquired another company, which changed their headcount. So they ran the numbers again, and found out they needed to spend another $3 million adjusting salaries to account for inherited inequities. Again, Benioff publicly announced these findings and their plans to close the gap.

Most CEOs of publicly traded companies would be terrified of this level of transparency.

Studies from Payscale show that Benioff made the right call.[13] They surveyed 71,000 employees to determine which factors most strongly correlate with employee satisfaction and engagement. An employer's ability to communicate clearly about compensation played a larger role in employee sentiment than traditional measures of employee engagement, such as opportunities for career advancement.

In fact, the study found that an employer's transparency around pay could actually have more of an impact than pay itself. Employees tend to think they are being paid unfairly, even when it isn't true. Payscale's study found that two-thirds of people who are being paid the market rate for their jobs believe they are being paid less than the market rate.

Even for employees who are being paid below market rate, Payscale found that if an employer can explain their pay decisions, this transparency can mitigate negative sentiment over lower pay. As Payscale's Chief Product Officer Dave Smith summarized in a *Harvard Business Review* article on this study, "If an employer pays lower than the market average for a position, but communicates clearly about the reasons for the smaller paycheck, 82 percent of employees we surveyed still felt satisfied with their work. Conversely, we found overpaying employees in an effort to retain them without having this larger conversation about pay doesn't ensure they are more satisfied. Our study showed it is more effective for employers to compensate top talent at market value and discuss how pay was determined than to pay them more than market value and keep company compensation practices shrouded in secrecy."[14]

Many employers I have worked with confide that they are hesitant to share their pay data or strategy with their employees because they don't want to "stir the pot." I assure them that I have yet to work with an organization where the pot wasn't already being stirred. Sharing pay data is actually more likely to relieve employees of negative perceptions they may be harboring and put these conversations to rest.

Greater transparency can actually save employers money and retain top talent.

So, How Do We Talk About This?

When consulting on communicating about pay, I consistently advise employers to focus on the "why." Remember, employees care more about why they're paid what they're paid than about the exact dollar value (within reason). They want to see that their employer values them enough to have put meaningful criteria behind how they are rewarded.

This "why" can be communicated in a few ways. The following three stages are essential to nurturing employee trust through pay conversations.

Communicate the results of your pay gap analyses. If you are wondering how in-depth you should go, the following points tend to cover enough without revealing individual employees' salaries:

- Aggregate of the gaps you found, including the percentage of employees impacted and the amount in total.
- Identification of the causes of any gaps.
- Targets to reduce any like-for-like gaps.
- Targets to reduce any organization-wide gaps.

Reach out to any groups you found that may have endured pay inconsistencies in the past and communicate the steps you will be taking to remedy those gaps. If a remediation plan was put in place, give your employees consistent status updates on your progress. Even if no remediation plan was needed, as you continue to check in on the status of pay equity in your organization, announce your findings to your employees to let them know you are proactively ensuring that gaps will not occur and persist without you detecting them.

Document and distribute your pay equity strategy. In addition to a pay rubric (outlined below), I also recommend sharing a strategy that includes your policies around the following:

- *Pay equity metrics and reporting commitment.* How often are pay equity metrics reported? To whom? Are different metrics reported to your management? To your board?
- *Policies of accountability.* Who is responsible for pay equity outcomes? Within a department? Across the organization? What roles do those who are held accountable play in setting pay equity targets?
- *Target date.* A date for adopting salary transparency, if you haven't yet.
- *Pay discussions.* Conversations about pay raises or bonuses should be separate from performance evaluations. Share what is going to be discussed ahead of time, including a pay rubric, and structure these conversations similarly for every employee.

Your pay equity strategy should also include the underlying policies that were discussed earlier in this chapter, especially if you are updating any of those policies and processes to become more equity-centered. Sharing that you are addressing policies that have an indirect impact on pay equity demonstrates that you are committed to sustaining pay equity for the long term and increases awareness around factors that can cause a pay gap.

Develop and share a standardized pay rubric. In addition to your pay equity strategy, employees should have access to a pay rubric that explains the criteria you use to make pay, bonus, and pay raise decisions. This rubric should include the following:

- Any index or database that you use, such as Payscale or Schwab Index, to determine market rates. Note why you have chosen that resource.
- The groupings of employees in your organization, the tiers in each group, and the pay range for each tier.
- The criteria you use to decide how much to pay new hires, how you award bonuses, and how you determine pay increases. These criteria give employees a clear understanding of what factors, such as education, sales performance, or years of experience, could explain why they are paid differently than their peers in seemingly similar roles.

Pay Equity Is Not One-and-Done

Conducting a pay gap analysis once only captures that moment in time. Continuing to evaluate pay regularly ensures that hidden gaps don't grow, identifies underlying policies that cause gaps over time, and helps identify where pay policies may be applied or communicated inconsistently. In addition, companies go through mergers, reorganizations, and other headcount-altering events. Reevaluating pay equity ensures that pay policies remain consistent, even in the face of these changes.

≈

Just as organizations' understanding of pay continues to evolve, so do their employees and their priorities. Some start families, start taking care of elders, and embrace other life shifts. How will your company shift with them?

CHAPTER 11

Family Matters

I've been one of Nike's most widely marketed athletes. If I can't secure maternity protections, who can?

—Olympian Allyson Felix

In the middle of the 2021 Olympics, Nike debuted a new video ad: a montage of active, pregnant women—mostly women of color—in states of sweaty glory. The ad asks, "What is an athlete?" and then shines the spotlight on expectant mothers overcoming obstacle after obstacle throughout their pregnancies. The ad ends by declaring pregnant women "The Toughest Athlete."

Just a few years earlier, Nike had told several Olympic runners their pregnancies meant that they weren't athletes at all.

In back-to-back exposés in the *New York Times*, Olympian runners Alysia Montaño, Kara Goucher, and Allyson Felix broke their NDAs to come forward with similar stories of how they were treated as Nike-sponsored athletes when they decided to become mothers.[1]

After Goucher became pregnant, she found out that Nike would not pay her until she started racing again. Even though she wasn't getting paid during her high-risk pregnancy, Goucher made more than a dozen unpaid appearances on Nike's behalf, in hopes of retaining the sponsorship after she gave birth. She even waited more than four months to announce her pregnancy just so that Nike could disclose it on Mother's Day. To start getting paid again as soon as possible, Goucher trained for, and ran, a half-marathon three months after her delivery. Even when her son became critically ill, she had to leave him in the hospital to participate in a race. Seven months after giving birth, Goucher raced the Boston Marathon, triggering chronic hip injuries, limiting her competitive career.

While Alysia Montaño was being widely celebrated as the "Pregnant Runner" for competing in the US championships while eight months pregnant, she was battling Nike behind the scenes for her pay and benefits. Because she didn't place in the top tier in some of the nation's most competitive races, while running pregnant, she lost her sponsored health insurance.

Allyson Felix's story may have garnered the most attention of the three. By 2018, Felix was a 6-time Olympic gold medal winner and 11-time world champion. That year, she decided to become a mother. Felix and her baby survived an emergency C-section at 32 weeks, necessitated by severe eclampsia that threatened her and her baby's life. When she tried to return to her sport, Nike told her that they were only willing to pay 30 percent of what they had paid her before pregnancy. Felix attempted to renegotiate the contract. Nike declined.

Within a few months of the *New York Times* reports, a congressional inquiry pressured Nike into putting protections in place for pregnant athletes, similar to the protections they already offered athletes who sustained injuries. Brooks, Nuun, and Altra all followed. Without Montaño, Goucher, and Felix breaking their NDAs, though, this might never have happened.

Fast-forward to the Tokyo Olympics in 2021. I was watching the women's track and field events and saw Nike's "Toughest Athlete" ad run twice in 30 minutes. The pre-race coverage for the women's 200 meters started, and Allyson Felix took her position at the starting blocks. For the last two years, skeptics had doubted that she could come back from an emergency C-section to compete, that qualifying, let alone contending for medals, was an impossibility. Black-and-white glamor photos of the athletes flashed across the screen. Felix's C-section scar was visible in most of them.

Felix did more than qualify. She returned to the games with a new sponsor—Athleta—and on her feet she wore spikes by Saysh, a company that Felix founded herself, with the slogan, "I KNOW MY PLACE (and it's in my own shoes)." Over the last two years, when she wasn't training, Felix was attending congressional hearings, discussing racial disparities in maternal mortality rates.

In partnership with her sponsor, Felix had personally paid to cover the costs of childcare for other Olympian mothers at the games that year. By the time she shot off the blocks, she had female athletes not just from the US, but from around the world, cheering for her.

Felix went on to medal in this race, and again as part of the US women's 400-meter relay team that took home the gold. By the end of the 2021 Olympics, Felix had surpassed Carl Lewis to become the most decorated American track-and-field athlete in Olympic history.

Felix proved Nike both wrong and right. She was even more valuable as an athlete after she became a mother, and she was living proof that mothers are often overlooked as The Toughest Athletes.

In our workplaces, they are often overlooked as The Greatest Employees.

The Mommy Track

It's no secret that women suffered the majority of COVID-related job losses. Women of color were hit the hardest, facing higher unemployment numbers than white women.[2] Even after employment bounced back for white women, the numbers still lagged for women of color.

Much of this "she-cession" was driven by the additional caretaking that working mothers had to take on when their homes turned into remote digital classrooms. One study found that working moms spent the equivalent of a full-time job overseeing the educational needs of their children in 2020, while continuing to work from home.[3] Balancing these responsibilities with work became impossible for too many.

And while the pandemic exacerbated these struggles, the tension between caretaking and career building is nothing new.

Approximately one million working women will become mothers this year. Although 75 percent of expectant mothers say they will be excited to go back to work after giving birth, 43 percent will leave the careers they were in. Of those who do return to the workforce, 50 percent will switch to a lower-paying job at a company they consider to be more family-friendly.[4]

The companies that lose new mothers pay a hefty price. They're not just losing an employee—they're losing someone who was likely to have been a top performer. Multiple studies have found that working mothers are more productive than their peers, and women with two kids are actually even more productive than women with one.[5]

Pay, however, does not seem to reflect this performance. According to a study published by *Business Insider*, the average American male employee receives a pay bump of more than 6 percent when he becomes a father. Conversely, women's earnings decrease by 4 percent for every child they have.[6] While many women do reduce their hours or take time away from work immediately after having children, this reduced productivity is the source of less than one-third of the salary reduction mothers experience every time they have a child. In addition, the motherhood penalty is found to be most severe for those who are already low-wage earners.[7]

The stigma around working mothers that causes these disparities can also keep them from being hired. In a landmark study conducted at Cornell, researchers responded to job openings with fictitious applications.[8] The ersatz applicants were similarly qualified, but some resumes made reference to children and parent-teachers associations and others did not. Women whose applications did not mention children were twice as likely to be called back. The researchers repeated the experiment with male applicants and found that men who referenced children were slightly *more* likely to be called back than men without. The researchers repeated the study with graduate students, asking them to pretend they were hiring managers and choose whom they would be likely to hire and how much they would offer them. Not only were they less likely to hire mothers, the starting pay they were willing to offer them was $11,000 lower than the pay they would offer women without children.

These inequities are a few of the reasons US mothers report the most stress among working mothers globally.[9] While working moms around the world face different challenges and barriers, workplaces in the US undeniably finish last among industrialized nations in one key comparison: access to paid leave.

Paid Leave—Not Just for Mothers

Of the 41 countries that comprise the Organization for Economic Cooperation and Development, the US is the only one that does not mandate paid parental leave.[10] And while the paid leave conversation often focuses on mothers, employers need to go beyond policies that permit maternity leave. Employees of all genders, as well as the employers they work for, can benefit from expanding the implementation of paid leave in the following ways.

Offer family leave, not just maternity leave. The benefits of spousal leave persist long after a child is born. The Institute for Labor Market Policy Evaluation found that expanding paternity leave could help close the earnings gap between working mothers and fathers. In heterosexual relationships, for every month of paternity leave a father takes, the mother's income increases by 6.7 percent.[11]

According to studies from McKinsey & Company, employers that offer paternity leave enjoy benefits that outweigh the costs. When interviewed about their experience taking leave, men said that the opportunity made them feel their employer had invested in them, and they were more likely to want to stay with that employer for the long term. They also stated that taking leave made them more invested in supporting and sponsoring their co-workers who were also parents.[12]

Having a culture of spousal leave in place could also have mitigated some of the she-cession. By giving time to both parents for taking care of a new child, cultural perceptions can shift to view both parents as caretakers. This more balanced approach to the domestic workload could have given mothers the time they needed to continue working through the pandemic.

Male leaders must model taking leave. In GEN's survey we ask, "If your company could do one thing to foster a sense of equity and inclusion, what would it be?" I'm always surprised by how consistently men state that they wish their employer would make it easier to take the leave they technically offer. "We have family leave for all genders, but if the execs don't take that leave, none of us feel like we can, either," writes one survey respondent.

"This organization makes a lot of noise about being one of the first to offer paternity leave, but no one actually feels comfortable using it," states another.

A 2017 Pew survey found that the median leave for new fathers is just one week, but even in companies that offered six weeks of paid paternity leave, fewer than half of dads actually took the full six weeks.[13] For paternity leave to have an impact, male leaders in the organization must actually take it, talk about it, and advocate for it. McKinsey & Company found the top three factors that men state would get them to take leave: (1) a work culture that encourages taking leave, (2) policy support from their employer, and (3) an unaffected promotion timeline.[14]

If you are a man in a visible position in your company, and you take leave, make sure to share what a positive experience it was when you return. I've seen leaders have a significant impact by taking 10 minutes at all-company meetings to talk about why they took leave, what they did during that leave, and the positive impact it had on their family and their ability to focus when they came back to work.

How much leave is the right amount of leave? While 80 percent of Americans support mandatory paid leave, not everyone is in agreement on the amount of time that makes sense.[15] The Gates Foundation made news in 2015 by announcing they would provide up to 52 weeks of paid leave to new parents. By 2019, the foundation updated its policy to cut the total leave time in half and replaced the other six months of leave with a $20,000 stipend to cover costs of childcare. This decision wasn't made just to benefit the bottom line. Research shows that a shorter leave can actually help employees.

A year off from work can hamper women's abilities to reintegrate into the workplace, return to senior roles, and maintain the same income they made previously.[16] Mothers deserve enough leave time to recover, and both parents should have adequate time to bond with their new child, but too much time away can make it difficult to return without struggling to catch back up. Even in companies like Netflix, where parents are offered a year of leave, most choose to take between four and eight months. Six months appears to be the magic number for benefiting from leave without falling behind. Considering that childcare costs, on average, over $1,200 a month in the US,[17] the stipend that the Gates Foundation offers provides the caretaking stability that parents need, without keeping them from returning to work.

Non-Parents Also Need Leave

While leave is often discussed as a benefit for new parents, other circumstances and life events can make it nearly impossible for employees to continue working without some accommodations.

The sandwich generation. The percentage of employees who are considered nonprofessional caretakers (meaning they care for a family member or loved one) has skyrocketed in recent years. As noted in chapter 3, 6 in 10 unpaid caregivers are also holding paying jobs.[18] As longer lifespans have become the norm, more adult children of retirees find themselves "sandwiched" between caring for their own young adult children, and retired parents living into their late eighties and nineties.

Most of these sandwiched caretakers are women. Because they spend more time on caretaking duties than men, 44 percent of female caregivers adjust their working patterns, with 9 percent stepping back from full time to part time, and 7 percent taking an indefinite leave of absence. On average, female caregivers sacrifice approximately $35,000 in annual income due to their caregiving responsibilities, and 16 percent of them move up their retirement date because they have no way to take time off work to care for loved ones and return to their jobs.[19]

Not only are employers that offer caretakers' leave more likely to retain their caretaking employees for the long term, they can also play a role in closing the wealth gap.

Domestic violence leave. The CDC reports that victims of domestic violence lose nearly 8 million days of paid work per year in the US, resulting in a $1.8 billion loss in productivity for employers.[20] Twenty-one percent of full-time employed adults report that they have been victims of domestic violence, and 74 percent of that group say they have been harassed at work by their abusers.[21] The CDC also reports that 85 percent of domestic violence victims are women.

In the US, many states and municipalities are expanding their paid leave laws to include leave for employees affected by domestic violence. In May 2018, New Jersey signed into law an updated version of their Paid Sick Leave Act to include leave for employees who are victims of domestic or sexual violence, or for leave when an employee's family member is a victim. Time off allows employees to seek medical attention, meet with a lawyer, file for a protection order, attend court hearings, or relocate, if needed.

To protect employees who are dealing with an ongoing threat, employers can also provide the following accommodations:

- Change the employee's work phone number.
- Remove the employee's name and number from automated phone messages and directories.
- Install caller ID.
- Train anyone in a receptionist role not to disclose to outside callers whether or not a certain employee is in the office.
- Inform co-workers, at the employee's request, if the employee has obtained a protection order against an individual who is not allowed within a certain distance of the employee's workplace.

Provide leave, flexible work arrangements, and other accommodations for employees with PTSD. Veterans, especially, may suffer from PTSD symptoms, including disrupted sleep patterns, panic attacks, anxiety when working with others, and difficulty concentrating on tasks. Employers can provide the following accommodations to allow those with PTSD to still perform successfully at their jobs:

- Provide private quiet spaces.
- Allow the employees to play soothing music through headphones while working.
- Allow longer or more frequent work breaks and provide backup coverage when needed.
- Allow the employee additional time to learn new responsibilities.
- Allow for time off for counseling, legal assistance, or medical appointments.
- Allow the employee to work from home part-time and support flexible work schedules.
- During onboarding, provide an opportunity for employees to state if particular smells or noises are triggering, and make efforts to remove these possible triggers from the employee's work environment.

Destigmatize Taking Leave

As mentioned in this chapter's section on paternity leave, providing a written leave policy does not necessarily normalize taking leave. To destigmatize leave, GEN has helped employers implement the following unusual but effective policies.

The Take 2 test. While leave policies technically allow workers to take time off and return, this does not address the perception that those who have been on leave have fallen behind. Administering a brief test to employees returning from extended leave keeps their competence from being called into question. For this test to mitigate stigma, companywide communication is key. While the test can assess some core skills, it does not need to be comprehensive. The assessment itself is actually less important than broadcasting that the employee has been assessed. Communicating visibly that all returning employees—including mothers, fathers, and those caring for elderly family members—have been "vetted" diminishes the stigma surrounding them as they return.

Develop a keep-in-touch plan for employees on leave. Keep-in-touch programs are not meant to compel employees on leave to communicate, but rather to provide structure around their preferences for being kept in the loop, while also respecting their time off. GEN's survey results show that women are 14 percent more likely to stay with their employer if they have a keep-in-touch program in place, and men are 34 percent more likely to feel comfortable taking leave if their employer has a keep-in-touch program. An effective keep-in-touch program should address the following phases:

- *Pre-leave*. Employees work with their managers to assess the work to be completed before going on leave, decide what frequency and method of communication is acceptable while they're on leave, and address any team concerns surrounding the work that is typically done by the employee.

- *Leave*. Employee and manager stay in touch according to the plan created during the pre-leave phase. The employee is informed about any organizational changes that may impact their experience or expectations when they do return to work.

- *Back to work*. Employee and manager reassess priorities and develop strategies to address new demands of work and parenting. The manager develops a communication plan to share with the rest of the team if any expectations for the employee's responsibilities or schedule need to change.

Make promotions accessible to employees on leave. When announcing a promotion opportunity, make sure to state that employees on leave are eligible. This encourages those on leave to apply and demonstrates that being out of the office for a short time is not a barrier to long-term career opportunities. If an employee on leave is promoted, when announcing this change, note that the employee was promoted while on leave.

Give Remote a Chance

After more than a year of letting their employees work entirely from home, many employers started floating "back to the office" plans in June 2021. Before the Delta variant sent most employees back home again, businesses got to gauge how their employees reacted to a range of new hybrid work models. Feelings about returning to the office were mixed, and noticeably different by demographic. While a majority of workers did not want to go back to five days of working in the office, the preference for remote work was far stronger among Black workers, according to the Remote Employee Experience Index.[22] This quarterly report, which tracks employee sentiment around workplace topics, found that 97 percent of Black employees wanted to continue a hybrid or full-time remote working model. Only 3 percent of Black respondents wanted to return to full-time in-office arrangements, compared to 21 percent of white respondents.

For many Black employees, working remotely offered relief from constantly code-switching and navigating biases. A *New York Times* article covering the results of the index quoted several employees of color who did not look forward to revisiting microagressions, such as co-workers touching their hair without their permission or being asked at work how they feel about the Black Lives Matter movement.[23] The prevalence of these feelings came through in the index's survey data. For Black employees, working remotely doubled their sense of belonging, increased their ability to manage stress by 64 percent, and improved their work–life balance by 25 percent.

While the option to work from home may afford benefits to underestimated individuals, it can also become a driver of inequities. As some offices reopened during 2020 and made it optional for employees to return, men were more likely to go back to the office on a full-time basis.[24] Even men who still wanted to stay home felt pressured to return because their male co-workers, and especially their managers, were returning. Because so many women were still tasked with supervising children, returning to the office was not as feasible for them, even if they wanted to.

This imbalance of in-person office demographics threatens to widen already existing gaps. Earning potential and career advancement are still highly correlated with in-person work, making women vulnerable to an "out of sight, out of mind" dynamic that can leave them behind. The *New York Times* reported similar visibility-related disparities were holding back employees of color as well.[25] To ensure that remote and flexible work policies have an equitable impact, they must be buoyed by the following supports.

Determine flexible work policies with employee participation. Give employees at all levels—not just managers—the chance to weigh in, and then use the intersectional data analysis methods from chapter 6 to ensure one group's interests are not overrepresented. After analyzing this employee feedback to drive your decision-making, share the rationale behind your flexible work policies with your employees. The more transparent you are around your decision-making process, the more likely your employees will be to buy in.

Make hybrid work models hybrid for everyone, including leaders. During the return-to-work decision-making rush, I worked with two organizations that implemented nearly identical return-to-the-office approaches. They simultaneously *required* and *limited* time back in the office. Employees were asked to choose two days a week that they would be in the office, for five hours each day. Any requests to work more or less than two days in the office had to be submitted for managerial approval. And the rules applied to everyone. Executives also had to limit their time in the office to two days a week, unless extenuating circumstances proved that they needed to be there more.

Out of a range of return-to-the-office approaches I witnessed, this one had the most success. It offered personal choice, by allowing employees to choose which days they were in the office, but it also provided enough structure for teams to collaborate in person. Requiring two days in the office also freed women from the expectation that they could always be the "default" caretaker. By requiring women to be present for two days, some heterosexual couples were impelled to navigate a more balanced approach to managing the caretaking workload at home. The shortened hours also allowed employees to commute at off-peak times and allowed parents to pick up children from school or daycare at reasonable hours.

Providing the option to request more time in the office also built equity into a flexible work culture by supporting employees for whom working from home was difficult or impossible. While working remotely did decrease stress for some, other individuals who did not have enough space or privacy needed an office to be productive.

Set targets and track participation. Just as KPIs are crucial for inclusive hiring and pay equity, they can also drive equity in flexible work culture. Gathering data on who is participating in flexible work arrangements can reveal imbalances between demographics or teams. This information can help you course-correct if policies have been implemented unevenly, or if certain groups feel they would be stigmatized for working from home. Setting a target for participation can overcome work-from-home stigma, signaling to managers that flexible work is more than a perk—it's a strategy that is meant to be taken seriously.

≈

So far, this book has covered the "what, why, and how" of policies and processes that can design equity-centered workplaces. But what about the "who"? Who are the leaders who decide to adjust these cultural levers? And how do we identify and promote decision-makers who are qualified to make these choices?

CHAPTER 12

Leadership Material

I will never forget my first interview in the financial sector.

The employment agency said I would only interview with the woman who could potentially become my boss, but during the meeting, a tall, broad-shouldered man opened her office door as he knocked and asked to steal me for a second. He walked me across the hall into what appeared to be a broom closet and asked me if I had plans to have kids soon.

I stuttered, "No, sir." He said, "Good, cuz the last thing we need around here is another mother."

I said nothing.

I got the job.

I soon learned that the man who had pulled me into the broom closet was the president of the firm. It was the sixth company he had captained in 10 years. I'll call him Rich.

My new role was going smoothly, but a few months in, my team hit a snag on a major project and missed a deadline. I scheduled a meeting with Rich, in his office, to discuss.

As I sat across from him, projecting my assessment over the expanse of his mahogany desk, I tried not to be distracted by the array of medals and plaques on display behind him. Framed between trophy cases of leadership awards, Rich seemed preoccupied, scrolling through his phone.

I continued, explaining how the project became delayed and how I thought we could get back on track. I was about to wrap up with an apology, but the moment I said the words "I'm sorry," he cut me off.

"Stop. Stop right there." Rich was suddenly riveted.

I waited in silence.

"Never apologize. Never let anyone hear you say you're sorry. You wanna get ahead? You'll never hear me say I'm sorry."

"What if. . .you make a mistake?" I ventured.

"Then, you know that. Not everyone needs to know that."

I was, again, at a loss for words.

I had been taught that accountability was key to leadership. But what did I know? I was conscious of the fact that I was new to this sector, in my mid-twenties, and learning the ropes. Maybe I was being naïve. Idealistic.

"We're good here," he dismissed me.

We only saw Rich a couple of days a week. He spent most of his time in his Malibu house, flying in for a day or two, then flying back. When he was in the office, I attempted to get questions answered around key projects, but his answers were often confusing. I would follow up with directors, who would roll their eyes and confirm that the information he gave me was incorrect. I didn't want to risk pushing back, though. I had seen him yell at employees, slam his fist on desks, and hang up the phone mid-conversation over disagreements. I wasn't going to invite that.

But his behavior had a flipside: When Rich wasn't yelling, he was charismatic. He appeared charmingly above the mundane and beyond reproach. He seemed so completely convinced of his every move that it was hard to think of him as anything but an authority figure. It felt impossible to question him.

A couple of years into my employment, the rumors started: The organization was in trouble, and investors were desperately looking for a buyer. Rich had stopped his semi-regular visits from SoCal, and we weren't hearing from him.

We were rudderless, anxious, without leadership when we needed it most. Our drift in limbo went on for months.

One morning an HR rep greeted me at my desk. We had been acquired. The purchasing company had already made an initial round of cuts. My job was temporarily safe, but my boss's was not.

The rep walked me to my boss's office. She had been given two hours and a cardboard box. I flashed back to my interview for the role, when Rich had said, "The last thing we need around here is another mother." I didn't know at the time that my boss was one of two mothers in the organization.

"I have a lot of people to meet with today, so you'll need to walk your supervisor to her car, get her badge from her, and bring it back."

I didn't know what to say. My soon-to-be-former boss had taken a chance on me, the nonprofit kid with no experience in finance, and now I was going to escort her to the parking garage and retrieve her badge.

I accompanied her through the office as she said her goodbyes. Other co-workers were also packing up, teary-eyed, blindsided. As we passed Rich's office, I spotted the top of his head. He was in for the first time in months, sequestered in his office with the door closed.

After everyone from the first round of cuts had left, Rich emerged. He announced that our business would be absorbed into a new parent company, and they were still deciding on a second round. He addressed a few details of the transition, then delivered his closing statement: "And finally, I wanted to say, don't worry about me. I'll be fine. The wife and I have a European junket planned. And when we get back I'll be taking the helm at a different firm."

The business had failed under Rich's watch. We had lost co-workers with no notice, and we didn't know if our own jobs were safe. But Rich had managed to ride his charisma into a seventh executive-level role.

Was that what leadership material looked like?

The Confidence-Competence Trap

Despite making up 47 percent of the workforce and graduating from college at higher rates than men, women still represent only 29 percent of senior managers, 22 percent of executive-level leaders, and 6 percent of CEOs.[1] Numbers for leaders of color are even more dismal. Although 12 percent of the US population is Black, Black employees hold only 3.2 percent of the senior leadership roles at large companies in the US and 0.8 percent of all Fortune 500 CEO positions.[2] The percentage of CEOs of color has actually decreased since 2016.

The problem isn't just that organizations appear to favor white men as leaders; it's that they often favor incompetent white men. In his provocatively titled book, *Why Do So Many Incompetent Men Become Leaders? (And How to Fix It)*, psychologist and chief talent scientist Tomas Chamorro-Premuzic analyzes thousands of 360-degree and multisource feedback evaluations. He finds that leaders like Rich are typical, not anomalous, because we are prone to mistake confidence in potential leaders for competence, especially in men. Additional studies find that highly talkative, charismatic, and even psychopathic individuals are more likely to be seen as leaders[3] than those who demonstrate more subtle but proven leadership strengths, such as strategic thinking or taking initiative.[4] Once these outwardly confident employees are promoted into leadership roles, though, they often prove ineffective.

Over-promoting stereotypically masculine traits, such as extraversion or bravado, means that we miss out on less gregarious individuals who may actually be better suited for leadership. Studies published in the *Harvard Business Review* found that women consistently outperform men in 17 of 19 core leadership skills, such as self-development and accountability, but still aren't seen, or promoted, as leaders.[5]

The result? Dissatisfied employees and misguided management.

Premuzic's studies find that most employees are dissatisfied with their managers, but most managers, especially male managers, see themselves as highly effective, with little awareness that their subordinates do not view them favorably. This perception gap, in itself, increases tension. In an interview with the *Harvard Business Review*, Premuzic notes, "Managers perform better when their self-views are in sync or aligned with other people's views on them, and they even do better when they see themselves in a more critical way than others see them."[6] He goes on to note that this is a particular area in which underestimated leaders are more likely to be in sync with their reports: "That's one area where women, again, have an advantage vis-à-vis men because they're more likely to be self-critical even if it is a sort of harsh and perfectionistic self-criticism that is harsher than (how) others see them."

The confidence that opens the door to leadership for many can also be a blinder that blocks the self-reflection required to be an effective leader.

Prizing confidence also thins the tightrope that underestimated individuals have to walk to advance into leadership roles. As explored in chapter 2, employees of color who attempt to speak up are seen as "pushy," women of color are at risk of being seen as too assertive, and women in general are seen as "talking too much," even when speaking less than their male peers. While speaking up and embracing extraversion is essential to being seen as a leader, these same traits are seen as off-putting in underestimated individuals.

Beyond diversity of race and gender, overvaluing confidence and charisma means that we miss out on diverse leadership styles proven to be effective across all backgrounds. Introverts, for example, hold some of the most undervalued leadership potential.

A 2018 study from Yale reveals that less talkative employees, who are often overlooked as potential leaders, seem to understand their peers better than their more chatty co-workers do.[7] Because introverts spend more time observing others and practicing reflection, they have a more accurate understanding of how people function in groups and what motivates them to work harder. Complementary studies find that introverts outperform extraverts in helping teams navigate conflicts and crises.[8] Like Trevor in chapter 4, they have often logged hours analyzing the relationships among members of the team and are able to focus on meeting others' needs rather than making their own voices heard. Extraverts, on the other hand, are more likely to prolong conflict within teams and increase, rather than decrease, interpersonal tension.

Missing out on these underestimated skills impacts the bottom line; for example, the 17 leadership competencies in which women excel are also highly correlated with employee retention, customer satisfaction, profitability, sales, and engagement.

So, how do we move from rewarding the stereotypically charismatic to recognizing and promoting typically unsung leadership potential?

Transparency: Not Just for Pay

In GEN's employee survey, respondents are most likely to check the "I don't know" boxes for questions related to promotions and advancement. Among national respondents, 72 percent of employees state that they do not know what steps they would need to take to advance in their workplace.

Leaders also struggle to articulate the promotion process in their organizations. When reviewing companies' promotional practices, I rarely see written processes or criteria for advancing employees into leadership roles.

While transparency is often associated with pay, it also has a crucial role to play in developing inclusive leadership and promotional strategies. Not only do clear, transparent criteria let employees know what steps they need to take to advance, they also force decision-makers to look for typically undervalued competencies that will make someone effective in a leadership role.

Without clear criteria, we are more prone to promote based on personality impressions, which are highly vulnerable to the confidence and charisma traps described earlier. We are also more likely to make the critical mistake of assuming that those who have performed well in their current role will perform well as leaders.

Multiple academic studies have found that organizations tend to promote based on what employees have done, without an evaluation of what they can do as leaders.[9] High-performing contributors, for example, are often promoted into management, even though the skills it took to excel in their contributing roles bear little resemblance to the skills needed to manage others. Just because an employee was successful in one role does not mean that same employee will succeed in leading others in similar roles.

To ensure that you are promoting for leadership competencies, rather than confidence or unrelated past performance, use the following guidelines to develop—and communicate—clear, transparent criteria.

Revisit job descriptions—for every role. Job descriptions tend to be forgotten after the initial hiring process. The same competency-based descriptions and hiring tools discussed in chapter 6 can also lead to more effective promotion decisions. Of the organizations GEN has worked with, those that had the most diverse leadership teams also had the clearest definitions of each job level, including expected competencies and behaviors, all the way up through directors on the board. Defining the expected skills for each role leads decision-makers to focus on the competencies they should promote so that confidence doesn't stand in for competence. Employees also gain a clear understanding of the steps they need to take to be promoted.

When defining criteria, keep the following principles in mind:

- Beware of using titles in place of competencies. Using titles may disproportionately exclude underestimated groups who have been overlooked for leadership roles in the past or have been given leadership-related tasks, but never given the title. In addition, although someone may have had a leadership title in the past, it does not necessarily mean that the candidate has been vetted for leadership skills.
- Think of your business's future leadership needs. Competencies should account for skills that go beyond past performance to demonstrating the

potential to lead businesses into the future. Can your leadership candidates understand an increasingly diverse employee and customer base? Have they shown skills, such as navigating complexity and facilitating conflict resolution, which are needed to lead a company through growth? Crafting competencies around adaptability can be more important than culture fit, which often becomes an anchor to the past rather than a catalyst to the future.

Communicate these criteria. While this seems like an obvious step, it can easily be overlooked. Your employees should have on-demand access to the competencies required for each role, and they should be reminded of them. Use one-on-ones, mentoring meetings, learning and development planning sessions, and performance evaluations to remind individuals aspiring to leadership what steps they need to take to advance. Intentionally including this information in meeting agendas helps guide ambitious employees and reminds managers of the skills they're looking for, by repeating them to employees.

You have set your criteria and communicated them, but how do you know what success looks like? What level of leadership diversity is good enough? The next step for achieving greater clarity: setting targets.

Which Came First: The Target or the Leader?

Quotas are complicated. In general, people are against them—until they're implemented.

The skepticism toward setting targets and quotas is understandable. Underestimated individuals can be stigmatized as diversity hires, undermining their credibility, even if they are highly qualified. Leaders often worry that setting quotas means they won't be able to fill roles if certain groups just are not adequately represented in the pipeline.

Despite these concerns, multiple case studies point to the same conclusion: over time, quotas work.

One of the earliest studies tracking the impact of quotas followed an amendment to India's self-governance act, the Panchyati Raj Act. The amendment, introduced in 1992, required at least 33.3 percent female representation in local village governments. Before this amendment was introduced, women held only 5 percent of government positions in India. Within 12 years, their share had risen to 40 percent. The quotas are no longer needed to maintain this more balanced representation.

Perhaps more important, this intervention changed people's perceptions of women as leaders.[10] Before the amendment was put in place, women were perceived as ill-suited for leadership and politics. Villagers who had been exposed only to male chiefs were particularly likely to assess women as unfit for government and were not willing to vote for them.

In a landmark study, researchers were able to track sentiment surrounding female leaders before and after the quotas were implemented, village by village. Because some villages adopted the amendment before others, researchers were able to assess how much attitudes toward female leaders changed as a result of the quota, rather than through a natural evolution of attitudes that could occur over time.

Among the villages that were early adopters, those who were initially skeptical of both the quota and women leaders overcame their biases against both. Villagers who were exposed to female chiefs, via the quota, changed their opinions, rating female and male leaders equally. Some even stated that the female chiefs they had been exposed to were more effective than the male chiefs. Skeptics in other villages who had not been exposed to female leaders, however, remained staunchly opposed.

Other countries took note. In 2003, Norway legislated a 40 percent minimum representation of each sex on the corporate boards of public and (larger) private companies.[11] Follow-up research found that changing the balance at the top triggered more diverse retention downstream. Women stayed in the companies longer, and the share of female managers increased. Because women could see that there were opportunities for them if they stayed, they were less likely to move on.

A study of large corporations in the US found similar positive associations between an increase in the number of female board directors and rising percentages of female executives and managers.[12]

After Norway's quotas proved successful, Germany, France, Iceland, Italy, Austria, Spain, Sweden, and the UK all followed suit. Female representation on boards in these countries now ranges between 25 percent and 40 percent. In the US, where attitudes toward quotas are hostile, female representation stays stuck at 18 percent.[13]

In all of these cases, when quotas were first being implemented, stakeholders were opposed to them. Over time, as targets were met, attitudes toward both new leaders and quotas shifted. Hostility gave way to a new understanding that standards did not have to be lowered to meet representation targets. Instead, companies got the push they needed to expand their recruiting and retention efforts. In addition, companies that implemented quotas actually found that they led to more professional standards for board selection than they had had before.

As one male CEO and director from Norway described, "In my opinion, what happened in Norway when affirmative action was introduced was that the entire recruitment process of boards was sharpened. The requirements were clarified, the election committee's responsibility was acknowledged. And the focus on the composition of the boards in general was improved. With that law, the importance of the board was upgraded, and the composition of the board. That is positive. And it might also be because you don't have to go far back before you see that the recruitment to boards and board members was heavily influenced by a sort of networking mentality, and the close network that you belonged to yourself."[14]

Some companies, and even entire states in the US, are starting to learn from this example, beginning to implement their own quotas. The success of these quotas, however, may be threatened by a too common mentality: the rule of the "One and Done."

One Is Not Done

In September 2018, California Governor Jerry Brown signed a bill into law that required public companies headquartered in California to name at least one female director to their boards by the end of 2019. That was the part that grabbed the headlines.

The fine print caught my attention: *The law further mandates that companies with five-member boards have at least two female directors by the end of 2021; corporations with six or more directors need at least three women. The penalties for failing to comply rise accordingly.* I read this and breathed a sigh of relief.

Often when I hear about quotas, they stop at the "One and Done" rule. One woman and one person of color ascend to a board position or the executive suite, and inclusive leadership initiatives are declared successful.

For that individual, and for the organization, having just one can be worse than having none.

Data tracking more than 2,000 management teams across the mutual fund sector compared the performance of homogeneous teams and mixed-sex teams. The study concluded that homogeneity won out. At first, this seems like an alarming conclusion for anyone working on advancing diversity initiatives. A close look at the data reveals an important nuance: In teams that were considered mixed-sex, women represented a very small minority of the group. Because women represent approximately 10 percent of fund managers, there was often only one female representative on mixed-sex teams.[15]

When underestimated individuals are the only representative, or represent a small minority, they are treated as tokens, which limits how they are perceived. Rather than being seen as specialists in their discipline, they are seen as specialists in their identity. The female stockbroker becomes the specialist on being female, not on trading. The Black creative director is the specialist in being Black, not in creative direction.

If these individuals' contributions are not taken at face value, it limits how much value they can add to the performance of the group. Therefore, a 10-person mixed-sex group in the mutual fund study was actually performing more like a 9-person group, despite the qualifications and efforts of the sole female.

In Iris Bohnet's book, *What Works: Gender Equality by Design*, she summarizes her analysis of multiple studies on tokenism: Underestimated individuals are highly aware that they may be written off as a diversity representative. Not only does this make them self-conscious about the ways they may be perceived, they also become hesitant to open doors for others who share their background, for fear that it may be seen as race-based or gender-based favoritism. For women, this is often described as "Queen Bee syndrome," a dynamic in which women who are "the only" feel the need to assimilate to the behaviors of their majority peers, rather than sponsor those of similar identities.

To overcome these dynamics, leadership groups must achieve a critical mass of underestimated individuals. Bohnet cites several studies which find that underestimated individuals stop being seen as stereotypes or tokens, and start being treated like individual experts or leaders, when there are more of them in a group.[16] With a larger presence, the comment from the one Black person is no longer representative of what all Black people think. Advice from the sole woman to mitigate risks isn't written off as stereotypically feminine risk aversion.

Additional studies released by the National Academies of Sciences of the United States of America conclude that the greater the diversity in a group, the more likely a phenomenon called "stereotype dispersion."[17] This term describes a perception shift in which majority members of a group progress from seeing more difference between themselves and minority members of a group, to seeing less difference, when more of those minority members are present. This change in perception can decrease tensions and allow groups to collaborate more effectively, unlocking the full potential of collective intelligence discussed in chapter 3.

When I present this evidence to organizations, the next questions are usually, OK, so how many is enough? If our workforce is evenly split female and male, do we need to have 50 percent representation? What if the pipeline just isn't balanced this way? What do we do about minority ethnic groups that represent less than 10 percent of the workforce?

Reaching Critical Mass: The Art of Setting Targets

While there is not a "perfect" number, stereotypes have far less impact when minority groups represent at least one-third of a group.[18] Once this threshold is met, underestimated individuals are more likely to be seen as credible, and they are less likely to adopt a scarcity mindset. Knowing there is room for "more than one" can make them feel free to sponsor others who look like them, and junior-level employees from underestimated backgrounds genuinely believe that there is room for them at the top.

For organizations that are facing unbalanced pipelines, this 33 percent target can seem out of reach. The advice I have for these organizations may sound counter to diversity goals: When possible, make your groups homogeneous. For example, if you need to split your leadership team into groups during an all-company meeting, don't attempt to maintain "mixed" groups if you will have just one underestimated individual in each group. If you're splitting thirty people into three groups, and you have three Black employees, do not put one Black employee in each of the three groups. You're better off having all three Black employees in a single group.

When I conduct workshops in majority-male environments, participants are often surprised when I end up grouping the women together. Without this intervention, however, they will be less likely to feel comfortable sharing their opinions honestly or having their contributions understood outside the frame of "the only." Once like individuals are able to share their perspectives in a mini-group with others with shared identities, they can present their conclusions, as a group, in front of others, returning diverse perspectives to the larger conversation.

While you probably will not convert all quota-averse skeptics, the following steps can foster buy-in as you start to set targets.

Decide on, and communicate, a rationale behind the target numbers you choose. I've seen organizations use three different target-setting heuristics that increased acceptance:

- *Pipeline-dependent.* Set representation targets that are in line with the demographics of graduating classes in your field, or are representative of the estimated population proportions in your sector. This logic is difficult to argue with.

- *Representative of the customer base.* Set targets that mirror the population you are trying to serve. Including more decision-makers that are familiar with the life experiences of your customers increases your chances of tailoring product development and marketing to their preferences.

- *Even representation at all levels of the business.* If women represent 50 percent of entry-level employees, for example, set targets at management, executive, and C-suite levels to match.

Communicate targets as part of a comprehensive leadership strategy and timeline. This strategy should include methods for identifying, recruiting, and developing diverse talent, as well as dates for tracking progress. For example, Markon Solutions, a GEN-certified company, stated the following in their inclusive leadership strategy: "Markon aims to identify 10 underrepresented candidates of excellence for leadership positions by January 2021, recruit 5 of them into a leadership track by the end of 2021, and add 3 underrepresented individuals to our leadership team by June 2022." This timeline was followed by the steps the company's current leadership team planned to take to reach these targets, including a mentorship matching program and a promotion-oriented training, education, and networking event series.

Stating the steps you will take to identify and develop leaders over the long term communicates that these individuals will be well-trained in leadership skills by the time they reach senior positions. This can help lessen "affirmative action" stigma by showing how thoroughly vetted and mentored these leaders are.

Once you have decided on your targets and communicated them, you may still be at a loss for exactly how to meet them. Just setting targets won't make your future leaders appear! To ensure you can meet your deadlines, start identifying talent early.

Identifying Leaders: Start at the Beginning

From the day entry-level employees join your company, you have a chance to identify future leaders.

One of the best ways to engage individuals with their own leadership potential is to encourage them to track their progress, starting early. Whether you facilitate this through frequent performance evaluations, mentorship and sponsorship meetings, or other one-on-ones, encourage junior-level underestimated employees to start tracking achievements. I urge my mentees to spend five minutes recording accomplishments at the end of each week in an achievement tracker. Capturing these small wins can demonstrate over time how they contributed to streamlining processes, making difficult decisions, or demonstrating other key leadership behaviors that should be promoted later.

Group meetings provide another early opportunity to spot employees with meaningful ideas or a proactive approach. Without inclusive practices, though, underestimated individuals may not have the same opportunities to make an impression. As discussed earlier in the second chapter, employees of color and female employees are more likely to have their talking points interrupted or their ideas appropriated.

The following inclusive meeting behaviors can help ensure that a diverse range of voices are heard and recognized.

Invoke the participatory pause. When soliciting feedback on an important topic, ask for a one- to two-minute reflection period before anyone raises a hand to respond. Even in diverse groups, men respond to questions more quickly than women do and are more confident in their answers, even when they know less about a topic than their peers and are more likely to be incorrect in their answer.[19] Because underestimated populations have been subject to "prove it again" biases that hold their answers to a higher standard, they may take longer to compose their responses before voicing their opinions.

Divide and confer. If a topic is being presented for feedback within a large group, provide time for participants to meet in subgroups (as small as pairs) first. Individuals who fear their opinions may not be welcome may feel more comfortable sharing with a peer or small group of peers first. Each subgroup should record their conclusions in a written format (such as a shared Google doc) before groups reconvene. This keeps this feedback from being buried once the larger group reunites. Organizations that practice this behavior report higher levels of collaboration, creativity, and productivity.

Provide lead time for review and space for open-ended feedback. Introverts' and internal processors' way of thinking through problems and presenting feedback runs counter to many workplace cultures. As we saw in chapter 4, they tend to consider all possibilities quietly before weighing in and often highlight the work of others ahead of their own. When given opportunities that honor how they perform, though, introverts—and their employers—can flourish. If possible, send materials or proposals out for review a day ahead of the meeting in which they will be discussed. In addition, solicit feedback through a survey that includes questions with open-ended responses, for these more introspective thinkers to document their feedback ahead of time.

The Application and the Nudge

Once you have started recognizing potential leaders, retaining them and recruiting them into the promotion process is key. To encourage engagement, create an open application process for promotions, encourage underestimated individuals to apply, and share why certain employees are promoted.

Open promotions to those who meet minimum requirements and select by the STAR method. When underestimated individuals tell me that they feel they have been passed over for a promotion, I ask if they received any feedback on why they weren't chosen. "I didn't even know the opportunity was available," most of them tell me. Promotions that are not formally communicated and open to all are implicitly exclusive. When a promotion opportunity arises, announce it to the entire company and state what the minimum requirements are for the position, relying on the competency-based job descriptions noted earlier in this chapter. Then, use the same blind resume reviews, structured interview processes, and STAR-assessment methods from the hiring chapter to debias your decision-making and select the best person for the role.

Encourage underestimated individuals to apply. As noted earlier in this chapter, men are more likely to assess themselves as qualified for leadership roles than women are. This confidence makes them more likely to believe they are qualified for promotions and apply, even if they do not meet all the minimum criteria. Women are more likely to wait until they are 100 percent sure they have met all of the qualifications.[20]

Encouraging all to apply, however, can have a big impact. Studies from the 2014 midterm elections give us an example of the success of the "nudge." Even though women are as good at fundraising as men and stand the same odds—or even slightly better—of winning, they are less likely to run for office. Being asked to run, though, changes that. Whether it makes them believe that they're qualified or counters doubts that bias may count them out, nudging can get women to take the next step forward. While men are encouraged to run more often than their equally qualified female peers, when women are encouraged to run, they become as likely to run for office as their male peers.[21]

When a promotion application process opens, be intentional about going through your list of underestimated individuals to see who may have met the qualifications for next steps and encourage them to apply. This signals to underestimated individuals that their application will be taken seriously, boosting the participation of highly qualified but previously underrepresented candidates.

Share why a candidate was chosen for promotion. Employees rarely experience transparency concerning the reasons an individual was chosen for advancement, but sharing this rationale can increase trust in the process. If the individual promoted is from an underestimated background, this can also lessen any stigma framing the promotion as an affirmative action choice. Sharing a promoted individual's qualifications and achievements bolsters their credibility against possible bias.

≈

We are closing in on the end of part 2. As we move into the final chapter, we return to first impressions. If I were a new employee, starting my first day, when I came into your office, what would I see?

CHAPTER 13

Blueprints for Inclusive Workspaces

In the early 1990s, Vienna was undergoing a period of rapid growth. The government had set a target of building 10,000 new apartments each year, the Iron Curtain had been lifted, and urban planners were competing to redesign the city. Eva Kail, a district planner in the city's strategic planning unit, knew this was a pivotal moment.[1]

Kail was noting the ways that the past had shaped how residents and visitors were experiencing the city 50 years later. Like most post–WWII European cities, Vienna had been designed by male planners for men like themselves who commuted between home and work by car or public transport. There was little to no accounting for other groups.

In 1991, Kail documented the legacy of this design by following eight people—among them a young girl, a wheelchair user, an urban mother, and an active retiree—and photographing their daily circulation. The photos told stories of Vienna residents who constantly adjusted to a city not meant for them. Benches were too few and far between for elderly citizens to enjoy a walk. Sidewalks and doorways into transit stations often weren't wide enough for a mother with a pram. Those carrying groceries had few covered places to rest with bags in the rain, and few streets had enough lighting for women to feel safe walking them at night.

Kail noted that most design flaws negatively impacted pedestrians, but those making trips by car rarely had a complaint. A follow-up survey led to a breakthrough revelation: two-thirds of car journeys were made by men, while two-thirds of journeys on foot were made by women.

The impact the photography exhibition made led to the creation of a new division of the city's strategic planning unit—the *Frauenboro*, which directly translates to "The Women's Office." "The Inclusion Office" may have been more appropriate, since the *Frauenboro* would go beyond gender to create design standards that made urban planning more inclusive for all.

Vienna's city government moved forward with selecting architects to assist with their massive, planned expansion in 1992, and Kail noticed that in 30 rounds of RFPs, no women had even been invited to pitch. She wasn't going to let history repeat itself. As the newly appointed head of the *Frauenboro*, Kail invited all the women architects she could find to apply.

Kail's female-led team directed a pilot project re-envisioning one of the districts in the city's expansion. A 357-unit housing structure that had been planned for the district would now include pram storage on every floor, wider stairwells for social but safe interactions, and a building height that was low enough to encourage "eyes on the street" visibility from windows—Jane Jacobs's widely accepted technique to discourage crime. Curb heights on this unit's block accommodated a range of mobilities for those transitioning from the bus to their flat.

The success of this pilot drew attention and a new term, "gender mainstreaming," was coined. The city government voted to expand the method to re-envisioning Mariahilf, a more central neighborhood. New lighting illuminated streets that residents had previously identified as inaccessible at night. A kilometer of sidewalk was widened, and unnecessary barriers were removed to accommodate strollers, the elderly who may have been walking with aids, and those in wheelchairs. Benches were added spaced closer together, and the timing of street lights was adjusted to be more pedestrian-friendly. Facilities for sports preferred by girls, such as volleyball and badminton courts, were added to parks next to the basketball courts, which were already crowded with boys.

Some of these elements of "gender mainstreaming" may seem quaint now, since they were implemented to bridge from a society in which men go to work and women run errands on foot with children. The principles underlying these guidelines, though, could be applied today to make our physical workspaces more inclusive for employees of all genders, mobilities, ages, and backgrounds. Just as sidewalks and parks were difficult to navigate for those who did not design them, our office spaces can feel unaccommodating to those who never see the blueprints.

Without inclusive design practices, even workplaces that seem inclusive in theory can build in bias. For an example, we return to Silicon Valley.

From Open Plans to Closed-Off Realities: The Inclusive Office Design Trend That Wasn't

In the early 2000s, the tech industry took an experimental step toward their vision of a meritocratic workplace: Silicon Valley embraced the open floor plan.

The intentions were egalitarian. Open office spaces would tear down walls and flatten hierarchies. Barriers between the executives and the rank and file would be eradicated! Without calling it a DEI initiative, equity and inclusion seemed central to this new approach.

From the outside, the spaces seemed to encourage movement and collaboration, giving employees more room to breathe, to be human. Traditional offices that fragmented the team became airier, light-filled spaces for all employees. For some groups, though, tearing down walls unintentionally created even higher barriers to advancement.

In a study conducted to explore how transforming workspaces transforms culture, researchers Alison Hirst of Anglia Ruskin University and Christina Schwabenland of the University of Bedfordshire discovered that these new wall-less realities improved the office experience for some, but limited interaction and focus for many, especially for women.[2]

The researchers had no intent to focus on gender. Analyzing the behavior of over 1,000 employees, though, repeatedly surfaced the same observations from women: Being on display made them feel more harshly judged for their appearance and emotions, and they were more vulnerable to around-the-clock interruptions.

One of the goals of the open floor plan was to promote movement and collaboration between departments. Hirst and Schwabenland found, however, that women avoided walking to parts of the floor that were predominately male. Previously, visiting these parts of the office space meant that they would be seen only by those on the periphery. Now, being the only woman walking through a sea of men unavoidably drew attention. Design meant to enhance mobility now inhibited it.

In general, women felt more self-conscious about their clothing, movements, and overall appearance. Many reported feeling pressure to change the way they dressed after the office opened up and flattened out. Men did not note any pressure to change their behavior, grooming, or movements about the office.

The feeling women had that they were on display was not "just in their heads."

The researchers learned that since the partitions came down, men in some teams had started to "rate" the attractiveness of female candidates as they walked into the office for interviews. "Visibility enabled these men to judge and rank women according to their sexual attractiveness," wrote Hirst and Schwabenland.

Women also felt increased pressure to be vigilant about hiding negative emotions. Without partitions, there was nowhere to hide on a bad day—and this had consequences.

Women don't need privacy because they are more likely to show negative emotions at work, but because they are more likely to be judged harshly for them. While women are stereotyped as being more emotional than men,[3] observations of over 2,000 employees found that men are 1.6 times more likely to show negative emotions when criticized, 2.4 times more likely than women to display negative emotions when their ideas are not heard, and 2.5 times more likely to display emotional distress after having a falling out with a co-worker.[4]

Despite the fact that men are more likely to display emotion, multiple studies have found that women are more likely than men to be punished or viewed negatively for being angry at work, while men may actually be rewarded for it.[5] Women of color and women with disabilities are even more likely to be seen as "too angry" or "emotional."[6] Some days, being able to hide in a cubicle or other closed-off space is the only way women can protect their reputation in the office.

Even when emotions aren't running high, being exposed leaves women vulnerable to other interactions that can derail their focus. One of the financial companies I worked for had an open floor plan, and I was one of few women in the office. Despite having my head down and earbuds in, I ended up fielding constant non-work-related interruptions. Men stopped by my desk multiple times a day to ask me what I thought they should buy their wives for their birthdays, what to wear to a holiday function, or to share their weekend plans. I was confused by these constant interruptions. I had no idea what someone should gift his wife for her birthday. I had never met her, but existing in the office while female made me the go-to person for these kinds of questions, at the expense of my focus.

Studies conducted by McKinsey & Company, surveying more than 65,000 employees at 423 companies, found that female senior leaders are 60 percent more likely than male leaders to be asked to provide this kind of emotional support and 26 percent more likely to help team members navigate work–life challenges.[7] Individuals who approach women with these kinds of questions often are unaware that they are part of a repeating phenomenon. This shadow work accumulates, robbing women of productive time and the kind of work that would allow them to advance. Casual conversation can help co-workers bond, but women bear the brunt of listening, consoling, and advice-giving, all at a cost to their careers.

Perhaps if the designers of US office spaces had had their own *Frauenboro* to guide them, these unintended consequences could have been avoided. Behavioral design holds the potential to translate Vienna's "gender mainstreaming" principles into "inclusion mainstreaming" designs for the future of work, starting today.

Return to Work: A Chance to Reimagine the Open Office Space

As of this writing, after COVID-19 drove workers to home offices, employers and employees are debating the *Return to the Office*. Women are not the only ones feeling anxiety over returning to an in-person environment. Employees of color are facing a return to Eurocentric dress codes and "Professionalism Standards" discussed in chapter 4, which raise the cost of being Black at work. In a survey conducted by Buzzfeed, many reported that they enjoyed the privacy of not being seen openly and potentially perceived as the "angry Black person." In a corporate America still reckoning with racial inequality, the in-person workplace puts pressure on many employees of color to behave like "Racism Wikipedia," answering their white co-workers' questions about race, while being careful not to make them uncomfortable.[8] These dynamics are exacerbated in open office environments.

Whether you have already returned to the office or are still debating it, there are several "inclusion mainstreaming" steps you can take to accommodate those who disproportionately face these kinds of challenges, especially in open office environments.

Red-yellow-green. One company that GEN certified implemented a color-coded "availability" system that took the emotional labor out of navigating the "casual conversation" interruption problem. On the back of every employee's chair they hung holders for the kinds of sliders that typically would have displayed their names. Instead of a name plate, though, employees could slide in one of three colored sliders. Red meant, "I'm doing work that requires deep focus. Please do not interrupt me unless it's an emergency." Yellow meant, "I'd be open to answering questions as needed, but please ask if it's a good time to talk." Green meant, "I'm working, but open for chit-chat, coffee breaks, and spontaneous collaboration!"

This method let employees who had commonly been interrupted in the past sustain their focus without constantly having to reassert their need to do so. Women reported higher levels of productivity after the color system was implemented, and some employees noted that having to change their behaviors made them more aware of this gendered dynamic. In a follow-up workshop, several employees noted that only when they were forced to wait or find someone else to talk to did they realize how often they had been leaning on particular individuals in the office. Women also expressed relief at no longer having to make sure they rejected interruptions in just the right way, to avoid offending anyone.

Make the open office optional, with movable partitions. I personally enjoyed this accidental design hack when one of my own office spaces was being remodeled. After our department was temporarily moved to an empty floor, to make it more "office-like," the facilities team rolled movable partitions next to our desks and chairs. Because workspaces set up with partitions were the default, introverts or those who needed more privacy didn't have to make a show by setting them up, while those who were more extraverted could remove them if they wanted to be socially available. Similar to the "red-yellow-green" system, the visual signals took the onus off employees to assert their need for space.

Provide private spaces. Introverts, the neurodivergent, workers who may be living with PTSD, and other underestimated individuals can all face unique challenges when working in open spaces. Providing the following private spaces can accommodate a range of needs that are not taken into account in "default" office designs:

- *Prayer rooms.* Some individuals may need space to practice daily prayer or to pray during holidays that are not typically protected by the US work calendar. For employees who typically have to work during fasting periods such as Ramadan or Yom Kippur, having a room like this can provide a much-needed low-blood-sugar mental break.

- *Nursing rooms.* Supporting new mothers should not stop at paid leave. Having a private space—that is not the janitor's closet—explicitly labeled for pumping eases the return to the office. In addition to exclusively reserving this space for new mothers, include refrigerators. GEN's survey responses include far too many stories from women who have had to pump, store their milk in the shared floor fridge, and find it gone when the fridge is cleaned out, or hear complaints from co-workers who do not find it appropriate to store breastmilk in a shared refrigerator. A mini-fridge in the nursing room solves these problems.

   New mothers are not the only ones who appreciate seeing a sanctioned space for them. Employees and candidates of all genders, including those with no intentions to become parents, perceive this amenity as a sign that the company goes beyond talk to accommodating the needs of all employees.

- *Quiet/focus rooms.* A room dedicated to quiet can be essential for introverts or those who are neurodivergent or working with PTSD. While I have seen quiet rooms in offices set up with candles or essential oils, the lingering scents from these can be disturbing to people who are allergic or to those who may be triggered by certain smells, and I advise against them. Finally, a Vacant/Occupied slider on the door can keep the quiet from being broken by someone knocking.

While these spaces may or may not be visually obvious while walking through a workplace, other signals, pictures, and symbols can stand out. Our co-workers' faces, for example, are not the only ones we see in the office. The pictures staring back at us are another design choice that can signal who belongs and who is still a guest.

Role Models Matter

If I walked through your office right now, what would I see on the walls? Landscapes? Quotations? Portraits?

Every day that I worked in an office in the financial sector, framed faces of white men kept watch over my desk. At the time I didn't think much of it. I assumed they were the faces of the company's previous directors or board members. Iris Bohnet's *What Works: Gender Equality by Design* introduced me to the studies mentioned below, which show I may have been underestimating the impact of those images.[9]

In a study conducted in the University of Washington's computer labs, researchers measured female students' association with careers in computer science.[10] One group of students was surveyed after they had been working in a computer lab decorated as it had been for years, with posters of male computer scientists or characters from *Star Wars* or *Star Trek*. The other group of students had been working in a lab with gender-neutral art, such as pictures of nature. In four different rounds of the experiment, the female students surrounded by gender-neutral art had heightened associations with women and careers in computer science. Changing the wall art to be more neutral or even feminine did not affect men's associations negatively.

Beyond signaling a sense of belonging, the kinds of role models we see or are reminded of can impact our performance. In a Swiss study, a picture of Hillary Clinton, Angela Merkel, or Bill Clinton—or no picture—was shown to 149 subjects, both male and female, before they were to deliver a speech.[11] Women who had a seen a picture of a female leader spoke for longer periods of time, and their speeches were rated higher in quality, both by external observers and the women themselves.

These same role modeling effects have been tested and verified across racial lines as well. The first time I remember seeing this dynamic in action was when I worked for the Edgar Martinez Foundation. The foundation's work focused on increasing the percentage of public school teachers in Washington State who were teachers of color. This work was driven by repeated studies showing a positive correlation between student achievement and having a teacher of the same racial background.[12]

When I shadowed several students of color who had Martinez Foundation teachers, I noticed their levels of confidence and enthusiasm rise as they went from classrooms with white teachers to classrooms with teachers of color. I will never forget the student who pulled me aside by the hand, pointed to the pictures of multiple heroes of color that their Martinez Foundation teacher had hung on the walls, and exclaimed, "I look like them!"

Beyond enhancing underestimated individuals' sense of confidence and belonging, increasing visibility of role models from underestimated backgrounds can actually diminish the biases others hold toward them. Studies focusing on the "reversibility" of prejudices found that increasing the presence of faces of other groups can reverse biases toward those groups over time.[13]

As cultural levers go, this is one of the easiest. You may not even have noticed the prevalence of male imagery or white faces decorating your walls until now, but replacing them with neutral artwork, or displaying resonant symbols, such as pictures of or quotes from diverse role models, can make underestimated employees feel an increased sense of belonging and confidence.

A Safer Workplace

The #TimesUp movement shed light on the harassment that women face from co-workers and supervisors. The kind of violence faced by women whose jobs require them to interact consistently with the public usually receives less attention, even though these kinds of roles pose much greater risk to women than to men. Women in public-facing roles often do not have access to the same level of protection offered to more male-dominated public-facing work. As documented in Caroline Criado Perez's *Invisible Women: Data Bias in a World Designed for Men,* nurses, for example, are subjected to more acts of violence than police officers or prison guards, and healthcare workers require time off from work due to violence four times more often than from other types of injury. The types of jobs in healthcare that are typically female-dominated, such as nursing, reported the most instances of injury by violence.[14]

These statistics are available only because outside researchers have documented them. Only 12 percent of the nurses in these studies who had been victims of on-the-job violence reported the incidents within their organizations. Most stated that there were no reporting structures, or they were told that violence was an assumed part of the job, so their complaints were not taken seriously.

These risks are not limited to healthcare. Women in the service industry are also far more likely than their male peers to be harassed, assaulted, or stalked. They, too, rarely have any means to report, and managers are hesitant to reprimand or remove customers who are behaving poorly.

Employers with public-facing employees can take a few of the following critical steps to help make the physical workplace safer for those who are often placed in vulnerable positions.

State your anti-harassment policy, visibly, from the point of entry. Whether your place of employment is a retail store, a hospital, or a restaurant, if there is a heightened chance of patients or customers harassing your employees, place signs at entryways boldly stating your zero-tolerance policy toward harassment. While this won't stop all bad behavior, you can discourage it by reminding customers that there are consequences; for example, "Anyone who harasses our employees will be removed and banned from the premises." In addition, limiting customer harassment limits multiple kinds of harassment. Studies published in the *Harvard Business Review* found that employees are less likely to harass other employees in establishments where customers are openly discouraged from doing so.[15] Post the procedures for reporting harassment clearly, in plain sight. This provides transparency around the process and serves as a subtle reminder that the organization takes complaints seriously.

Require only first names on badges. During one of my breaks home from college, I worked as a server in a hotel restaurant where name badges were required. Social media had exploded, from Myspace to Facebook, and it was easy to find someone if you had both their first and last names. Multiple male customers took advantage of this and sent me unwanted messages over these platforms. At the time I worried that telling them to stop would cause them to make false complaints to my manager, or worse.

Protecting the identity of healthcare workers is especially important for their safety, as well. Patients who feel they were mistreated or family members who have suffered a loss can take it out on employees, and displaying their identity can put them at great risk. Unless it is absolutely critical to have a last name on display, first names create the same level of rapport, while increasing safety.

Different emergencies, different alarms. In settings such as healthcare centers, staff are accustomed to hearing color-coded alarms for different kinds of emergencies, but not all hospitals and clinics have a coded alarm in place for cases when employees are being harassed or assaulted. As Perez points out in one case study, "In one instance, the patient call bell, bathroom assist bell, Code Blue for respiratory or cardiac arrest, and staff emergency alarms all made the same sound in the nurse's station."[16] A *specific* alarm for harassment can eliminate confusion over which alarm is signaling which emergency and drive the appropriate urgent response.

A panic button can also be a lifesaver in bars and restaurants. While several states now have laws against allowing only one person to close an establishment after a certain hour, many bars are still being closed at the end of the night by a lone woman. The panic button can mean the difference between someone assaulting a bartender and that would-be assailant fleeing out the door.

Tips on tipping. This may not seem like a "workplace design" cultural lever, but this best practice can be integrated into your menu. In restaurants where the tip is "built into" the pricing or automatically added on as a percentage of the bill, servers are less likely to be harassed by customers.[17] Customers in optional tipping environments are more likely to assume that servers will put up with harassment or even play into flirting that goes too far to earn their tip. When a tip is included, this licensing of inappropriate behavior is gone. If you decide to include this best practice, state it clearly at the top of your menu.

Gender-neutral restrooms. Finally, for employees who may identify as transgender or nonbinary, marking restrooms as gender neutral can make the workplace safer for them, emotionally and physically. Binary restrooms become a difficult choice for those who are going through transitions or have completed transitions but have not yet "outed" themselves to their co-workers. In service establishments in particular, this step can reduce transphobic violence.[18]

≈

You have come to the end of part 2 of this book, and you have covered a lot. You've gone from hiring the right person for the job to ensuring that performance is evaluated fairly. You've learned what you can do so that underestimated individuals have equal opportunities to rise into leadership roles. You know what cultural levers you can adjust in your business today to design bias out and equity in.

In the final three chapters, we turn toward the future. Part 3 explores how artificial intelligence could exacerbate the impact of bias rather than save us from it. We discuss the classic DEI pitfalls and how to avoid them. Finally, we propose some DEI principles to live by as our workforce continues to evolve in ways no one can totally envision.

Summary of Part 2

Chapter 6: Help Wanted—Inclusive Recruiting

Unconscious bias in job descriptions can drive strong applicants away from even considering an opportunity.

Be aware of masculine-coded and feminine-coded terms in job advertisements. Since most candidates' first impressions come from the job title, using words such as "journeyman" can have a significant impact on whether or not they apply. Other words, for example, "blacklisting" and "cakewalk," have racially biased connotations and can embed racial bias.

Instead of asking for a degree from an elite university, requiring a degree in a specific field is more inclusive.

Require only actual requirements. Do you need someone with five years of leadership *experience*, or do you need someone with leadership *skills*? Advertise for *competencies* and look for transferable skills, such as the ability to solve complicated problems.

If your organization is taking specific steps to create an equity-centered work environment, note it in your job description. Stick to the specifics you offer, such as flexible work arrangements or paid leave. This information encourages underestimated groups to apply.

Show the number of applicants you've received for a posting. Again, underestimated applicants will be far more likely to apply.

Don't post only on LinkedIn. To appeal to a more diverse pool of applicants, promote your job openings where underestimated individuals are more likely to see them.

Debias the selection process by adopting a clear procedure for blind resume reviews. If you work with an outside recruiter, ask if they conduct blind reviews.

Chapter 7: The Best Person for the Job—Merit-Based Hiring

Debias interviewing and scoring:

- Define the competencies you are looking for and create interview questions based on the STAR (Situation-Task-Action-Result) framework.
- Before beginning the interviews, decide on the exact wording of each question and the weighting of the responses.
- Schedule interviews for approximately the same time of day.
- Before beginning an interview, give the candidate advance notice that you will be following a structured interview process and explain what to expect regarding your questioning and scoring.
- In interviews, ask the same questions of every candidate in the same order.
- After interviewing all candidates, each member of the selection committee should individually write final notes, compare the scoring of all candidates, and write down one top candidate before reuniting with the rest of the committee to discuss. Scoring candidates privately sidesteps the "HiPPO effect"—a tendency to conform to the Highest Paid Person's Opinion (HiPPO) in the room.
- When evaluating the candidates, compare them directly to one another, rather than discussing each candidate separately. When applicants are explicitly compared to one another, your selection committees will be more likely to choose a candidate based on performance rather than subjective judgment.

Assessment tests can be helpful when they have been vetted for bias and are used appropriately. Here are levers you can adjust to level the playing field:

- Do not ask multiple candidates to take the test in a room together at the same time.
- Allow candidates to adjust the temperature in the room.
- Do not penalize test-takers for guessing, and state this at the beginning of the test.

Chapter 8: It's Who You Know— Protégés and Professional Development

Men are less likely to mentor women than they were before the #MeToo movement, and white people are less likely to mentor people of color than they were before the Black Lives Matter movement. White men's mentors are far more likely to be in senior roles than mentors of women or people of color. While mentors have an impact on career advancement for employees of all backgrounds, men benefit much more. The critical variable: the seniority of the mentor.

When women and employees of color have access to mentors in senior roles, they advance more quickly, are rewarded with higher compensation, and have higher levels of job satisfaction. Closing the mentorship seniority gap catalyzes career advancement and pay equality for employees of all backgrounds. It starts with intentional matching that includes the following:

- An inventory of potential mentors and mentees.
- Matching mentees to more than one mentor, and letting the mentee choose.
- Early KPI tracking.

If you are a senior leader, you typically have intense demands on your time. Focus mentoring meetings for optimum value:

- Understand your mentee's holistic career goals, or define those goals if your mentee is not sure yet.
- Identify blind spots or opportunities for improvement, provide constructive feedback, and point your mentee to resources.
- Ask about your mentee's preferences regarding feedback and coaching.

If you choose to mentor someone of a different gender or who comes from a different background than your own, two suggestions:

- Be transparent and visible about whom you are mentoring.
- Use the same structure for mentees of all backgrounds, but acknowledge difference.

Mentorship and sponsorship are often used interchangeably, but they require different levels of commitment. Sponsorship means verbally advocating on your sponsee's behalf and connecting them to your network. To sponsor underestimated individuals in your organization, communicate your plans to become a sponsor and allow candidates to apply informally. If you don't have time to provide ongoing sponsorship or mentorship but still want to further the professional development of underestimated employees, focus one-on-ones on this single question: What are your career goals?

Women are less likely to be invited to opportunities to grow their technical and business-critical skills. If you are about to forward a training announcement to the "perfect employee," send it to all the employees in your department instead. After underestimated employees complete the training, ask if they would be willing to share their experience with others through a presentation or summary in your company newsletter.

Make sure that your networking events are inclusive. Here are some keys:

- Try to schedule networking events during the workday.
- Make sure your food choices are inclusive.
- Encourage sober socializing. (Women who are seen drinking may be perceived as more intoxicated than they are, and their character may be called into question.)
- Require attendance from senior leaders.
- Track who is attending and who is not. If your events appear homogeneous, distribute a survey to see what would make underestimated employees more likely to attend.

Chapter 9: Exceed Expectations—The Performance Evaluation

Unconscious bias in performance evaluations can make or break careers.

One way to limit the effect of such bias is to conduct more frequent reviews. In businesses that conduct shorter but more frequent reviews, the perceived performance gap between women and men is nearly nonexistent.

Women's performance evaluations tend to be shorter and focus more on skills that are not as promotable as men's. The feedback women receive is also likely to be vague, lacking specific directives for improvement or clear connection to business outcomes. Men are more likely to receive longer performance reviews focused on the technical aspects of their jobs.

One way to counter this trend is to replace the common "open box" on performance reviews—a comment field, usually prefaced by a generic question such as "How did this employee succeed?" or "How did this employee not meet expectations?" Instead of the box, apply structured criteria. Investing the time to develop meaningful criteria is crucial to optimizing performance:

- Quantify competencies.
- Document examples.
- Tie performance to progress toward individual goals.
- Tie performance to business outcomes.
- Include everything, even office "housework."

What you do before and after the evaluation can make or break the success of your carefully selected criteria:

- Share the criteria in advance of evaluations.
- Ensure that managers do not see employees' self-evaluations before evaluating them.
- Ban personality words like "cold," "warm," "aggressive," and "likeable."
- Audit evaluations for bias by comparing the results by demographic.
- Check evaluations for *performance support bias*, a bias in which overconfidence in a certain group's abilities gives them more access to opportunities.

Chapter 10: The Physiology of Pay

Pay does not exist in a vacuum. To close your pay gap for the long term, you must close opportunity gaps in hiring, evaluations, and promotions as well.

Relying on referrals with no standards or checks can hurt your efforts to build a diverse workforce and progress toward pay equity. Keys to making your referrals work for all:

- Use the standardized hiring practices in chapter 7 to avoid giving special treatment to referrals.
- Consider an "extra" bonus for diversity referrals.
- Collect data around referrals and analyze it to help catch opportunity gaps.

Salary negotiations can reward employees who are great negotiators but who may not be more deserving of higher wages than their peers. These guidelines can help to debias the process:

- Clearly state the salary range of the job.
- Offer every candidate the chance to negotiate.
- Do not ask for salary histories or expectations.

Use employee self-evaluations wisely. When self-evaluations are allowed to influence pay decisions, managers may reward aggrandized self-perceptions rather than actual performance.

Not all gap analyses are created equal. These guidelines will help to ensure an accurate audit:

- Group together employees who perform comparable work. Analyze each of these groups separately.

- Choose controls (the factors that explain why employees in the same grouping may be paid different amounts) that are relevant to skill, effort, risk, or accountability and not related to gender, race, age, or other demographic characteristic.

- Choose an accurate measure of central tendency (median or mean), and analyze your data with an intersectional lens.

- Measure total compensation, including commissions, bonuses, and any other rewards.

If you discover a pay gap, be transparent about it and what you will do to correct it. An employer's ability to communicate clearly about compensation has been shown to play a larger role in employee sentiment than traditional measures of employee engagement. Sharing pay data is likely to relieve employees of negative perceptions they may be harboring.

When communicating about pay, focus on the "why." Employees care more about *why* they are paid what they're paid than about the exact dollar value (within reason). Essentials for pay conversations:

- Communicate the results of pay gap analyses, including causes discovered and targets to reduce the gaps.

- Document and distribute your pay equity strategy, including your pay equity metrics and policies of accountability.

- Share a standardized pay rubric with the criteria behind pay, bonus, and raise decisions.

Conducting a pay gap analysis once captures a moment in time. Continuing to evaluate pay regularly ensures that hidden gaps don't grow as your company evolves.

Chapter 11: Family Matters

In 2020, the year of COVID, women lost a million more jobs than men. Women of color were hit the hardest, facing higher unemployment numbers than white women.

Much of this "she-cession" was driven by the additional caretaking that working mothers had to take on. The companies that lost new mothers lost someone who was likely to have been a top performer. Multiple studies have found that working mothers are more productive than their peers.

Employees and employers can benefit from expanding paid leave in the following ways:

- Offer family leave, not just maternity leave.
- For paternity leave to have an impact, male leaders must model taking leave.
- The amount of leave should be substantial, but not too long. A year off can hamper women's abilities to reintegrate into the workplace or return to senior roles.

Parents are not the only employees who may require leave. More adults find themselves "sandwiched" between caring for their own children and parents living into their late eighties and nineties. Employers that offer caretakers' leave are more likely to retain their caretaking employees.

Twenty-one percent of full-time employed adults report that they have been victims of domestic violence, and over four-fifths of domestic violence victims are women. Time off allows employees affected by domestic violence to seek medical attention, meet with a lawyer, file for a protection order, attend court hearings, or relocate, if needed. Accommodations such as these can allow them to perform successfully:

- Provide private, quiet workspaces and more frequent work breaks.
- Allow the employee additional time to learn new responsibilities.
- Offer a flexible work schedule and time off for counseling, or legal or medical appointments.
- During onboarding, provide an opportunity for employees to state if particular smells or noises are triggering and try remove those triggers from the work environment.

To destigmatize taking leave, consider these unusual but effective policies:

- Develop a keep-in-touch plan for employees on leave.
- Make promotions accessible to employees on leave.
- Administer a brief test to employees returning from extended leave, to prevent their competency from being called into question.

Many employees prefer the flexibility of remote or hybrid work options. Earning potential and career advancement are still highly correlated with in-person work, however, making underestimated groups more vulnerable to an "out of sight, out of mind" dynamic that can leave them behind. To ensure an equitable impact, provide the following supports:

- Determine flexible work policies with employee participation, giving employees at all levels, not just managers, the chance to weigh in.
- For everyone to feel comfortable participating, leaders need to model hybrid work.
- Set targets and track participation. Gathering data on who is participating in flexible work arrangements can reveal imbalances between demographics or teams.

Chapter 12: Leadership Material

We are prone to mistake confidence in potential leaders for competence, especially in men. Most employees are dissatisfied with their managers, but most managers, especially male managers, see themselves as highly effective.

Overvaluing confidence and charisma means that we miss out on diverse leadership styles proven to be effective across all backgrounds. Introverts, for example, may hold some of the most undervalued leadership potential. To move from rewarding the stereotypically charismatic to recognizing and promoting typically unsung leadership potential, define clear, transparent criteria that let employees know what steps they need to take to advance.

- Revisit job descriptions, clearly defining the expected skills for every role. Beware of using titles in place of competencies, and consider your future leadership needs.
- Communicate your criteria for advancement using one-on-ones to remind individuals aspiring to leadership of the steps they need to take to advance.

Although skepticism over quotas is strong in the US, multiple case studies point to the same conclusion: Over time, quotas work. To implement quotas for underestimated employees effectively, leadership groups must achieve a critical mass of underestimated individuals. While there is not a "perfect" number, stereotypes have far less impact when minority groups represent at least one-third of a group. For organizations that are facing unbalanced pipelines, this 33 percent target can seem out of reach. In this case, the organization must set a target.

The following steps can foster buy-in:

- Communicate the rationale behind the target numbers you choose: pipeline-dependent, representative of the customer base, or representation at all levels of the business.

- Communicate targets as part of a comprehensive leadership strategy and timeline.

Group meetings provide another early opportunity to spot potential leaders. These inclusive meeting behaviors can help ensure that a diverse range of voices are heard and their contributions are recognized:

- Invoke a one- to two-minute reflection period before accepting feedback.
- If a topic is being presented for feedback within a large group, provide time for participants to meet in subgroups first.
- Provide lead time for review and space for open-ended feedback.

Once you have started recognizing potential leaders, retaining them and recruiting them into the promotion process is key. Actions to encourage engagement:

- Open promotions to all who meet minimum requirements. Select by the STAR method.
- Encourage underestimated individuals to apply.
- Share the reasons that a candidate was chosen for promotion.

Chapter 13: Blueprints for Inclusive Workspaces

Without inclusive design practices, even workplaces that seem inclusive in theory can build in bias. Open office spaces, for example, were well-intended, but they robbed women of the productive time and focus needed to advance. Employees of color also preferred more privacy over too-open spaces where they had experienced being perceived as the "angry Black person."

Several "inclusion mainstreaming" steps can moderate these effects:

- Consider a red-yellow-green color-coded "availability" system to counter the "casual conversation" interruption problem.
- Make the open office optional with movable partitions to accommodate introverts, extraverts, and all personality types in between.
- Provide private spaces (prayer room, nursing room, quiet/focus room).

The kinds of role models we see or are reminded of can affect our performance. Consider your wall art. Are the images homogeneous, or can all of your employees relate?

Workers in healthcare and service industries are disproportionately exposed to threats and violence, and these workers are disproportionately female. The following steps can make the workplace safer for those who are placed in vulnerable positions:

- State your anti-harassment policy, visibly, from the point of entry.
- Require only first names on badges.
- In settings such as healthcare centers, provide a specific, recognizable alarm for harassment situations.
- In bars and restaurants, provide a panic button for workers.
- Also in food service, employ built-in tipping and state it clearly on your menu.
- Provide gender-neutral restrooms to combat transphobic violence.

Finally, we look ahead in part 3, "Zooming Back Out—The Big Picture."

PART 3

Zooming Back Out—
The Big Picture

CHAPTER 14

AI Won't Save Us (Unless We Save It First)

"Fairness is a statistical concept."

—Heather Krause, Founder of We All Count

"Algorithms are human agency and interests, encoded."

—University of Sussex Researcher Tony Roberts

In 2015, T.J. Fitzpatrick was attending a science fiction convention at an Atlanta Marriott. In the convention center restroom, when he went to wash his hands, nothing came out of the soap dispenser. He assumed it was empty. T.J. went to the next one, and the next, until he had held his hands under all 10 soap dispensers. Then his friend Larry came in, and T.J. decided to wait for him. When Larry went to wash his hands, the soap worked on the first try.

T.J. tried again—still no success. For Larry, it worked every time.

T.J. was Black, and Larry was white.

They laughed about it, recorded a quick split-screen take of their experiences, and shared the videos out to social media. It may have been the first time a soap dispenser went viral. Suddenly it was clear that this was a trend outside of the Atlanta Marriot. "Oh my God, I thought it was just me," commented a Black woman. Thousands of similar comments rolled in from people of color who had experienced the mysterious case of the "racist soap dispenser" in other places.

Touchless dispensers use near-infrared technology that emits light from an LED bulb, which a person's hands then reflect to a triggering sensor. Because darker skin absorbs more light than lighter skin, in many of these dispensers, too little light is reflected to trigger the sensor.

The dispensers rely on artificial intelligence. Like many other "smart" devices in our lives, though, the algorithms behind them are not DEI-intelligent.

The more reliant we become on AI, the more frequently we see inanimate objects behave with prejudice. Google's PR department spent years apologizing for a photo-labeling system that misidentified Black people as gorillas. Nikon's "smart" digital cameras got poor reviews for repeatedly flashing "Did someone blink?" messages when photographing Asian people. Voice recognition software, trained by men, is more consistently accurate in understanding male voices than female voices. Object-detection software has failed to recognize dark-skinned individuals in virtual reality games, and more dangerously, in the models designed to prevent self-driving cars from hitting pedestrians.

These mishaps provide compelling arguments for diverse product development teams. If Nikon had tested its camera on Asian audiences, if women were involved in training voice recognition software, if Black employees were in the room as UX specialists, these biased designs could have been avoided.

Unfortunately, biased algorithms can also block the same people who could make AI more inclusive from getting in the door.

Bias for—and in—Action

Amazon has core "Leadership Principles" that are relentlessly emphasized internally and externally. One of these core principles is a "Bias for Action." They define it as follows:

Speed matters in business. Many decisions and actions are reversible and do not need extensive study. We value calculated risk taking.[1]

In 2014, Amazon's machine learning team decided to take one of these calculated risks by automating parts of their recruiting and hiring processes.

It was an opportunity that seemed prime for machine learning assistance. Recruiters and HR professionals usually had to spend weeks sorting through resumes to determine which applicants met even the minimum requirements for a role. Machine sorting could save time and potentially make the selection process fairer. After all, machines aren't wooed by applicants with charismatic cover letters or glowing recommendations.

The team leaned into their Bias for Action principles and instituted a machine-learning-based recruiting system. It was structured similarly to Amazon's shopping frameworks—the system "scored" applicants from 1 to 5 stars, just as consumers could score products they had purchased.

A year in, the machine learning team realized they had a problem.[2]

The system was downgrading resumes that included the word "women" or otherwise indicated that the applicant was a woman. Resumes that were submitted by graduates of women's colleges, for example, or that included the term "women's chess club" were rated less favorably, compared to resumes of similar caliber that were clearly submitted by men.

This biased sorting was a result of the ways that machines "learn" in the algorithm development process. To learn how to hire, for example, Amazon's machines were fed 10 years of hiring history, which informed algorithms that would determine whom to accept or reject. Hundreds of thousands of resumes marked "accepted" or "rejected" were scanned, interpreted, and sorted into a framework for what "hirable" looked like. Because Amazon had disproportionately hired men, especially for technical roles, men were coded as hirable. Even the language men used in their resumes was considered more desirable; applicants who used more male-coded language were scored higher compared to applicants who listed similar accomplishments but used female-coded language.

Despite the risks posed by AI-driven hiring tools, 56 percent of managers plan to embrace AI-based hiring practices by 2022.[3] Today 72 percent of resumes are rejected without ever being seen by a human eye.[4]

But when it comes to employment, employers aren't limiting their use of AI to hiring.

Algorithmic Attrition

In *Weapons of Math Destruction*, Cathy O'Neil shares examples of several data tools, algorithms, and platforms that companies use to triage their retention efforts. Which employees are worth putting energy into keeping? Several startups, including one named Gild, are devoted to helping employers answer this question. But instead of rating employees' retention worthiness by evaluating their skills or accomplishments, Gild evaluates their social capital. How much "clout" do employees have? What would be the social cost of losing certain individuals?

O'Neil explains Gild's method by giving us a fictional software developer, Pedro, who lives in Sao Paulo. Every night after getting home from work, Pedro has dinner and then quickly jumps online, spending hours communing with fellow coders by gaming or solving coding problems on sites like GitHub. Even though Pedro doesn't know it, Gild's model will "reward" his level of engagement with others, especially with those who have large online coding networks. If Pedro's online contacts are influencers with hundreds of thousands of followers, his "social capital" score skyrockets.

These connections don't always find each other by working together on coding problems, though. For example, many of them also frequent Japanese manga websites—male-dominated online comic book communities that oversexualize women in their comics and cartoons. Gild's algorithm doesn't discriminate, though. If high-profile coders are connecting en masse, and Pedro is there, Pedro's score goes up.

As you might imagine, most female coders don't dwell on manga sites. They also have reason to avoid massive online coding communities like GitHub. As detailed in chapter 3, their work is not treated the same as male-generated code on these open-source platforms. In 2015, the harassment campaign known as Gamergate targeted women in the video gaming industry, subjecting them to relentless harassment, threats, and stalking, in some cases so severe that they had to leave their homes.[5]

Female coders may hone their skills outside online communities, or in safer female coding and gaming groups, which don't rank as highly in social capital indexes. Do they not deserve for employers to invest in their retention?

The Half-Life of Encoded Bias

As our society becomes increasingly dependent on AI, a pernicious assumption is spreading that software will allow us to escape the influence of bias. It's easy to believe that math will cut through messiness, that depending on "objective" algorithms will free us from prejudice. The mathematical models that underpin AI and machine learning, however, hold immense power, and commensurate risk.

In an interview on the *Racism at Work* podcast, Harry Gaskell, Chief Innovation Officer at Ernst & Young UK and chair of the Employers Network for Equality & Inclusion, discusses the social consequences of encoded bias. Despite spending most of his life working with statistical models, Gaskell himself is astounded by their staying power. Reflecting on algorithms he played a role in creating, he calls for urgency in reigning in algorithmic bias:

> *There's nothing in AI that we can't control if we choose to control it,*
> *but we need to get there quickly. I started coding things nearly 35 years*
> *ago now and some of those systems, that me and my colleagues built*
> *35 years ago, we thought they would probably have a 5- or 10-year*

shelf life, that we'd write them and that they would be replaced by other things pretty quickly. Actually some of them are still in use today, it embarrasses me to say. Particularly in industries that have been around for a while, like banking, they're still using code that is 20, 30, 40, 50 years old.

My worry is that if we're not careful we might start building AI which is around for decades that was never built using. . .ethics, social responsibility, accountability, reliability. . .If we build stuff not using those principles and those things also have lives of decades, I really worry that we're going to bake bias into systems that'll be very difficult to get out. The sooner we get our act together. . .the sooner we eliminate bias from systems, the better it's going to be.[6]

While his message is intended as a warning, the first part of Gaskell's statement gives me hope:

There's nothing in AI that we can't control if we choose to control it. . .

The potential that AI holds to build a fairer society does not have to be a false hope. It is already creating positive outcomes for many. AI that was originally created to sort boutique baked goods has been reengineered to recognize cancer cells, increasing the odds of early detection and survival.[7] NASA machine learning lead engineer Anirudh Koul and I shared the Seattle TEDx stage in 2018. Anirudh showed numerous examples of ways that AI could contribute to a more equitable society. Koul had drawn on his experience building hands-free dictation features in Microsoft Office for those with motor impairments to create Seeing AI, an app that helps blind and low-vision communities navigate spaces using their smartphones.

If we make the right choices, AI could help us build more equity-centered workplaces as well. As Gaskell notes, however, it won't just happen. We have to code fairness in, starting now.

The Fairness Standards

Amazon has a final core principle in its list: "Success and Scale Bring Broad Responsibility."

AI adoption is accelerating and will likely continue to do so.[8] Meanwhile, we have little to no regulation of how employers can or should use it. There are no US standards for due diligence, transparency, or accountability. In this new AI Wild West, companies like Amazon will have to uphold their "Broad Responsibility" by implementing—and adhering to—standards of algorithmic fairness.

The idea of standards is nothing new to developers and statisticians. For example, Gaskell points out in his podcast interview that IBM has coding standards for naming, platform portability, and safe function-calling practices.[9] To ensure that automated intelligence is inclusive and equations are equitable, developers should answer questions that would determine whether their code meets standards of fairness.

Before exploring some of the questions that could test mathematical models for fairness, I want to acknowledge that I am not a developer or a professional statistician. I have heavily leaned on the work of data scientists, ethicists, and thought leaders such as Cathy O'Neil, Heather Krause, and Tony Roberts for the frameworks that follow. I highly recommend exploring their work for a deeper understanding of these concepts.

Who (or What) Is Missing?

The absence of a group can matter more than its presence. Data and Society fellow and NYU faculty member Mimi Onuoha captured this idea in a combined data project and mixed-media installation titled *The Library of Missing Datasets*. In collaboration with others, Onuoha created a physical repository—mainly old metal filing cabinets—of data sets that do not exist yet, but should. In her words:

> *Missing data sets are my term for the blank spots that exist in spaces that are otherwise data-saturated. My interest in them stems from the observation that within many spaces where large amounts of data are collected, there are often empty spaces where no data live. Unsurprisingly, this lack of data typically correlates with issues affecting those who are most vulnerable in that context.*[10]

Onuoha and her team have posted lists of some of these missing data sets on GitHub, inviting crowdsourced creation of data repositories that would cross the data sets off the "missing" list. Examples include the following:

- Number of Americans without bank accounts.
- Employment/unemployment numbers that include the incarcerated.
- Demographics of bitcoin buyers.
- Royalties that Spotify pays each of its artists per play per song.

Workplaces have missing data sets as well, and if people are not accounted for when a mathematical model is created, they will not be included when the model is implemented. For example, homogeneous companies that are trying to diversify may lack data about the very people they want to hire and retain. Employers can also be missing data around their processes, or the behaviors of applicants, that could optimize their algorithms for fairness.

If Onuoha listed these kinds of missing data sets for employers, they could include the following:

- Words different genders use to describe the same jobs.
- Demographic breakdown of resume reviewers over the last 10 years.
- Which interview questions have been asked to which demographics of applicants.
- The interviewer/interviewee demographic pairing of candidates who have been hired.

The categories that an algorithm allows for can also allow certain demographics to go statistically missing. Individuals who have transitioned from one gender to another, for example, have lost years of medical records because methods for tracking transgender individuals were never built into medical record-keeping systems. Similar problems follow transgender and nonbinary employees and applicants. If your hiring algorithm codes for binary gender options only, nonbinary applicants' resumes may never reach you. Employees who transition during their tenure with an organization can risk losing data that was previously linked to their employee profile by a certain gender.

As Mimi Onuoha notes, data sets are not the results of our realties: "Datasets are the results of their means of collection." Which leads to the next question—*who* is behind the means of collection?

Who Is Creating the Model?

This question is important for two reasons. The first, and more obvious, is that diverse teams are more likely to provide diverse insights, which decreases the odds of designing racist soap dispensers and sexist voice recognition software.

The second reason is less obvious, but psychology professionals have given it a name: the "interviewer effect."[11] Several studies have shown that participants in research studies alter their opinions or their perceptions depending on the demographic of the person interviewing them.

I mentioned data ethicist Heather Krause earlier in this chapter. Krause is the chief data scientist at Datassist, and the founder of We All Count, a project dedicated to equity in data science.[12] In experiments conducted by the We All Count team, researchers compared how subjects responded to questions about whether they approved or disapproved of men hitting their wives. They compared the following pairs of interviewers and interviewees:

- Male respondent, male enumerator, both urban.
- Male respondent, male enumerator, both rural.
- Female respondent, female enumerator, both urban.
- Female respondent, female enumerator, both rural.
- Male respondent, female enumerator, both urban.
- Male respondent, female enumerator, both rural.
- Female respondent, male enumerator, both urban.
- Female respondent, male enumerator, both rural.

They found that respondents in the second variation (male respondent, male enumerator, both rural) were the most likely to state that this kind of violence against women was okay. Respondents in the third variation (female respondent, female enumerator, both urban) were least likely to say it was okay. Women speaking to women enumerators were 7 to 12 percent more likely to reject violence against women than women speaking to male enumerators.[13]

The interviewer effect encourages participants to take social norms into account when responding to an interviewer, and it could influence testing how people interact with automation.[14] For example, if an interviewer asks a diverse range of individuals about their experience with a hiring platform, women might be less likely to criticize the experience to a male interviewer, or a person of color might be less likely to give negative feedback to a white evaluator.

To avoid building a model based on feedback tainted by the interviewer effect, try to match interviewers' demographics to those of your participants. If your testing has already been conducted, note the demographic pairings of the interviewers and interviewees who interacted. As I explain later in this chapter in "Debiasing Your Data," you can use this information to employ several different statistical solutions that account for the interviewer effect in your population, and compensate for it in your algorithm.

Are You Evaluating Impact Through an Equity Lens?

To determine whether a model is fair, you have to test it. Even if you test it with diverse audiences, though, that does not guarantee you are evaluating

FIGURE 14.1   Adopted from We All Count

through an equity lens. Krause gives us two examples of how our embedded worldview can give us different mathematical evaluations of the same event.

Example 1: Whose average is it, anyway?

Let's pretend you are evaluating the impact of class size on student learning. You are presented with the three classrooms shown in figure 14.1.[15] The first classroom has one student in it, the second has three students in it, and the third has five students.

What is the average class size in this school?

Most readers would say "three." And they would be correct.

The average class size is also four. It depends on whom you ask.

If you ask the *teachers*, one says "one," the second says "three," the third says "five." Add that up, divide by three, and your average is three. But whose experience are we actually evaluating? How does the math change if we ask the students?

In the first classroom, the one student says "one"; in the second classroom, there are three students who all say "three"; and in the third classroom, five students all say "five." Adding all of these responses totals 35. Divide by nine, and your student-perceived average is almost four.

Even basic math that we learn by fourth grade has an embedded worldview. We are more inclined to solve for the average from the teacher's point of view because we put the locus of power on authority figures.

Similarly, when testing the impact of hiring or retention models on employees, ask yourself from whose point of view you are mathematically assessing impact—the employee? The manager? Co-workers? Who is affected, and therefore should be the locus of evaluative power?

Example 2: Beware the randomized control trial trap.

Randomized control trials (RCTs) are often hailed as the gold standard of research methods. Heather Krause disagrees, at least contextually. "Randomized control trials are the very best. . .randomized control trials," she states in several presentations. RCTs are the gold standard of finding one specific answer: the estimate of the *average* effect of an action, policy, or other intervention on a population.

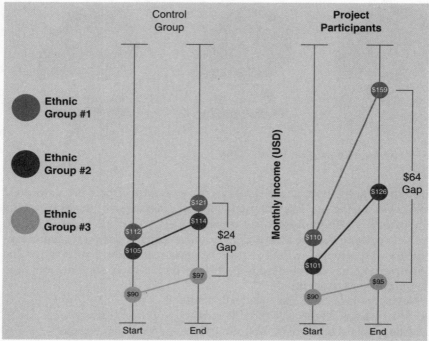

FIGURE 14.2 Adopted from We All Count

For example, if a city government is trying to determine whether a new policy increased income for the population of a certain neighborhood, an RCT can tell them that the population experienced an average increase of $27 after the policy was implemented.

What if we evaluated that data with an equity lens?

Let's say the people included in this project identify as members of three distinct ethnic groups, who started at different income levels, and experienced their incomes increasing at different rates throughout the project, as shown in figure 14.2.[16]

For the overall group, the average income increase was $27. But when we break it down, there is more to this story. Average income for the first ethnic group increased by $5. The second group saw an average increase of $25, and the third, $49. That's a 45 percent increase for the group that started in the most privileged position, and only a 6 percent increase for the poorest group. In fact, it appears this project widened the overall income gap between groups.

Similarly, you could discover that the representation of women in your organization is 15 percent below the representation of women in the pipeline for your industry, so you institute a change in hiring processes. Over a year, you see the gap close. What you may not see, however, is that you've increased the share of white women by 20 percent and lost 5 percent women of color by focusing more on gender at the expense of losing focus on race. Or, perhaps the entire increase is accounted for by hiring more women into departments where women were already overrepresented. RCTs will not reflect this.

To evaluate with an equity lens, you have to look beyond the results of an RCT.

Debiasing Your Data

Even when you find a source of potential bias in your model, you can't always change the data set or circumstances you're working with. If you are forced into accepting that biases will persist in your model, multiple statistical methods exist for estimating the *effects* of the biases and adjusting your algorithms to compensate for them. I will not derive full mathematical explanations of how to do that here; however, We All Count (accessible at WeAllCount.com) provides extensive resources on techniques such as propensity score matching, and building mixed-effects models with an interaction effect for the biasing characteristics.

In addition, if there are particular characteristics that you know will bias how a model evaluates job applicants, you can "blind" applications or resumes before an algorithm is applied to them. In fact, AI can be the solution to the AI problem! Platforms such as Gapjumpers and Blendoor have been developed to scrub names and demographic information from resumes, cover letters, and other job application materials. You can use these to remove biasing characteristics from application materials before running them through an automated sorting process.

Finally, beware of using proxies to attempt to fix incomplete or skewed data sets. Chapter 9 on pay equity explains the potential dangers of substituting, for example, age as a proxy for experience. In industries and roles where switching careers is common, age is not representative of years of experience.

If you discover a missing data set that you wish you had access to, it can be tempting to use a proxy. Instead, I recommend making the effort to locate data sets from outside your organization that describe the group you are trying to understand. The Black Futures Lab, for example, launched the Black Census Project in 2018 to provide data on the experiences, views, and backgrounds of Black Americans.[17] We All Count features more of these resources, including a wealth of powerful data equity tools for any employers looking to hire from, understand better, or simply respect Indigenous communities in the US.

Transparency

In her book, Cathy O'Neil lists three key traits that separate simple, harmless algorithms from weapons of math destruction. The first is transparency. Algorithms that are opaque or invisible have more potential to harm vulnerable groups. When nobody knows the variables that comprise a model, nobody knows who is being left out, who may benefit, and who may be harmed.

Transparency also levels the playing field. In chapter 6, I told the story of my friend, Aaron, who took a personality test to apply for an accounting job. I didn't discuss Aaron's competition. Applicants with the means to pay career coaches would have had a greater chance to "game" that test. Career coaching industries are now built on knowing which companies use which tests, what they ask, and, as in video gaming, how to "win." The less transparent you are about your hiring algorithms, the more likely you are to accept applicants who have been keyword-coached and miss out on applicants with superior qualifications but less access to AI coaching.

To foster transparency, I recommend including a condensed version of what Krause refers to as a "data biography" with all algorithm-based models. This data biography should be available to anyone interacting with the algorithm and should include the following.

The elements of your equation. What + What = What? Let users know exactly what factors comprise your mathematical model and how they are weighted.

How the data is used. Most data lives long beyond its original purpose. The EU has regulated this fact of data life through their General Data Protection Regulation (GDPR) standards, which require businesses to disclose how data is stored, used, and eventually destroyed. Businesses can model ethical data usage by mirroring this standard, stating whether the data will be used for any purpose other than its originally intended use.

Who created the mathematical model. In his interview, Gaskell emphasizes that transparency is essential beyond the algorithm itself. Knowing who created the model fosters accountability and highlights any possible motivations or biases that could have been embedded by the designer.

Data sets and specific definitions. Describe the data sets that were used to build your algorithm and provide specific definitions that are methods-based. For example, if you say that you built an algorithm based on a data set in which 20 percent of respondents were Black, does that mean. . .

- That others identified them as Black?
- That they self-identified as Black?
- That they self-identified as Black by writing it in?
- That they self-identified as Black by picking it from a list that included White, Hispanic, Asian, Middle Eastern, Black, and other? Could they pick only one option or multiple options?

These versions of "Black respondents" all have different embedded meanings.

How the model was evaluated (and reevaluated and adjusted). How was the model tested? How often is it retested? When was the last time it was adjusted based on findings from impact evaluations?

≈

This chapter may have seemed to miss an obvious and important workplace-related AI theme: job automation. Looking forward, AI won't just determine who is selected for jobs, it will select which jobs will still exist at all.

Automation is just one aspect of a future of work that is unknown to us. It's easy to wonder if it's even possible to create a DEI strategy now that will still be relevant in an uncertain future.

No matter what your future of work will look like, 10 core DEI principles can help guide your way.

CHAPTER 15

DEI Principles to Live By

Between 15 and 30 percent of jobs in the developed world are estimated to be taken over by machines, disembodied AI, or robots in the next 10 to 20 years.[1] In his book, *Evil Geniuses: The Unmaking of America*, Kurt Andersen cites these pre-pandemic estimates in his chapter on the future of work, warning us that manual labor jobs aren't the only ones at risk of automation. Engineers, radiologists, and even lab assistants may all find themselves competing against machines in the future workplace.

Automation isn't the only force reshaping the future of work. As chapter 3 highlighted, the future workforce will be increasingly female, non-white, neurodivergent, and LGBTQ-identifying with each passing year. We will also be facing a mass retirement of baby boomers; every day, 10,000 more turn the "official retirement age" of 65,[2] and *Forbes* estimates that 75 percent of baby boomers plan to retire early, taking with them decades of institutional knowledge.[3]

Even the concept of the physical workplace is no longer a given. The hybrid workplace is likely here to stay, with Twitter, Facebook/Meta, and Amazon all announcing in 2021 that their employees can work from home indefinitely.

In the face of these shifts and the unknowns we are yet to encounter, crafting a DEI strategy can feel daunting. How can you know that the policies you implement today will be relevant even a year from now?

Ambiguity should not stop you from developing a DEI strategy. It should be a reason to start.

In March 2020, the pandemic sent much of the US into lockdown, and employers went into crisis mode, cutting costs wherever possible. DEI initiatives were some of the first casualties in companies that treated them as optional "extras." In contrast, businesses that had integrated DEI best practices into their overall business strategy retained the diversity of their workforce, and many outperformed their competition in the crisis.[4]

At GEN, we kept in touch with all certified organizations, staying "on call" to support them in case they were struggling to sustain their DEI strategy in this time of crisis. We were pleasantly surprised that none of them seemed to experience DEI emergencies. Over a year and a half later, not only did all GEN-certified businesses survive—they thrived. Even ones that were in hard-hit industries, such as event production, managed to grow their employee base and promote underestimated individuals into leadership positions during the pandemic. Because DEI was *already* integrated into every part of how these employers conducted business, they didn't have to treat it as an "extra." It wasn't a cost center—it was a built-in competitive advantage.

When creating, implementing, and communicating your strategy, these 10 core DEI principles can help it survive the unknown.

Stage 1: Creating Your DEI Strategy

In your strategic plan, anticipate transitions, prepare to retain, and rely on your data.

1. Don't over-automate the underestimated. Pre-plan transition safety nets.

Just as underestimated individuals can be passed over for promotions or mentorship, they are also at risk of being overlooked during workforce transformations, unless a DEI transition plan is in place. High-profile employees are more likely to have a safe landing pad, leaving behind those without safety nets.

In crafting your DEI strategy, note which jobs you think are most likely to be automated and the demographics most likely to be impacted. Are they disproportionately jobs belonging to underestimated individuals? If so, you can build a retention safety net by looking at what new opportunities will be created by automation. While AI means the elimination of some roles, it also means there will be increased demand for other skills. Similar to the way cashiers became checkout assistants, corporate workplaces may see machine-to-human translator roles appear, or a heightened demand for systems thinkers who can help predict how automating one workflow will impact processes downstream. Identifying underestimated individuals who have these skills, or training for them, starting now, will ensure that they have a safety net, and that your organization will continue to benefit from their insights going forward.

2. Don't create a recruiting strategy without a retention strategy.

Once you have developed a recruiting strategy, it can be tempting to run with it and assume you'll get the rest of your DEI strategy in place soon after. At GEN, if an employer comes to us asking for a recruiting strategy, we will insist that they also create a retention, equity, and inclusion strategy. Your recruiting strategy may bring employees from diverse backgrounds through the door, but these individuals may quickly discover that the culture is not ready for them. In the time it takes for an employer to develop a retention strategy, some employees may already be planning their exit.

Not only will having a complete DEI strategy in place help with retention, it will help with recruitment. As noted in chapter 6, candidates are now asking employers to share the exact steps they are taking to prioritize DEI. By having a retention strategy in place, you will be ready to share how you go beyond talk to meaningful action.

At GEN we recommend that retention, equity, and inclusion strategies address at least the following key elements:

- *Performance evaluations.* Are they standardized? How do you safeguard against bias? How often are they conducted? Do self-evaluations impact decisions around pay and promotions?
- *Pay equity.* Do you perform pay gap audits? Are they based on total compensation, including commissions, bonuses, and stock options? How often are audits conducted? Do you take an intersectional approach?
- *Promotions.* How are promotional decisions made? Can anyone apply? How transparent is the decision-making process? Do you compare promotion frequencies by demographics? Are employees on leave eligible for promotions?
- *Professional development/ongoing education.* What opportunities do you offer? Is your mentorship based on intentional matching? How do you ensure equal access to professional development opportunities for employees of all backgrounds? Are networking events offered during work hours?
- *Flexibility/leave/remote work.* What are your flexible work policies? Are they determined with employee input? Do you offer paid parental and caretaker leave for all genders? Is taking leave modeled and encouraged by leadership?
- *Vendor/procurement policy.* Do you ask potential vendors what their DEI policies are? Do you prefer to work with vendors who have a diverse leadership team?

- *DEI evaluation and reporting policy.* How do you track progress toward DEI goals? To whom is it reported? How often? How is it incorporated into your holistic business strategy?

3. Act on data, not best guesses.

When business leaders contact GEN because the DEI strategy they created isn't working, we tend to find gaps in the following areas:

- What leaders think employees want versus what employees (especially underestimated employees) actually want.
- The access to opportunities that one group of employees experiences versus the access to opportunities that underestimated employees experience.

We are living in an age when it is easier than ever to collect, analyze, and act on data. No matter how well you think you know your culture or how open you believe employees are with one another, test your assumptions. Your strategy should be driven by data, not best guesses. Crafting a data-smart DEI strategy means collecting data that answer the two following questions:

- *What are the quantifiable differences between different populations' lived experiences in their workplace?* For example, do equal percentages of women and men, or white employees and employees of color, report being asked about their career goals in the last 12 months, being invited to a networking event, or having a conversation about pay? The more specific you are in finding the gaps in experiences, the more effective you can be in tackling these challenges in your DEI strategy. Sometimes gaps surface that employees themselves aren't aware of. For example, women may not state that there is a gap between the frequency with which managers ask different genders about their career development goals because they may not have been aware that men are asked more often. Asking what employees have or have not experienced, and then comparing their answers, can pinpoint exactly where you have hidden gaps in processes.
- *What do employees, of all backgrounds, want?* It may seem obvious, but this crucial step is often overlooked in crafting DEI strategy: Ask employees what they want. When assessing companies for certification, GEN measures the gap between what employees say they want and what an organization actually offers, and we often find that employers have made incorrect assumptions. Even if paid leave and flexibility top the list for what women want nationally, that doesn't mean that these are the priorities for women in your organization. You won't know unless you ask. When analyzing this employee feedback, aggregate and pay attention

to the responses from underestimated employees, whose answers may be in the minority, but which can hold the keys to retaining and supporting them.

Stage 2: Implementing Strategy

As you implement your plan, keep a long-term perspective, leverage experts, let everyone in the company own DEI, and stay alert at the intersections.

4. Think long term and set expectations.

One of the headlines I was thrilled to see in 2020 came from a tech giant that had released its diversity numbers. Rather than announcing, "We've Reached Pay Equity!" or "We Lead in Diversity!" the press release read, "We are at the starting line. We have a long way to go."

As the first chapters of this book explored, most organizations' default settings have been programmed by one group, for one group, for decades. For this reason, GEN is yet to work with an organization that was beyond the starting line when they came to us. Without an intentional pause-and-reset, why would they be?

Recognizing and communicating that you are at the starting line sets expectations that change will not happen overnight. It also demonstrates to underestimated employees that you are taking your approach to DEI seriously, rather than treating it like a one-off event or a marketing campaign.

Keeping a long-term perspective also means accepting that not everyone will immediately be on board. Just as people tend to be quota-averse until quotas are implemented, DEI efforts may not win over all of your employees until they see results. Often, employees need to see greater diversity lead to organizational success before they can believe it. Until then, stay the course. If you are not immediately seeing results, and even if you are experiencing setbacks, remember that making up for years, or decades, of institutional bias takes time.

5. DEI is not kickball. Work with data-smart experts.

Companies that do not rely on expertise often take what I refer to as the Kickball Approach: DEI becomes a fun extracurricular, similar to the company kickball team or party-planning committee. Everyone gathers in the break room on a Wednesday afternoon, contributes their best DEI-related ideas, and they run with the one that sounds like the most fun. As explored in chapter 4,

DEI practitioners must have a range of skills and knowledge—from supply chain management to statistical analysis—to be successful. This multidisciplinary expertise cannot be matched by the Kickball Approach.

If you do not have a DEI expert in-house, find a qualified one to work with you, at least on a consulting basis. When evaluating practitioners to partner with, ask what kinds of metrics they use, and look for measurements that go beyond representation. As chapter 5 explored, tracking upstream measures of success—such as equitable access to professional development opportunities—is essential to driving downstream indicators of success, such as diverse representation. If candidates do not measure lead indicators, look for someone who does.

6. DEI does not belong to HR.

As we learned in chapter 14, even jobs that seem to have little to do with DEI can perpetuate bias, in the workplace and beyond. Taking the following steps can help account for the impact each role has on equity and inclusion:

- *Make DEI part of every job description.* Equity and inclusion should be core competencies for every role, as they relate to the role. Revisiting chapter 6 on recruiting, when drafting competency-based job descriptions, write equity and inclusion into them. This could mean requiring an understanding of DEI-related terms, such as *intersectionality*, as well as more role-specific skills, such as auditing algorithms for bias.

- *Make sure that leaders and non-HR employees visibly communicate their approach to equity and inclusion.* Leaders from across business centers should be vocal about how their approach to their work is equity-centered, so that DEI is perceived as an integrated part of business strategy rather than as a siloed HR initiative.

7. Evaluate—and reevaluate—with an intersectional lens.

New forces that shape the future of work will impact underestimated groups differently and will require evolving approaches to DEI. Transforming your DEI strategy in alignment with an evolving workplace requires finding out what's working, what's not, and adjusting accordingly—with an intersectional lens. As chapter 5 explored in depth, employees who live at the intersection of multiple underestimated identities—being a woman and being Latinx, for example—don't often have a "frame" for their experiences. Experiencing the workplace as a Latinx person *or* as a woman is not the same as experiencing the workplace as both, at the same time. Unless we intentionally take an intersectional approach to understanding and acting on employee feedback, the unique experiences of employees living at the intersections will be missing from the data.

Stage 3: Communicating Your Strategy

Now that you have implemented your DEI strategy, communicate your changes clearly and without condescension, and if you make a mistake, acknowledge it.

8. DEI is a choice; it is not "in your DNA."

If there is one phrase I would ask companies to stop using, it would be "DEI is in our DNA." It may be well intended, but it keeps underestimated voices from being heard and undermines otherwise effective DEI strategies. Employees who have felt excluded do not feel encouraged to speak up if an employer has pushed the narrative that their workplace is inherently, unquestionably, inclusive. Being told "DEI is in our DNA" can make employees feel like the problem is "in their head," or that their concerns simply will not be taken seriously.

Implying that DEI naturally occurs within your organization also minimizes the intentionality and effort that you have chosen to invest in your strategy. Instead, communicate the steps you have taken as an organization to ensure that equity is integrated into your business practices. Here are a few examples from GEN-certified companies.

"At Evia Events, we measure what matters, and we're transparent! As examples, we track promotion timelines and participation rates in professional development opportunities by gender and race to ensure employees are receiving equal access. This gives us the information we need to course-correct if we identify imbalances."

"Nia Impact Capital extended its leave policies to cover domestic violence survivors and now allows new parents to return on a part-time, flexible schedule until ready to return full-time."

"At Markon Solutions, we know that diverse leadership doesn't just happen on its own. So, we've developed an inclusive leadership strategy for diverse representation that includes a method for identifying, recruiting, and developing diverse talent, starting with entry-level employees."

"BSW Wealth offers a custom workplace setup, paid paternity and maternity leave, and company-paid healthcare for dependents."

9. DEI is not charity.

A few years ago, GEN partnered with an employer whose leadership team wanted to better understand why women were leaving the company faster than other employees. We spent months conducting surveys and interviewing employees, pinpointing exactly where the gaps were in their experiences and what they needed to feel a greater sense of belonging. The leadership team committed to an action plan and prepared to present next steps to their employees. During their all-company meeting, I watched proudly as their CEO shared what he had learned through this process, where they had made mistakes in the past, and what they were going to change going forward. He went through a timeline and accountability plan and was nearing the end of the presentation. Then, he closed with the line, "We're really excited to finally be lifting you ladies up."

I watched the confidence deflate. Heads shook. Eyes rolled.

This one statement reinforced an inequitable power dynamic, making him a hero who was reaching down to lift up employees "in need."

When employers communicate about DEI like it's a charity campaign, it makes underestimated employees feel like "problems" to be "fixed."

If you find yourself phrasing your DEI initiatives in ways that seem "charitable" or "helping," try these framings instead:

"We want to reach our full potential, and we can't do that if we're not including everyone."

"We realize that our business started off with imbalanced representation, and now we want to more closely represent those we serve."

"We have learned that different groups of employees have had different experiences and access to opportunities here. We're leveling the playing field going forward by taking the following steps. . ."

10. You're going to mess up. It's okay—as long as you make it okay.

I've had the opportunity to study critical race theory, learn from respected DEI practitioners, and research best practices, and I still mess up. I have accidentally left people out, and said things I wish I could take back. I've learned that three steps are essential to helping everyone move forward:

- *Take accountability: Name your mistake.* The first step to regaining trust and confidence is showing that you see what you have done wrong. If there is a particular person, or group of people, who have been on the receiving end of your mistake, apologize to them for *your actions*, and take care not to apologize for *their feelings*. As an example, I often hear people say, "I'm sorry you feel hurt." This is not accountability. An apology that helps everyone move forward sounds more like, "I apologize for leaving you out. . .using the wrong pronoun. . .not considering how this would make you feel." Demonstrating that you can recognize your actions makes it easier for others to believe you can do better next time.

- *Acknowledge any harm done.* Again, without apologizing for someone else's feelings, acknowledge any hurt you may have caused. Noting that your actions may have caused pain, disappointment, or distrust shows that you understand the impact of your mistake.

- *Commit to (educated) action.* In stating what steps you will take to do better in the future, it is important to note how you plan to educate yourself in doing so. Please do not expect your co-workers or peers to invest time and emotional labor in educating you. If they choose to do so, be sure to thank them. Otherwise, plenty of resources exist—and are listed at the end of this book, in the Notes section—to further your own learning journey. Once you have taken time to figure out your next steps, communicate what you will do differently in the future.

≈

Reviewing these principles and the steps in earlier chapters may make you look back at the past and think about what your company could have done differently. I often wonder, if the financial company I was working for years ago had embraced some of these principles, if I still would have walked away from that dinner in Chicago. . .

CHAPTER 16

Hold the Door

Another world is not only possible. She is on her way. On a quiet day, I can hear her breathing.

—Arundhati Roy

Like most people living in Seattle at the time, I took a few photos during the George Floyd protests. Over a year later, I find myself looking at them and thinking about what that summer stood for. I've noticed something that didn't quite catch me then. With the right filter applied, these photos could have been my parents and their friends at protests in the sixties and seventies. As a child of activist boomers, I was brought up with the stories of how that generation championed the rights of those who were considered "outsiders" in race, gender, custom, and belief. Growing up with these stories, decades ago, was inspiring.

Now, though, looking at protest photos from 2020, I'm reminded of a phrase I learned when I was working in international development: constructive impatience.

Nobel laureate economist Amartya Sen coined this term decades ago, in his book, *Development as Freedom*. He continues to praise the "virtue of impatience" in discussing global inequality today: "I think impatience is the most important virtue that we have to cultivate. I think [we have] suffered a lot from being super-patient with inequality and injustice on one side and absurdity on the other."

This quote from a speech Sen gave in 2019 loops in my head as I look at photos and headlines from 2020's summer of unrest. The protest signs could have been taken straight out of my parents' storage. The corporate statements of solidarity could have been from years ago. I find it hard not to wonder if the photos we will take 10, 20, or 30 years from now will document the same costs of untimely patience. Will we still be trying to politely train our way out of bias? Will companies be copying and pasting today's PR statements? Will another intern, like Sanaika, be wondering, "How is the world going to progress?"

I thought back to that dinner in Chicago. Walking out the door, when you don't know what's on the other side, or what tools you'll need to be successful, is scary.

We have the tools now.

What else will it take?

Walking Away

Something happened after I left that dinner in Chicago that I wouldn't find out about until years later. I got a call one day from a woman who had been at the table that night. We'll call her Erin. She said she had seen the TED talk and wanted to reach out to tell me something.

"That night, after you walked out. . .I don't know if anyone ever told you this, but I walked out too, after you. I thought I might catch you, but by the time I got outside, you were already gone."

"I had no idea. I wish I had known," I told her.

"I just. . .I didn't know how to tell you without it sounding braggy, and I wish I had stood up when you did. But, honestly, I don't think I would have walked out if you hadn't done it first."

The conversation veered into talking about past employers and how similar—and stalled—their DEI initiatives had been. When we were working for them, we didn't see anything wrong, maybe because our employers hadn't provoked a "Chicago dinner moment." We knew now, though, that the same dynamic had been playing out there. It was just more subtle and consistent. They had all been stuck in some version of DEI samsara, moving through the same motions of recruiting underestimated individuals, encouraging them to *lean in*, and training employees to be reborn unbiased. The fact that it didn't work never seemed to matter. The cycle would start all over again. Because no one knew any better, this approach was "enough." We settled for it.

"It was like DEI Groundhog Day," Erin joked.

We had both also witnessed times, though, when someone would have their "stand up and leave the table" moment. While they weren't usually as dramatic as the evening Erin and I experienced, they all shared a similar sentiment: "I'm not even sure what's on the other side of this door, but let's find out what else is possible."

We talked about wishing we could discover what that common element was, the change agent that summoned enough *constructive impatience* to push open the door. What could activate that in others?

Beacons

People fell in love with the 2016 Cubs and the 2002 Oakland *Moneyball* A's for the same reason: They pushed our perceptions of what was possible. Billy Beane didn't just give us a fun baseball data trick. He showed us a new, practical way of doing things that could push an entire team, as a collective, past their own ideas of what they thought was possible. Watching them push past their limits made us want to push past our own.

I've seen individuals—and organizations—have the same impact when they walk away from outdated approaches to DEI that they know aren't working. Erin realized that she didn't have to stay at the table when she saw someone else walk away first. She had an example to follow. Markon Solutions set another example. They're a change agent—a beacon.

A 300-employee government contracting firm, Markon pairs professional services with large government and defense projects. Their profile isn't usually what people think of when they hear "DEI Champion." Markon Vice President Ray Carney and his team knew that they couldn't perform at their best, though, if they were leaving people out. They launched their GEN certification efforts just before the pandemic hit the US. We continued working together remotely, through the lockdown, and they never let up. It wasn't always easy. Because they were taking a systemic approach, there were more change management challenges than other DEI initiatives had presented in the past.

Success at Markon depends on finding qualified candidates and hiring them quickly. Honoring this rapid recruiting with an equity strategy meant finding ways to attract applicants from diverse backgrounds, conduct blind resume reviews, and embrace structured interview practices, all while keeping a competitive hiring pace. There were other challenges, too: Markon's equity strategy had to comply with government regulations specific to their industry, and we needed to manage how their new processes would affect their relationships with some of their partners. Markon proved that none of these challenges were insurmountable.

Other businesses in their industry were watching. Since Markon announced their certification, we've received multiple inquiries from employers in the same industry. We asked them what made them decide to reach out.

"We heard about Markon getting certified. We weren't sure if this made sense for us, but if they did it, we should, too. . .and hearing that guy, Ray, talk about it made us feel like we could."

If Markon became a beacon for aspiring equity-centered employers, Ray became an unlikely beacon of what a DEI leader can look like. In his forties, white, straight, able-bodied, educated, and married with kids in a DC suburb, Ray appears to have nothing to gain personally from a DEI initiative. I admit that I initially wondered if he was going to be personally invested enough to see this through. I underestimated him. Over time, I would come to see Ray as one of the most compelling, relentless advocates of workplace equity that I've met. In the face of pushback from skeptical stakeholders and questions from nervous employees, he consistently reasserted his belief that this choice meant raising Markon's standards, not lowering them.

I got to meet with members of the 10-person task force that Markon had assembled to tackle the certification. Four of them were white men. All of them spoke to the role that Ray played in giving them the push they had needed to support these efforts more publicly.

One task force volunteer explained, "Seeing someone like him, who in many ways is like me, be so vocal about this. . .it made it easier for me to join in. I knew I wouldn't be alone in it."

After celebrating Markon's certification, I spent some one-on-one time with Ray. I wanted to understand what motivated him to push for the GEN approach so strongly, even in the face of resistance. Did he also have activist parents? Was there an event in his life that had moved him to care about this? Was he an undercover liberal in a largely conservative industry?

"Not at all," he said. "It just made so much sense. If we didn't do this, we wouldn't be getting the most out of all our people. We'd be selling ourselves short." Ray joked about how people are always surprised to find out he identifies as a Republican after they hear him advocate so ardently for equity and inclusion in the workplace.

To Ray, changing Markon's approach to DEI wasn't a political choice or a social stance. It was a choice to leave old limits behind. And by setting an example, Ray allowed others to see that DEI, done right, is its own lever to push an entire organization to its full potential. It is a means to finding out what else, in our collective self, is possible.

Ray boasts constantly about earning the GEN Certification. In a photo on his LinkedIn page, he beams, holding a GEN plaque, and his caption reads, "One of the proudest moments of my career. . .We hope to see others follow in our footsteps!"

With the processes and methods in this book, the practical steps toward equity that you can take now, you are also in a position to be a beacon for change. Before you set your own example for others, though, there is one last—and first—lever you will need to adjust.

The First—and Last—Cultural Lever

When Erin and I walked away from dinner that night, we weren't just walking away because someone had said something racist. We were walking away from a room where "no response" was an acceptable response. We were walking away from the idea that the status quo was all we were capable of, and toward the promise that something else was possible, on the other side of the door.

I didn't know that night when I opened the door, that I had just pulled the first lever. It was the same lever that Erin would pull after me, and that Ray would pull when he first reached out to GEN: We all made a choice. And others were watching.

I remember the weight of that door. I think it even crossed my mind briefly, that in heels, with a purse and coat in hand, I was about to botch the exit. Once I gave the door that first pull, though, it swung smoothly on its fulcrum, the levers in the hinges rotated, redirecting the momentum, clearing the path.

I didn't know that my choice had made it easier for someone else to walk through.

You've read the book. You have the tools. Making the choice to walk through the door is the first lever you have to pull. When you walk out of the old room, others may see you and shout, "Hold the door!"

I'll see you there.

Summary of Part 3

Chapter 14: AI Won't Save Us (Unless We Save It First)

As our society becomes increasingly dependent on AI, a pernicious assumption is spreading that software will allow us to escape the influence of bias. This is often not the case. If we code fairness in, though, AI could help us build more equity-centered workplaces. Failure to do so can embed bias into these systems for years, or decades.

To ensure that automated intelligence is inclusive and equations are equitable, developers should answer questions that would determine whether their code meets standards of fairness:

- *Who, or what, is missing?* The categories that an algorithm allows for can also allow certain demographics to go statistically missing.
- *Who is creating the model?* Diverse teams are more likely to provide diverse insights, which decreases the odds of exclusive designs. In addition, to avoid building a model based on feedback tainted by the *interviewer effect*, match interviewers' demographics to those of your participants.
- *Are you evaluating impact through an equity lens?* Be aware of the point of view of your model and don't rely only on randomized control trials.

Even when you find a source of potential bias in your model, you can't always change the data set or circumstances you're working with. Two mitigations can help to counter this potential:

- "Blind" applications or resumes by removing biasing characteristics before an algorithm is applied to them.
- Instead of using a proxy for a missing data set, find data sets from outside your organization that describe the group you are trying to understand.

One key trait that separates harmless algorithms from "weapons of math destruction" is transparency. To foster transparency, include a "data biography" with algorithm-based models. This information should be available to anyone interacting with the model and should include the following:

- The elements of your equation: What + What = What?
- How the data is used.
- Who created the mathematical model.
- Data sets and specific definitions.
- How the model was evaluated (and reevaluated and adjusted).

Chapter 15: DEI Principles to Live By

In the face of rising AI, a rapidly transforming workforce, workspaces in transition, and other unknowns that we are yet to encounter, crafting a DEI strategy can feel daunting. How can you know that the policies you implement today will be relevant even a year from now?

When creating, implementing, and communicating your strategy, these 10 core DEI principles can help it survive the unknown:

1. Don't over-automate the underestimated.
Pre-plan transition safety nets.

While AI means the elimination of some roles, it also means there will be increased demand for other skills. Identify underestimated individuals who have these skills, or train for them, starting now.

2. Don't create a recruiting strategy without a retention strategy.

Your recruiting strategy may attract employees from diverse backgrounds, but what is your strategy to retain them? Retention, equity, and inclusion strategies must address at least the following key elements:

- *Performance evaluations* that are standardized and safeguarded against bias.
- *Pay equity* ensured by pay gap audits, based on total compensation, and conducted over time, not just once.
- *Promotion process* that is transparent and open to all.
- *Professional development/ongoing education* with equal access to opportunities for employees of all backgrounds.
- *Flexibility/leave/remote work policies* determined with employee input and including paid leave for all genders.
- *Vendor/procurement policy* that includes awareness of vendors' DEI policies.
- *DEI evaluation and reporting policy*, incorporated into your holistic business strategy, that includes how you track and report progress toward DEI goals.

3. Act on data, not best guesses.

Your strategy should be driven by data, not best guesses. Crafting a data-smart DEI strategy means collecting data that answer the following two questions:

- What are the quantifiable differences between different populations' workplace experiences?
- What do employees, of all backgrounds, want?

4. Think long term and set expectations.

As you implement your DEI strategy, keep a long-term perspective. Remember that making up for what may be years, or decades, of institutional bias takes time.

5. DEI is not kickball. Work with data-smart experts.

DEI practitioners must have a range of skills and knowledge, from supply chain management to statistical analysis, to be successful. If you do not have a DEI expert in-house, find a qualified consultant—one who measures lead indicators—to work with you.

6. DEI does not belong to HR.

DEI is the job of everyone in the company. Make DEI part of every job description, and make sure that leaders and non-HR employees visibly communicate their approach to equity and inclusion.

7. Evaluate—and reevaluate—with an intersectional lens.

New forces that shape the future of work will affect underestimated groups differently. Transform your DEI strategy in alignment with an evolving workplace by finding out what's working, what's not, and adjust accordingly—with an intersectional lens.

8. DEI is a choice; it is not "in your DNA."

Implying that DEI naturally occurs within your organization can make employees feel like their concerns will not be taken seriously and minimizes the effort that you have chosen to invest in your DEI strategy. Instead, communicate the steps you have taken to ensure that equity is integrated into your business practices.

9. DEI is not charity.

Be aware not to communicate about your DEI initiative in a way that implies it is like a charity campaign. Doing so can make underestimated employees feel like "problems" to be "fixed." Your DEI implementation is about your company reaching its full potential.

10. You're going to mess up. It's okay—as long as you make it okay.

Odds are good that you will make missteps in your journey toward an equitable workplace. If you do, three steps are essential to helping everyone move forward:

- *Take accountability: Name your mistake.* The first step to regaining trust and confidence is showing that you see what you have done wrong.
- *Acknowledge any harm done.* Without apologizing for someone else's feelings, acknowledge any hurt you may have caused.
- *Commit to (educated) action.* In stating what steps you will take to do better in the future, it is important to note how you plan to educate yourself in doing so.

Chapter 16: Hold the Door

With the processes and methods in this book—the practical steps toward equity that you can take now—you are in a position to be an agent for change. When you open the door to a future of inclusion, others will follow.

Notes

Language Guide

1. John Eligon, "A Debate Over Identity and Race Asks, Are African-Americans 'Black' or 'black'?" *New York Times*, June 26, 2020, https://www.nytimes.com/2020/06/26/us/black-african-american-style-debate.html.

Chapter 1: Beyond Good Intentions

1. "Being Black in Corporate America: An Intersectional Exploration" (Center for Talent Innovation, 2019), https://coqual.org/wp-content/uploads/2020/09/CoqualBeingBlackinCorporateAmerica090720-1.pdf; Neysa Dillon-Brown, "Women And Minorities Are Still Underrepresented in the Boardroom," Corporate Board Member, February 20, 2019, https://boardmember.com/women-minorities-underrepresented-board/.
2. Lareina Yee, Alexis Krivkovich, Eric Kutcher, et al., "Women in the Workplace 2016" (LeanIn.Org and McKinsey & Company, 2016), https://womenintheworkplace.com/2016.
3. Jessica Guynn, "Here's Why Women, Blacks and Hispanics Are Leaving Tech," *USA Today*, July 9, 2020, https://www.usatoday.com/story/tech/news/2017/04/27/toxic-workplaces-technology-women-minorities-retention/100977038/.
4. "Generations of Progress for Women and Girls Could Be Lost to COVID Pandemic, UN Chief Warns," *UN News*, United Nations, August 31, 2020, https://news.un.org/en/story/2020/08/1071372.
5. Brittany Chambers, "How The Coronavirus Has Resulted in the Highest Job Loss for Women: Erasing a Decade of Progress," *Forbes*, May 12, 2020, https://www.forbes.com/sites/brittanychambers/2020/05/12/how-the-coronavirus-has-resulted-in-the-highest-job-loss-for-women-erasing-a-decade-of-progress/?sh=69fa558e192a.
6. Quentin Fottrell and Jeanette Settembre, "In the #MeToo Era, 60% of Male Managers Say They're Scared of Being Alone With Women at Work," *MarketWatch*, June 16, 2019, https://www.marketwatch.com/story/men-are-afraid-to-mentor-female-colleagues-in-the-metoo-era-heres-what-not-to-do-2019-05-20.
7. Laura Morgan Roberts and Anthony J. Mayo, "Toward a Racially Just Workplace," *Harvard Business Review*, November 14, 2019, https://hbr.org/2019/11/toward-a-racially-just-workplace.
8. Martin Abel, "Why Female Bosses Get Different Reactions Than Men When They Criticize Employees," The Conversation, September 10, 2020, https://theconversation.com/why-female-bosses-get-different-reactions-than-men-when-they-criticize-employees-145970.
9. Evan W. Carr, Andrew Reece, Gabriella Rosen Kellerman, and Alexi Robichaux, "The Value of Belonging at Work," *Harvard Business Review*, December 16, 2019, https://hbr.org/2019/12/the-value-of-belonging-at-work.

10. Frank Dobbin, Daniel Schrage, and Alexandra Kalev, "Rage Against the Iron Cage: The Varied Effects of Bureaucratic Personnel Reforms on Diversity," *American Sociological Review* 80, no. 5 (2015): 1014–1044, doi: 10.1177/0003122415596416.

11. Frank Dobbin and Alexandra Kalev, "Why Diversity Programs Fail," *Harvard Business Review*, July–August 2016, https://hbr.org/2016/07/why-diversity-programs-fail.

12. Erica Goode, "At Energy-Minded U.S. Hotels, They'll Turn the Lights Off for You," *New York Times*, May 9, 2016, https://www.nytimes.com/2016/05/10/business/hotel-energy-efficiency-carbon-footprint.html.

13. Wikipedia, s.v. "List of Cognitive Biases," last modified July 14, 2021, 14:01 (UTC), https://en.wikipedia.org/wiki/List_of_cognitive_biases.

14. Hannah Valantine, "The Science of Diversity and the Impact of Implicit Bias," National Institutes of Health, 2017, https://diversity.nih.gov/sites/coswd/files/images/2017-12/implicit_bias_talk_for_toolkit_pdf_508c_0.pdf.

15. Kathleen Melymuka, "Why Women Quit Technology," *Computerworld*, June 16, 2008, https://www.computerworld.com/article/2551969/it-careers-why-women-quit-technology.html.

16. The term "Weapons of Math Destruction" was coined by former Wall Street quantitative analyst and current mathematician, data scientist, author, and data ethicist Cathy O'Neil.

Chapter 2: "But We've Always Done It This Way. . ."

1. The IAT measures the strength of unconscious associations between concepts (e.g., Black people, gay people) and evaluations (e.g., good, bad) or stereotypes (e.g., athletic, clumsy). The main idea is that responding is easier when closely related items share the same response key. "Implicit Association Test (IAT)," Project Implicit, 2011, https://implicit.harvard.edu/implicit/takeatest.html; "About the IAT," Project Implicit, 2011, https://implicit.harvard.edu/implicit/iatdetails.html.

2. "From Love to Voting: Who Really Decides, You or Your Brain?" CBC DOCS, https://www.cbc.ca/natureofthings/features/my-brain-made-me-do-it-who-decides.

3. Linnea Dunne, "So You Think You Were Hired on Merit? Gender Quotas and the Perception Gap," *Linnea Dunne* (blog), August 21, 2017, http://www.linneadunne.com/2017/08/21/think-hired-merit-gender-quotas-perception-gap/.

4. Shari Kendall and Deborah Tannen, "Gender and Language in the Workplace," ed. Ruth Wodak, *Gender and Discourse* (1997): 81–105, https://time.com/wp-content/uploads/2017/06/d3375-genderandlanguageintheworkplace.pdf.

5. Susan C. Herring, "Gender and Participation in Computer-Mediated Linguistic Discourse" (paper, Annual Meeting of the Linguistic Society of America, Philadelphia, January 9–12, 1992), https://files.eric.ed.gov/fulltext/ED345552.pdf.

6. Janet Holmes, "Language Myth # 6: Women Talk Too Much," PBS, 2005, http://www.pbs.org/speak/speech/prejudice/women/.
7. Iris Bohnet, *What Works: Gender Equality by Design* (Cambridge, MA: Belknap Press, an Imprint of Harvard University Press, 2016), 62–63.
8. Benjamin Artz, Amanda H. Goodall, and Andrew J. Oswald, "Do Women Ask?" *Industrial Relations: A Journal of Economy and Society* 57, no. 4 (2018): 611–636, https://onlinelibrary.wiley.com/doi/abs/10.1111/irel.12214.
9. Benjamin Artz, Amanda Goodall, and Andrew J. Oswald, "Research: Women Ask for Raises as Often as Men, but Are Less Likely to Get Them," *Harvard Business Review*, June 25, 2018, https://hbr.org/2018/06/research-women-ask-for-raises-as-often-as-men-but-are-less-likely-to-get-them.
10. Morela Hernandez and Derek R. Avery, "Getting the Short End of the Stick: Racial Bias in Salary Negotiations," *MIT Sloan Management Review*, June 15, 2016, https://sloanreview.mit.edu/article/getting-the-short-end-of-the-stick-racial-bias-in-salary-negotiations/.
11. Ashleigh Shelby Rosette, Christy Zhou Koval, Anyi Ma, and Robert Livingston, "Race Matters for Women Leaders: Intersectional Effects on Agentic Deficiencies and Penalties," *The Leadership Quarterly* 27, no. 3 (2016): 429–445, https://doi.org/10.1016/j.leaqua.2016.01.008.
12. As measured by the percentage of Black women enrolled in college in relation to other race-gender groups. "Black Women Are Ranked the Most Educated Group by Race & Gender," HBCU Buzz, March 4, 2014, https://hbcubuzz.com/2014/03/black-women-are-ranked-the-most-educated-group-by-race-gender/.
13. Zuhairah Washington and Laura Morgan Roberts, "Women of Color Get Less Support at Work. Here's How Managers Can Change That," *Harvard Business Review*, March 4, 2019, https://hbr.org/2019/03/women-of-color-get-less-support-at-work-heres-how-managers-can-change-that.
14. "The State of Black Women in Corporate America" (LeanIn.Org and McKinsey & Company, 2020), https://media.sgff.io/sgff_r1eHetbDYb/2020-08-13/1597343917539/Lean_In_-_State_of_Black_Women_in_Corporate_America_Report_1.pdf.
15. Daniel A. Effron, Jessica S. Cameron, and Benoît Monin, "Endorsing Obama Licenses Favoring Whites," *Journal of Experimental Social Psychology* 45, no. 3 (2009): 590–593, https://doi.org/10.1016/j.jesp.2009.02.001.
16. Carol Kulik, Molly Pepper, Loriann Roberson, and Sharon Parker, "The Rich Get Richer: Predicting Participation in Voluntary Diversity Training," *Journal of Organizational Behavior* 28, no. 6 (2007): 753–769, https://www.researchgate.net/publication/227677080_The_rich_get_richer_Predicting_participation_in_voluntary_diversity_training.
17. Tessa L. Dover, Brenda Major, Cheryl R. Kaiser, "Members of High-Status Groups Are Threatened by Pro-Diversity Organizational Messages," *Journal of Experimental Social Psychology* 62 (2016): 58–67, https://doi.org/10.1016/j.jesp.2015.10.006.
18. Tessa L. Dover, Brenda Major, and Cheryl R. Kaiser, "Diversity Policies Rarely Make Companies Fairer, and They Feel Threatening to White Men," *Harvard Business Review*, January 4, 2016, https://hbr.org/2016/01/diversity-policies-dont-help-women-or-minorities-and-they-make-white-men-feel-threatened.

Chapter 3: Why Should We Care?

1. "Women in the Workforce: United States (Quick Take)," Catalyst, October 14, 2020, https://www.catalyst.org/research/women-in-the-workforce-united-states/.
2. William H. Frey, "The Millennial Generation: A Demographic Bridge to America's Diverse Future" (Brookings, January, 2018), https://www.brookings.edu/wp-content/uploads/2018/01/2018-jan_brookings-metro_millennials-a-demographic-bridge-to-americas-diverse-future.pdf.
3. "Older People Projected to Outnumber Children for First Time in U.S. History," US Census Bureau, March 13, 2018, release no. CB18-41, https://www.census.gov/newsroom/press-releases/2018/cb18-41-population-projections.html.
4. "Understanding Neurodiversity at Work," Headstart, September 25, 2020, https://www.headstart.io/insights/neurodiversity-at-work-and-its-untapped-commercial-potential/.
5. Bailey Reiners, "The Cold, Hard Truth About Ageism in the Workplace," Built In, May 12, 2021, https://builtin.com/diversity-inclusion/ageism-in-the-workplace.
6. Lynn Friss Feinberg, "The Dual Pressures of Family Caregiving and Employment: Six in 10 Family Caregivers Are in the Labor Force" (AARP Public Policy Institute, 2016), https://www.aarp.org/content/dam/aarp/ppi/2016-03/The-Dual-Pressures-off-Family-Caregiving-and-Employment.pdf.
7. Jeffrey M. Jones, "LGBT Identification Rises to 5.6% in Latest U.S. Estimate," Gallup, February 24, 2021, https://news.gallup.com/poll/329708/lgbt-identification-rises-latest-estimate.aspx.
8. "What Workforce Diversity Means for Gen Z," Monster, 2020, https://hiring.monster.com/employer-resources/recruiting-strategies/workforce-planning/workforce-diversity-for-millennials/.
9. "2017 Cone Communications CSR Study" (Cone Communications, 2017), https://www.conecomm.com/2017-cone-communications-csr-study-pdf.
10. "In an Increasingly Diverse Market, Brands Can Drive Growth With Multicultural Marketing," Living Word Insights, December 4, 2020, https://livingword.co.uk/in-an-increasingly-diverse-market-brands-can-drive-growth-with-multicultural-marketing/.
11. Katia Savchuk, "Do Investors Really Care About Gender Diversity?" Stanford Business Insights, September 17, 2019, https://www.gsb.stanford.edu/insights/do-investors-really-care-about-gender-diversity.
12. "Tesla Exempt Solicitation," Tesla, Inc., June 17, 2020, https://www.sec.gov/Archives/edgar/data/1318605/000121465920005699/p612202px14a6g.htm.
13. Greg Iacurci, "Money Invested in ESG Funds More Than Doubles in a Year," *CNBC*, February 11, 2021, https://www.cnbc.com/2021/02/11/sustainable-investment-funds-more-than-doubled-in-2020-.html.
14. Sheryl Estrada, "'Just Going Through the Motions': Employers Fail to Make DEI a Business Function, Report Finds," HR Dive, February 18, 2021, https://www.hrdive.com/news/just-going-through-the-motions-employers-fail-to-make-dei-a-business-fun/595293/.
15. "How Much Does It Cost to Defend an Employment Lawsuit?" Workforce.com, May 14, 2013, https://www.workforce.com/news/how-much-does-it-cost-to-defend-an-employment-lawsuit.

16. Reiners, "The Cold, Hard Truth."

17. Allison Scott, Freada Kapor Klein, and Uriridiakoghene Onovakpuri, "Tech Leavers Study" (Kapor Center for Social Impact, 2017), https://mk0kaporcenter5ld71a.kinstacdn.com/wp-content/uploads/2017/08/TechLeavers2017.pdf.

18. Steve Henn, "When Women Stopped Coding," *NPR, Planet Money,* October 21, 2014, https://www.npr.org/sections/money/2014/10/21/357629765/when-women-stopped-coding.

19. J. Terrell, A. Kofink, J. Middleton, C. Rainear, E. Murphy-Hill, C. Parnin, and J. Stallings, "Gender Differences and Bias in Open Source: Pull Request Acceptance of Women Versus Men," *PeerJ Preprints* 4 (February 2016), https://peerj.com/preprints/1733v1.pdf.

20. Dexter Thomas, "Perspective: Forbes Deleted a White Tech Writer's Article That Called Silicon Valley a 'Meritocracy'," October 8, 2015, https://www.latimes.com/business/technology/la-forbes-tech-meritocracy-20151007-htmlstory.html.

21. Corinne A. Moss-Racusin, John F. Dovidio, Victoria L. Brescoll, Mark J. Graham, and Jo Handelsman, "Science Faculty's Subtle Gender Biases Favor Male Students," *Proceedings of the National Academy of Sciences* 109, no. 41 (October 2012): 16474–16479, https://doi.org/10.1073/pnas.1211286109.

22. Ernesto Reuben, Paola Sapienza, and Luigi Zingales, "How Stereotypes Impair Women's Careers in Science," *Proceedings of the National Academy of Sciences* 111, no. 12 (March 2014): 4403-4408, https://doi.org/10.1073/pnas.1314788111.

23. Elizabeth Weise and Jessica Guynn, "Black and Hispanic Computer Scientists Have Degrees From Top Universities, but Don't Get Hired in Tech," *USA TODAY,* July 20, 2020, https://www.usatoday.com/story/tech/2014/10/12/silicon-valley-diversity-tech-hiring-computer-science-graduates-african-american-hispanic/14684211/.

24. Anita Woolley, Christopher Chabris, Alex Pentland, Nada Hashmi, and Thomas Malone, "Evidence of a Collective Intelligence Factor in the Performance of Human Groups," *Science* 330, no. 6004 (October 2010): 686–688, https://doi.org/10.1126/science.1193147.

25. Katherine W. Phillips, "How Diversity Makes Us Smarter," *Scientific American,* October 2014, https://www.scientificamerican.com/article/how-diversity-makes-us-smarter/.

26. Timothy Au, "Diversity in the Workforce Leads to More Innovation and Patents, New Study Finds," *IAM,* February 15, 2018, https://www.iam-media.com/strategy/diversity-workforce-leads-more-innovation-and-patents-new-study-finds.

27. Matthew Syed, *Rebel Ideas: The Power of Diverse Thinking* (New York: Flatiron Books, 2021).

Chapter 4: Shifting to a Systemic Perspective

1. "Cardiology's Problem Women," *The Lancet* 393, no. 10175 (2019): 959, https://doi.org/10.1016/S0140-6736(19)30510-0.

2. "Applying Behavioral Science to End Poverty and Enhance Equity" (World Bank Group, Mind, Behavior, and Development Unit (eMBeD)), https://documents1. worldbank.org/curated/en/744191532458732002/pdf/128784-eMBeD-Brochure-DIGITAL.pdf.

3. "Is the Modern Workplace Designed for Men?" RTE, March 8, 2018, https:// www.rte.ie/lifestyle/living/2018/0307/945722-is-the-modern-workplace-designed-for-men/.

4. Alexandra Topping, "Sexism on the Covid-19 Frontline: 'PPE Is Made for a 6ft 3in Rugby Player'," *Guardian*, April 24, 2020, https://www.theguardian. com/world/2020/apr/24/sexism-on-the-covid-19-frontline-ppe-is-made-for-a-6ft-3in-rugby-player?fbclid=IwAR24nN-_jD3iG5Z6lrt6BJPZq60_PY4TfrxJ-rPEcLxtabdFNPSdz7aHU6g.

5. Jessica Hester, "Offices Aren't Designed for Women in General," CityLab, August 4, 2015, https://www.citylab.com/life/2015/08/offices-arent-designed-for-women/ 400406/; Anne B. Hoskins, "Occupational Injuries, Illnesses, and Fatalities Among Women," *Monthly Labor Review* (Bureau of Labor Statistics, October 2005), https:// www.bls.gov/opub/mlr/2005/10/art4full.pdf.

6. Pam Belluck, "Chilly at Work? Office Formula Was Devised for Men," *New York Times*, August 3, 2015, https://www.nytimes.com/2015/08/04/science/chilly-at-work-a-decades-old-formula-may-be-to-blame.html.

7. Dawn Onley, "U.S. Circuit Court Rules It Is Legal to Refuse Jobs to People with Dreadlocks," *TheGrio*, March 3, 2019, https://thegrio.com/2019/03/03/u-s-companies-dreadlocks-jobs/.

8. Sylvia Ann Hewlett, Maggie Jackson, Ellis Cose, and Courtney Emerson, "Vaulting the Color Bar: How Sponsorship Levers Multicultural Professionals into Leadership" (Center for Talent Innovation, 2012), https://coqual.org/wp-content/ uploads/2020/09/36_vaultingthecolorbar_keyfindings-1.pdf.

9. Margaret Shih, Todd L. Pittinsky, and Amy Trahan, "Domain-Specific Effects of Stereotypes on Performance," *Self and Identity* 5, no. 1 (2006): 1–14, https://doi .org/10.1080/15298860500338534.

10. Kieran Snyder, "The Abrasiveness Trap: High-Achieving Men and Women Are Described Differently in Reviews," *Fortune*, August 26, 2014, https://fortune .com/2014/08/26/performance-review-gender-bias/.

11. Roy F. Baumeister and John Tierney, *Willpower: Rediscovering the Greatest Human Strength* (Penguin Press, 2011).

12. Daniel Engber, "Everything Is Crumbling," *Slate*, March 6, 2016, http://www .slate.com/articles/health_and_science/cover_story/2016/03/ego_depletion_an_ influential_theory_in_psychology_may_have_just_been_debunked.html.

13. Veronika Job, Carol S. Dweck, and Gregory M. Walton, "Ego Depletion—Is It All in Your Head? Implicit Theories About Willpower Affect Self-Regulation," *Psychol Sci* 21, no. 11 (November 2010): 1686–1693, https://doi. org/10.1177/0956797610384745; Walter Mischel, *The Marshmallow Test: Why Self-Control Is the Engine of Success* (Back Bay Books, 2015).

14. Baumeister and Tierney, *Willpower*.

15. Atul Gawande, *The Checklist Manifesto: How to Get Things Right* (Henry Holt and Company, 2009), 28–37.

Chapter 5: Inclusion at the Intersections

1. Name changed.
2. Kimberlé Crenshaw, "The Urgency of Intersectionality," TEDWomen 2016, October 2016, https://www.ted.com/talks/kimberle_crenshaw_the_urgency_of_intersectionality?language=en.
3. Renee Morad, "It's 2021 and Women Still Make 82 Cents for Every Dollar Earned by a Man," *NBC News*, March 23, 2021, https://www.nbcnews.com/know-your-value/feature/it-s-2021-women-still-make-82-cents-every-dollar-ncna1261755.
4. Alice Truong, "When Google Increased Paid Maternity Leave, the Rate at Which New Mothers Quit Dropped 50%," Quartz, February 8, 2016, https://qz.com/604723/when-google-increased-paid-maternity-leave-the-rate-at-which-new-mothers-quit-dropped-50/.
5. American Homefront Project, "In a Little-Discussed Program, VA Helps Veterans Deal With Race-Based Stress," *Colorado Public Radio News*, September 8, 2020, https://www.cpr.org/2020/09/08/in-a-little-discussed-program-va-helps-veterans-deal-with-race-based-stress/#:~:text=Studies%20have%20shown%20that%20veterans,pressures%20of%20returning%20from%20war.

Chapter 6: Help Wanted—Inclusive Recruiting

1. Sara A. Begley, Julia Y. Trankiem, and Sarah T. Hansel, "Employers Using Personality Tests to Vet Applicants Need Cautious 'Personalities' of Their Own," *Forbes*, October 30, 2014, https://www.forbes.com/sites/theemploymentbeat/2014/10/30/employers-using-personality-tests-to-vet-applicants-need-cautious-personalities-of-their-own/?sh=39595e4d3bd0.
2. Roy Maurer, "Recruiting Is Top HR Concern in 2021," SHRM, January 5, 2021, https://www.shrm.org/resourcesandtools/hr-topics/talent-acquisition/pages/recruiting-is-top-hr-concern-2021.aspx.
3. Courtney Seiter, "Why We Removed the Word 'Hacker' from Buffer Job Descriptions," *Open Culture* (blog), *Buffer*, March 13, 2015, https://buffer.com/resources/job-descriptions-diversity/.
4. Danielle Gaucher, Justin Friesen, and Aaron C. Kay, "Evidence That Gendered Wording in Job Advertisements Exists and Sustains Gender Inequality," *Journal of Personality and Social Psychology* 101, no. 1 (July 2011): 109–128, http://gender-decoder.katmatfield.com/static/documents/Gaucher-Friesen-Kay-JPSP-Gendered-Wording-in-Job-ads.pdf.
5. Gaucher, Friesen, and Kay, "Gendered Wording," 109–128.

6. Available at https://www.ongig.com/text-analyzer#/.

7. David Pilgrim, "Brown Paper Bag Test," Ferris State University Jim Crow Museum, February 2014, https://www.ferris.edu/HTMLS/news/jimcrow/question/2014/february.htm.

8. "Amazon Engineers Accomplish Inside Wiki for Unconsciously Racist Phrases," *News Himalaya*, June 24, 2020, https://newshimalaya.com/2020/06/24/amazon-engineers-accomplish-inside-wiki-for-unconsciously-racist-phrases/.

9. Logan Whiteside, "Google Doesn't Care Where You Went to College," *CNN Business*, April 9, 2015, https://money.cnn.com/2015/04/09/technology/google-people-laszlo-bock/index.html.

10. Tara Sophia Mohr, "Why Women Don't Apply for Jobs Unless They're 100% Qualified," *Harvard Business Review*, August 25, 2014, https://hbr.org/2014/08/why-women-dont-apply-for-jobs-unless-theyre-100-qualified.

11. "The Mom Success Factor: Valuing the Role of Moms as Managers and Colleagues in Organizations" (WerkLabs, 2020), https://f.hubspotusercontent00.net/hubfs/5134751/WerkLabs/WerkLabs_TheMomProject_MomSuccessFactor_October2020.pdf.

12. Claudia Dale Goldin, "A Grand Gender Convergence: Its Last Chapter," *American Economic Review* 104 (2014): 1091–1119.

13. Cassie Sanchez, "How to Write a Job Description in 2020: Best Practices from Half a Billion Job Postings," Textio, April 24, 2020, https://textio.com/blog/how-to-write-a-job-description-in-2020-best-practices-from-half-a-billion-job-postings/28706464272.

14. Robin Smyton, "Telling Job Seekers How Many Other People Have Applied Increases Applications, Could Boost Diversity," Phys.org, April 23, 2018, https://phys.org/news/2018-04-job-seekers-people-applications-boost.html.

15. Sandra L. Hofferth, Sarah M. Flood, and Matthew Sobek, American Time Use Survey Data Extract Builder: Version 2.6 (data set), University of Maryland and University of Minnesota, 2017, https://doi.org/10.18128/D060.V2.6.

16. Alison L. Booth and Patrick Nolen, "Gender Differences in Risk Behaviour: Does Nurture Matter?" *Economic Journal* 122 (2012): 56–78; Marie-Pierre Dargnies, "Men Too Sometimes Shy Away from Competition: The Case of Team Competition," *Management Science* 58 (2012): 1982–2000.

17. Jens Manuel Krogstad, "Social Media Preferences Vary by Race and Ethnicity," Pew Research Center, February 3, 2015, https://www.pewresearch.org/fact-tank/2015/02/03/social-media-preferences-vary-by-race-and-ethnicity/.

18. "The Hispanic Job Search: Methods, Preferences and Outlook," *Refuel Agency* (blog), January 23, 2020, https://www.refuelagency.com/blog/hispanic-job-search/.

19. Debby Carreau, "The Ugly Truth Behind Why Men Are More Likely to Get Noticed by Job Recruiters, According to New LinkedIn Study," CNBC Make It, March 8, 2019, https://www.cnbc.com/2019/03/08/linkedin-study-reveals-why-men-are-more-likely-to-get-noticed-by-job-recruiters-than-women.html.

20. Kazi Zainab Khanam, Gautam Srivastava, and Vijay Mago, "The Homophily Principle in Social Network Analysis," *Proc. ACM Meas. Anal. Comput. Syst.* 37, no. 4, article 111, May 2020, https://arxiv.org/pdf/2008.10383.pdf.

21. Monica Beyer, "Gender Bias: The Résumé Edition," HR Daily Advisor, May 15, 2019, https://hrdailyadvisor.blr.com/2019/05/15/gender-bias-the-resume-edition/.

22. Everett J. Mitchell II and Don Sjoerdsma, "Black Job Seekers Still Face Racial Bias in Hiring Process," LiveCareer, September 2, 2020, https://www.livecareer.com/resources/careers/planning/black-job-seekers-face-racial-bias-in-hiring-process.
23. Eryn J. Newman, Mevagh Sanson, Emily K. Miller, Adele Quigley-McBride, Jeffrey L. Foster, Daniel M. Bernstein, and Maryanne Garry, "People With Easier to Pronounce Names Promote Truthiness of Claims," *PLoS ONE* 9, no. 2 (February 26, 2014), https://doi.org/10.1371/journal.pone.0088671.
24. Costanza Biavaschi, Corrado Giuliettiand, and Zahra Siddique, "IZA Discussion Paper No. 7725: The Economic Payoff of Name Americanization," IZA Institute of Labor Economics, November 2013, http://ftp.iza.org/dp7725.pdf.

Chapter 7: The Best Person for the Job—Merit-Based Hiring

1. Scott Highhouse, "Stubborn Reliance on Intuition and Subjectivity in Employee Selection," *Industrial and Organizational Psychology* 1 (2008): 333–342, https://blogg.hrsverige.nu/wp-content/uploads/2010/04/Stubborn1.pdf.
2. Filip Lievens, Scott Highhouse, and Wilfried De Corte, "The Importance of Traits and Abilities in Supervisors' Hirability Decisions as a Function of Method of Assessment," *Journal of Occupational and Organizational Psychology* 78, no. 3 (2005): 453–470, https://doi.org/10.1348/096317905X26093.
3. Valentina Zarya, "Venture Capital's Funding Gender Gap Is Actually Getting Worse," *Fortune*, March 13, 2017, http://fortune.com/2017/03/13/female-founders-venture-capital/.
4. Julie Weeks, "Women, Especially Women of Color, Are Fueling Business Startup Activity," American Express, April 6, 2016, https://www.americanexpress.com/en-us/business/trends-and-insights/articles/women-especially-women-of-color-are-fueling-business-startup-activity/.
5. Dana Kanze, Laura Huang, Mark A. Conley, and E. Tory Higgins, "We Ask Men to Win and Women Not to Lose: Closing the Gender Gap in Startup Funding," *Academy of Management Journal* 61, no. 2 (2018): 586–614, https://doi.org/10.5465/amj.2016.1215.
6. *APA Dictionary of Psychology*, s.v. "regulatory focus theory," https://dictionary.apa.org/regulatory-focus-theory.
7. Dana Kanze, Laura Huang, Mark A. Conley, and E. Tory Higgins, "Male and Female Entrepreneurs Get Asked Different Questions by VCs—and It Affects How Much Funding They Get," *Harvard Business Review*, June 27, 2017, https://hbr.org/2017/06/male-and-female-entrepreneurs-get-asked-different-questions-by-vcs-and-it-affects-how-much-funding-they-get.
8. Rolf Bax, "The Worst Job Interview Questions, Revealed," *Resume.io* (blog), updated August 10. 2021, https://resume.io/blog/the-worst-job-interview-questions-revealed.
9. *Encyclopedia Britannica*, s.v. "halo effect," October 9, 2019, https://www.britannica.com/science/halo-effect.

10. Uri Simonsohn and Francesca Gino. "Daily Horizons: Evidence of Narrow Bracketing in Judgment From 10 Years of M.B.A. Admissions Interviews," *Psychological Science* 24, no. 2 (February 2013): 219–224, https://doi.org/10.1177/0956797612459762.

11. Balazs Szatmari, "We Are (All) the Champions: The Effect of Status in the Implementation of Innovations," *ERIM Ph.d. Series Research in Management*, December 16, 2016, http://hdl.handle.net/1765/94633.

12. Iris Bohnet, Alexandra van Geen, and Max Bazerman, "When Performance Trumps Gender Bias: Joint vs. Separate Evaluation," *Management Science* 62, no. 5 (September 29, 2015): 1225–1234, http://dx.doi.org/10.1287/mnsc.2015.2186.

13. "PI Behavioral Assessment™ Certified in the European Federation of Psychologists' Associations' (EFPA) Test Review Model," The Predictive Index, 2021, https://www.predictiveindex.com/news-press/news/pi-behavioral-assessment-certified-in-the-european-federation-of-psychologists-associations-efpa-test-review-model/.

14. Frank L. Schmidt and John E. Hunter, "The Validity and Utility of Selection Methods in Personnel Psychology: Practical and Theoretical Implications of 85 Years of Research Findings," *Psychological Bulletin* 124, no. 2 (1998): 262–274, https://static1.squarespace.com/static/5b100920b105987b3e97fd32/t/5b36404a6d2a73fcad279e22/1530282064466/Schmidt+and+Hunter+article.pdf.

15. Stephen M. Garcia and Avishalom Tor, "The N-Effect: More Competitors, Less Competition," *Psychological Science* 20 (2009): 871–877.

16. Michael Inzlicht and Talia Ben-Zeev, "A Threatening Intellectual Environment: Why Females Are Susceptible to Experiencing Problem-Solving Deficits in the Presence of Males," *Psychological Science* 11 (2000): 365–371.

17. Tom Y. Chang and Agne Kajackaite, "Battle for the Thermostat: Gender and the Effect of Temperature on Cognitive Performance," *PLoS ONE* 14, no. 5 (May 22, 2019), https://doi.org/10.1371/journal.pone.0216362.

Chapter 8: It's Who You Know— Protégés and Professional Development

1. Jena McGregor, "#MeToo Backlash: More Male Managers Avoid Mentoring Women or Meeting Alone With Them," *Washington Post*, May 17, 2019, https://www.washingtonpost.com/business/2019/05/17/metoo-backlash-more-male-managers-avoid-mentoring-women-or-meeting-alone-with-them.

2. Jillesa Gebhardt, "How #MeToo Has Impacted Mentorship for Women," Survey-Monkey Inc., 2019, https://www.surveymonkey.com/curiosity/mentor-her-2019/.

3. Stephanie Bradley Smith, "How a Lack of Sponsorship Keeps Black Women Out of the C-Suite," *Harvard Business Review*, March 5, 2021, https://hbr.org/2021/03/how-a-lack-of-sponsorship-keeps-black-women-out-of-the-c-suite.

4. Nancy M. Carter and Christine Silva, "Mentoring: Necessary but Insufficient for Advancement," Catalyst, 2010, https://www.globalambassadors.org/sites/default/files/Mentoring_Necessary_But_Insufficient_for_Advancement_Final_120610.pdf.

5. "The Sponsor Dividend," Center for Talent Innovation, 2019, https://coqual.org/wp-content/uploads/2020/09/CoqualTheSponsorDividend_KeyFindingsCombined090720.pdf.

6. Jena McGregor, "Nearly Three-quarters of Executives Pick Protégés Who Look Just Like Them," *Washington Post*, January 9, 2019, https://www.washingtonpost.com/business/2019/01/09/nearly-three-quarters-executives-pick-proteges-who-look-just-like-them/.

7. Hugh Welsh, "Sponsorship Has More Promise for Executive Diversity Than Mentorship," *Entrepreneur*, May 27, 2016, https://www.entrepreneur.com/article/274525.

8. Kathy Gurchiek, "Multicultural Women Benefit from Male Support in the Workplace," SHRM, July 19, 2017, https://www.shrm.org/ResourcesAndTools/hr-topics/behavioral-competencies/global-and-cultural-effectiveness/pages/multicultural-women-benefit-from-male-allies-in-the-workplace.aspx.

9. Emily T. Amanatullah and Michael W. Morris, "Negotiating Gender Roles: Gender Differences in Assertive Negotiating Are Mediated by Women's Fear of Backlash and Attenuated When Negotiating on Behalf of Others," *Journal of Personality and Social Psychology* 98 (February 2010): 256–267, https://psycnet.apa.org/buy/2010-00584-007.

10. Jeffrey Pfeffer, Christina T. Fong, Robert B. Cialdini, and Rebecca R. Portnoy, "Overcoming the Self-Promotion Dilemma: Interpersonal Attraction and Extra Help as a Consequence of Who Sings One's Praises," *Personality and Social Psychology Bulletin* (October 2006), https://journals.sagepub.com/doi/abs/10.1177/0146167206290337.

11. "The Sponsor Dividend," Center for Talent Innovation, 2019, https://coqual.org/wp-content/uploads/2020/09/CoqualTheSponsorDividend_KeyFindingsCombined090720.pdf.

12. Abigail R. Riemer, Sarah J. Gervais, Jeanine L.M. Skorinko, Sonya Maria Douglas, Heather Spencer, Katherine Nugai, Anastasia Karapanagou, and Andreas Miles-Novelo, "She Looks Like She'd Be an Animal in Bed: Dehumanization of Drinking Women in Social Contexts," *Sex Roles* 80 (2019): 617–629, https://www.wpi.edu/news/study-finds-both-men-and-women-take-negative-view-women-who-drink.

Chapter 9: Exceed Expectations—The Performance Evaluation

1. Can be accessed at https://benschmidt.org/profGender/.

2. Scott Jaschik, "Rate My Word Choice," *Inside Higher Ed,* February 9, 2015, https://www.insidehighered.com/news/2015/02/09/new-analysis-rate-my-professors-finds-patterns-words-used-describe-men-and-women.

3. Kerry Chavez and Kristina M.W. Mitchell, "Exploring Bias in Student Evaluations: Gender, Race, and Ethnicity," *Political Science and Politics* 53, no. 2 (2019): 270–274, doi:10.1017/S1049096519001744.

4. Emma A. Renström, Marie Gustafsson Sendén, and Anna Lindqvist, "Gender Stereotypes in Student Evaluations of Teaching," *Frontiers in Education* 5 (2021), https://www.frontiersin.org/articles/10.3389/feduc.2020.571287/full.

5. Anne Boring, "Gender Biases in Student Evaluations of Teaching," *Journal of Public Economics* 145 (January 2017): 27–41.

6. Heather Laube, Kelly Massoni, J. Sprague, and Abby Ferber, "The Impact of Gender on the Evaluation of Teaching: What We Know and What We Can Do," *National Women's Studies Association Journal* 19, no. 3 (2007): 87–104.

7. Kristina M. W. Mitchell and Jonathan Martin, "Gender Bias in Student Evaluations," *PS: Political Science & Politics* 51, no. 3 (2018): 1–5, https://www.cambridge.org/core/journals/ps-political-science-and-politics/article/gender-bias-in-student-evaluations/1224BE475C0AE75A2C2D8553210C4E27.

8. Frances Trix and Carolyn Psenka, "Exploring the Color of Glass: Letters of Recommendation for Female and Male Medical Faculty," *Discourse and Society* 14, no. 2 (2003): 191–220, https://www.jstor.org/stable/42888558.

9. Shelley J. Correll and Caroline Simard, "Research: Vague Feedback Is Holding Women Back," *Harvard Business Review*, April 29, 2016, https://hbr.org/2016/04/research-vague-feedback-is-holding-women-back.

10. Eric Luis Uhlmann and Geoffrey L. Cohen, "Constructed Criteria: Redefining Merit to Justify Discrimination," *Psychological Science*, June 1, 2005, https://journals.sagepub.com/doi/abs/10.1111/j.0956-7976.2005.01559.

11. Lori Nishiura Mackenzie, JoAnne Wehner, and Shelley J. Correll, "Why Most Performance Evaluations Are Biased and How to Fix Them," *Harvard Business Review*, January 11, 2019, https://hbr.org/2019/01/why-most-performance-evaluations-are-biased-and-how-to-fix-them.

12. "Q: What Is an h-index? How Do I Find the h-index for a Particular Author?" University of Texas MD Anderson Center Research Medical Library, January 22, 2020, https://mdanderson.libanswers.com/faq/26221.

13. Adapted from the OECD Competency Framework, available at https://www.oecd.org/careers/competency_framework_en.pdf.

14. Joan C. Williams and Marina Multhaup, "For Women and Minorities to Get Ahead, Managers Must Assign Work Fairly," *Harvard Business Review*, March 5, 2018, https://hbr.org/2018/03/for-women-and-minorities-to-get-ahead-managers-must-assign-work-fairly.

15. Shelley J. Correll, "Constraints Into Preferences: Gender, Status, and Emerging Career Aspirations," *American Sociological Review* 69, no. 1 (February 2004): 93–113, https://doi.org/10.1177/000312240406900106.

16. Shelley J. Correll and Caroline Simard, "Research: Vague Feedback Is Holding Women Back," *Harvard Business Review*, April 29, 2016, https://hbr.org/2016/04/research-vague-feedback-is-holding-women-back.

17. Janice Fanning Madden, "Performance-Support Bias and the Gender Pay Gap Among Stockbrokers," *Gender & Society* 26, no. 3 (June 2012): 488–518, https://doi.org/10.1177/0891243212438546.

Chapter 10: The Physiology of Pay

1. "The Impact of Job Referrals: Effects on Pay, Engagement, Diversity" (Payscale, 2017), https://www.payscale.com/content/whitepaper/wp_ImpactofJobReferrals.pdf.
2. Lydia Frank, "How to Use Employee Referrals Without Giving Up Workplace Diversity," *Harvard Business Review*, March 15, 2018, https://hbr.org/2018/03/how-to-use-employee-referrals-without-giving-up-workplace-diversity.
3. Cat Zakrzewski, "Intel Doubles Up on Hiring Women and Minorities," *Wall Street Journal*, August 3, 2015, https://www.wsj.com/articles/BL-DGB-42906.
4. Laura Kray, "Gender Bias in Negotiators' Ethical Decision Making" (IRLE Working Paper No. 102-11, March 2011), http://irle.berkeley.edu/workingpapers/102-11.pdf.
5. Jacquelyn Smith, "Here's Exactly How Much Money to Ask for in a Salary Negotiation," *Business Insider*, September 16, 2016, https://www.businessinsider.com/how-much-money-to-ask-for-in-a-pay-negotiation-2016-9; Melissa Phipps, "Interview Question: 'What Are Your Salary Expectations'," The Balance Careers, July 17, 2021, https://www.thebalancecareers.com/interview-questions-about-your-salary-expectations-2061235.
6. See, e.g., Hannah Riley Bowles, Linda Babcock, and Kathleen L. McGinn, "Constraints and Triggers: Situational Mechanics of Gender in Negotiations," *Journal of Personality and Social Psychology* 89, no. 6 (2005): 955–956, https://dash.harvard.edu/bitstream/handle/1/38036097/Bowles%20Babcock%20McGinn%202005.pdf?sequence=1.
7. Andreas Leibbrandt and John A. List, "Do Women Avoid Salary Negotiations? Evidence from a Large-Scale Natural Field Experiment," *Management Science* 61, no. 9 (September 8, 2014): 2016–2024, https://doi.org/10.1287/mnsc.2014.1994.
8. James E. Bessen, Chen Meng, and Erich Denk, "Perpetuating Inequality: What Salary History Bans Reveal About Wages" (SSRN, June 2020), http://dx.doi.org/10.2139/ssrn.3628729.
9. Claire Cain Miller, "As Women Take Over a Male-Dominated Field, the Pay Drops," *New York Times*, March 18, 2016, https://www.nytimes.com/2016/03/20/upshot/as-women-take-over-a-male-dominated-field-the-pay-drops.html.
10. Dick Grote, "Let's Abolish Self-Appraisal," *Harvard Business Review*, July 11, 2011, https://hbr.org/2011/07/lets-abolish-self-appraisal.html.
11. Robert W. Eichinger, Michael M. Lombardo, and Lominger Limited, Inc., "Knowledge Summary Series: 360-Degree Assessment," *Human Resource Planning*, 2003, https://www.kornferry.com/content/dam/kornferry/docs/article-migration/Knowledge%20Summary%20Series-%20360-Degree%20Assessment%20.pdf.
12. Marc Benioff, *Trailblazer: The Power of Business as the Greatest Platform for Change* (Currency, 2019).
13. Jingcong Zhao, "Improving Employee Satisfaction: Proven Tips From Research," Payscale, November 14, 2018, https://www.payscale.com/compensation-today/2018/11/employee-satisfaction-research.
14. Dave Smith, "Most People Have No Idea Whether They're Paid Fairly," *Harvard Business Review*, December 2015, https://hbr.org/2015/10/most-people-have-no-idea-whether-theyre-paid-fairly.

Chapter 11: Family Matters

1. Allyson Felix, "Allyson Felix: My Own Nike Pregnancy Story," *New York Times*, May 22, 2019, https://www.nytimes.com/2019/05/22/opinion/allyson-felix-pregnancy-nike.html.
2. Meredith Covington and Ana H. Kent, "'The She-Cession' Persists, Especially for Women of Color," *St. Louis Fed on the Economy* (blog), December 24, 2020, https://www.stlouisfed.org/on-the-economy/2020/december/she-cession-persists-women-of-color.
3. Chabeli Carrazana, "Moms Spent the Equivalent of a Full-Time Job on Child Care Last Year—While Working at the Same Time," The 19th, August 3, 2021, https://19thnews.org/2021/08/moms-child-care-pandemic-full-time-job/.
4. "Back-to-Work: The Billion Dollar Opportunity for Companies" (Maven, 2021), https://www.mavenclinic.com/back-to-work-whitepaper.
5. Matthias Krapf, Heinrich W. Ursprung, and Christian Zimmermann, "Parenthood and Productivity of Highly Skilled Labor: Evidence from the Groves of Academe," *Journal of Economic Behavior & Organization* 140 (August 2017): 147–175, https://doi.org/10.1016/j.jebo.2017.05.010.
6. Aaron Taube, "Men Earn More Money After Having a Kid, While Women Earn Less," *Business Insider*, September 8, 2014, https://www.businessinsider.com/men-earn-more-money-after-having-a-kid-2014-9.
7. Rachel Nania, "More Than College Tuition: 'We Have a Child Care Crisis in This Country'," WTOP, February 13, 2017, https://wtop.com/parenting/2017/02/more-than-college-tuition-we-have-a-child-care-crisis-in-this-country/.
8. Shelley J. Correll, Stephen Benard, and In Paik, "Getting a Job: Is There a Motherhood Penalty?" *American Journal of Sociology* 112, no. 5 (March 2007): 1297–1339, https://www.journals.uchicago.edu/doi/abs/10.1086/511799?journalCode=ajs.
9. Caitlyn Collins, *Making Motherhood Work: How Women Manage Careers and Caregiving* (Princeton, New Jersey: Princeton University Press, 2019).
10. Gretchen Livingston and Deja Thomas, "Among 41 Countries, Only U.S. Lacks Paid Parental Leave," Pew Research Center, December 16, 2019, https://www.pewresearch.org/fact-tank/2016/09/26/u-s-lacks-mandated-paid-parental-leave/.
11. Elly-Ann Johansson, "The Effect of Own and Spousal Parental Leave on Earnings" (Institute for Evaluation of Labour Market and Education Policy (IFAU) Working Paper 2010:4, March 22, 2010), https://www.ifau.se/globalassets/pdf/se/2010/wp10-4-The-effect-of-own-and-spousal-parental-leave-on-earnings.pdf.
12. "A Fresh Look at Paternity Leave: Why the Benefits Extend Beyond the Personal," McKinsey & Company, March 5, 2021, https://www.mckinsey.com/business-functions/organization/our-insights/a-fresh-look-at-paternity-leave-why-the-benefits-extend-beyond-the-personal.
13. Renee Stepler, "Key Takeaways on Americans' Views of and Experiences with Family and Medical Leave," Pew Research Center, March 23, 2017, https://www.pewresearch.org/fact-tank/2017/03/23/key-takeaways-on-americans-views-of-and-experiences-with-family-and-medical-leave/.
14. Francesca Colantuoni, Wahi Diome-Deer, Karl Moore, Shaibyaa Rajbhandari, and Gila Tolub, "A Fresh Look at Paternity Leave: Why the Benefits Extend Beyond

the Personal," McKinsey & Company, March 5, 2021, https://www.mckinsey.com/business-functions/organization/our-insights/a-fresh-look-at-paternity-leave-why-the-benefits-extend-beyond-the-personal.

15. Juliana Menasce Horowitz, Kim Parker, Nikki Graf, and Gretchen Livingston, "Americans Widely Support Paid Family and Medical Leave, but Differ Over Specific Policies," Pew Research Center, March 23, 2017, http://www.pewsocialtrends.org/2017/03/23/americans-widely-support-paid-family-and-medical-leave-but-differ-over-specific-policies/.

16. Claire Cain Miller, "With Paid Leave, Gates Foundation Says There Can Be Too Much of a Good Thing," *New York Times*, January 25, 2019, https://www.nytimes.com/2019/01/25/upshot/paid-parental-leave-sweet-spot-six-months-gates.html.

17. Colin Seeberger, "CAP Report Analyzes Costs of Child Care for Infants and Toddlers, Need for Increased Public Support," Center for American Progress, November 15, 2018, https://www.americanprogress.org/press/release/2018/11/15/460972/release-cap-report-analyzes-costs-child-care-infants-toddlers-need-increased-public-support/.

18. Lynn Friss Feinberg, "The Dual Pressures of Family Caregiving and Employment: Six in 10 Family Caregivers Are in the Labor Force" (AARP Public Policy Institute, May 2016), https://www.aarp.org/content/dam/aarp/ppi/2016-03/The-Dual-Pressures-off-Family-Caregiving-and-Employment.pdf.

19. "The Cost of Caregiving Falls Disproportionately on Women," RBC Wealth Management, 2021, https://www.rbcwealthmanagement.com/us/en/research-insights/the-cost-of-caregiving-falls-disproportionately-on-women/detail/.

20. "Costs of Intimate Partner Violence Against Women in the United States" (Centers for Disease Control and Prevention, National Center for Injury Prevention and Control, March 2003), https://www.cdc.gov/violenceprevention/pdf/ipvbook-a.pdf.

21. Roy Maurer, "When Domestic Violence Comes to Work," SHRM, July 7, 2021, https://www.shrm.org/resourcesandtools/hr-topics/risk-management/pages/domestic-violence-workplace-nfl-ray-rice.aspx.

22. Sheela Subramanian and Tina Gilbert, "A New Era of Workplace Inclusion: Moving From Retrofit to Redesign," *Future Forum* (blog), March 11, 2021, https://futureforum.com/2021/03/11/dismantling-the-office-moving-from-retrofit-to-redesign/.

23. Ruchika Tulshyan, "Return to Office? Some Women of Color Aren't Ready," *New York Times*, June 23, 2021, https://www.nytimes.com/2021/06/23/us/return-to-office-anxiety.html.

24. Hannah Hickok, "Are Men-Dominated Offices the Future of the Workplace?" *BBC*, May 6, 2021, https://www.bbc.com/worklife/article/20210503-are-men-dominated-offices-the-future-of-the-workplace.

25. Nelson D. Schwartz, "Working from Home Poses Hurdles for Employees of Color," *New York Times*, September 6, 2020, https://www.nytimes.com/2020/09/06/business/economy/working-from-home-diversity.html.

Chapter 12: Leadership Material

1. "2020 Gender Equality in the U.S." (Equileap, Global & Special Reports, December 2020), https://equileap.com/wp-content/uploads/2020/12/Equileap_US_Report_2020.pdf.

2. "Share of Companies in the United States with Racially and Ethnically Diverse CEOs from 2004 to 2018," Statista, August 2019, https://www.statista.com/statistics/1097600/racial-and-ethnic-diversity-of-ceos-in-the-united-states/.

3. Eric W. Dolan, "New Study Finds People Who Speak More Are More Likely to Be Viewed as Leaders," PsyPost, July 17, 2021, https://www.psypost.org/2021/07/new-study-finds-people-who-speak-more-are-more-likely-to-be-viewed-as-leaders-61540.

4. K. Landay, P.D. Harms, and M. Credé, "Shall We Serve the Dark Lords? A Meta-analytic Review of Psychopathy and Leadership," *Journal of Applied Psychology* 104, no. 1 (2019): 183–196, http://dx.doi.org/10.1037/apl0000357.

5. Jack Zenger and Joseph Folkman, "Research: Women Score Higher Than Men in Most Leadership Skills," *Harvard Business Review*, June 25, 2019, https://hbr.org/2019/06/research-women-score-higher-than-men-in-most-leadership-skills.

6. Tomas Chamorro-Premuzic and Alison Beard, "Why Are We Still Promoting Incompetent Men?" March 12, 2019, in *Harvard Business Review IdeaCast*, podcast, MP3 audio, 25:27, https://hbr.org/podcast/2019/03/why-are-we-still-promoting-incompetent-men.

7. Bill Hathaway, "Study: Sad, Lonely People More Likely to Be 'Natural' Social Psychologists," YaleNews, March 15, 2018, https://news.yale.edu/2018/03/15/study-sad-lonely-people-more-likely-be-natural-social-psychologists.

8. "People Love Working with Extraverts, Until the Going Gets Tough," Association for Psychological Science, November 18, 2016, http://www.psychologicalscience.org/news/minds-business/people-love-working-with-extraverts-until-the-going-gets-tough.html.

9. James A. Fairburn and James M. Malcomson, "Performance, Promotion, and the Peter Principle," *The Review of Economic Studies* 68, no. 1 (January 2001): 45–66, https://doi.org/10.1111/1467-937X.00159; Alan Benson, Danielle Li, and Kelly Shue, "Research: Do People Really Get Promoted to Their Level of Incompetence?" *Harvard Business Review*, March 08, 2018, https://hbr.org/2018/03/research-do-people-really-get-promoted-to-their-level-of-incompetence.

10. Neema Kudva and Kajri Misra, "Gender Quotas, the Politics of Presence, and the Feminist Project: What Does the Indian Experience Tell Us?" *Signs* 34, no. 1 (Autumn 2008): 49–73, https://doi.org/10.1086/589239; Raghabendra Chattopadhyay and Esther Duflo, "Women as Policy Makers: Evidence from a Randomized Policy Experiment in India," *Econometrica* 72 (2004): 1409–1443; Lori Beaman, Raghabendra Chattopadhyay, Esther Duflo, Rohini Pande, and Petia Topalova, "The Power of Political Voice: Women's Political Representation and Crime in India," *American Economic Journal: Applied Economics* 4 (2012): 165–193.

11. Margarethe Wiersema and Marie Louise Mors, "What Board Directors Really Think of Gender Quotas," *Harvard Business Review*, November 14, 2016, https://hbr.org/2016/11/what-board-directors-really-think-of-gender-quotas.

12. Fidan Ana Kurtulus and Donald Tomaskovic-Devey, "Do Female Top Managers Help Women to Advance? A Panel Study Using EEO-1 Records," *ANNALS of the American Academy of Political and Social Science* 639 (2012): 173–197.

13. Wiersema and Mors, "Gender Quotas."

14. Wiersema and Mors, "Gender Quotas."

15. Michaela Bar, Alexandra Niessen, and Stefan Ruenzi, "The Impact of Work Group Diversity on Performance: Large Sample Evidence from the Mutual Fund Industry" (SSRN, September 2007), http://dx.doi.org/10.2139/ssrn.1017803.

16. Iris Bohnet, *What Works: Gender Equality by Design* (Cambridge, Massachusetts: Harvard University Press, 2016).

17. Xuechunzi Bai, Miguel R. Ramos, and Susan T. Fiske, "As Diversity Increases, People Paradoxically Perceive Social Groups as More Similar," *Proceedings of the National Academy of Sciences* 117, no. 23 (June 2020): 12,741–12,749, https://doi.org/10.1073/pnas.2000333117.

18. Rosabeth Moss Kanter, "Some Effects of Proportions on Group Life: Skewed Sex Ratios and Responses to Token Women," *American Journal of Sociology* 82 (1977): 965–990; Michelle Duguid, "Female Tokens in High-Prestige Work Groups: Catalysts or Inhibitors of Group Diversification?" *Organizational Behavior and Human Decision Processes* 116, no. 1 (2011): 104–115, https://doi.org/10.1016/j.obhdp.2011.05.009.

19. Jennifer J. Lee and Alice M. Mccabe, "Who Speaks and Who Listens: Revisiting the Chilly Climate in College Classrooms," *SAGE Journals* 35, no. 1 (February 2021): 32–60, https://doi.org/10.1177/0891243220977141; M.A. Lundeberg, P.W. Fox, and J. Punćcohaf, "Highly Confident But Wrong: Gender Differences and Similarities in Confidence Judgments," *Journal of Educational Psychology* 86, no. 1 (1994): 114–121, https://doi.org/10.1037/0022-0663.86.1.114.

20. Tara Sophia Mohr, "Why Women Don't Apply for Jobs Unless They're 100% Qualified," *Harvard Business Review*, August 25, 2014, https://hbr.org/2014/08/why-women-dont-apply-for-jobs-unless-theyre-100-qualified.

21. Jennifer L. Lawless and Richard L. Fox, "Men Rule: The Continued Under-Representation of Women in U.S. Politics" (Women & Politics Institute, January 2012), https://www.american.edu/spa/wpi/upload/2012-men-rule-report-web.pdf.

Chapter 13: Blueprints for Inclusive Workspaces

1. Elle Hunt, "City with a Female Face: How Modern Vienna Was Shaped by Women," *Guardian*, May 14, 2019, https://www.theguardian.com/cities/2019/may/14/city-with-a-female-face-how-modern-vienna-was-shaped-by-women; Noele Illien, "How Vienna Built a Gender Equal City," BBC, May 24, 2021, https://www.bbc.com/travel/article/20210524-how-vienna-built-a-gender-equal-city.

2. Alison Hirst and Christina Schwabenland, "Doing Gender in the 'New Office'," *Gender, Work and Organization* 25, no. 2 (2017): 159–176, https://uobrep.openrepository.com/handle/10547/622118.

3. Ashby Plant, Janet Hyde, Dacher Keltner, and Patricia Devine, "The Gender Stereotyping of Emotions," *Psychology of Women Quarterly* 24, no. 1 (March 2000): 81–92, https://doi.org/10.1111/j.1471-6402.2000.tb01024.x.

4. Terri Simpkin, "Mixed Feelings: How to Deal With Emotions at Work," Totaljobs, January 8, 2020, https://www.totaljobs.com/advice/emotions-at-work.

5. Christopher K. Marshburn, Kevin J. Cochran, Elinor Flynn, and Linda J. Levine, "Workplace Anger Costs Women Irrespective of Race," *Frontiers in Psychology* 11 (November 2020), https://doi.org/10.3389/fpsyg.2020.579884.

6. Rachel Thomas, Marianne Cooper, Kate McShane Urban, et al., "Women in the Workplace 2021," (LeanIn.Org and McKinsey & Company, 2021), https://wiwreport.s3.amazonaws.com/Women_in_the_Workplace_2021.pdf.

7. Thomas, "Women in the Workplace."

8. Venessa Wong, "These People of Color Are Anxious About Racist Microaggressions When They Return to the Office," BuzzFeed News, June 29, 2021, https://www.buzzfeednews.com/article/venessawong/workers-returning-office-racism.

9. Iris Bohnet, *What Works: Gender Equality by Design* (Cambridge, Massachusetts: Harvard University Press, 2016).

10. Sapna Cheryan, Victoria C. Plaut, Paul G. Davies, and Claude M. Steele, "Ambient Belonging: How Stereotypical Cues Impact Gender Participation in Computer Science," *Journal of Personality and Social Psychology* 97, no. 6 (December 2009): 1045–1060, https://doi.org/10.1037/a0016239.

11. Ioana M. Latu, Marianne Schmid Mast, Joris Lammers, and Dario Bombari, "Successful Female Leaders Empower Women's Behavior in Leadership Tasks," *Journal of Experimental Social Psychology* 49, no. 3 (2013): 444–448, https://doi.org/10.1016/j.jesp.2013.01.003.

12. Christopher Redding, "A Teacher Like Me: A Review of the Effect of Student-Teacher Racial/Ethnic Matching on Teacher Perceptions of Students and Student Academic and Behavioral Outcomes," *Review of Educational Research* 89, no. 4 (2019): 499–535, https://doi.org/10.3102/0034654319853545.

13. S. Sangrigoli, C. Pallier, A-M Argenti, VA Ventureyra, and S. de Schonen, "Reversibility of the Other-Race Effect in Face Recognition During Childhood," *Psychological Science* 16, no. 6 (June 2005): 440–444, https://pubmed.ncbi.nlm.nih.gov/15943669/.

14. Caroline Criado Perez, *Invisible Women: Data Bias in a World Designed for Men* (New York: Abrams Press, 2019), 138–139.

15. Stefanie K. Johnson and Juan M. Madera, "Sexual Harassment Is Pervasive in the Restaurant Industry. Here's What Needs to Change," *Harvard Business Review*, January 18, 2018, https://hbr.org/2018/01/sexual-harassment-is-pervasive-in-the-restaurant-industry-heres-what-needs-to-change.

16. Perez, *Invisible Women*, 141–142.

17. Johnson, "Sexual Harassment."

18. Beatriz Pagliarini Bagagli, Tyara Veriato Chaves, and Mónica G. Zoppi Fontana, "Trans Women and Public Restrooms: The Legal Discourse and Its Violence," *Frontiers in Sociology* 6 (March 2021), https://doi.org/10.3389/fsoc.2021.652777; "Transgender Teens With Restricted Bathroom Access at Higher Risk of Sexual

Assault," Harvard T.H. Chan School of Public Health, May 7, 2019, https://www
.hsph.harvard.edu/news/hsph-in-the-news/transgender-teens-restricted-
bathroom-access-sexual-assault/.

Chapter 14: AI Won't Save Us (Unless We Save It First)

1. "Leadership Principles," https://www.amazon.jobs/en/principles.
2. Jeffrey Dastin, "Amazon Scraps Secret AI Recruiting Tool That Showed Bias Against Women," Reuters, October 10, 2018, https://www.reuters.com/article/us-amazon-com-jobs-automation-insight-idUSKCN1MK08G.
3. "The Changing Face of HR" (The Sage Group, 2020), https://online.sageintacct.com/rs/473-QSL-641/images/changing-face-hr-research-HR-People-Mgt.pdf.
4. Cathy O'Neil, *Weapons of Math Destruction: How Big Data Increases Inequality and Threatens Democracy* (New York: Crown Publishing, 2016).
5. Caitlin Dewey, "The Only Guide to Gamergate You Will Ever Need to Read," *Washington Post*, October 14, 2014, https://www.washingtonpost.com/news/the-intersect/wp/2014/10/14/the-only-guide-to-gamergate-you-will-ever-need-to-read/.
6. Harry Gaskell and Binna Kandola, "Episode 5: AI—Is It Bias, and What Does That Mean for the Workplace?" November 19, 2019, in *Racism at Work*, podcast, MP3 audio, 45:06, https://pearnkandola.com/diversity-and-inclusion-hub/guides-and-tools/racism-at-work-podcast-episode-5-ai-bias/.
7. James Somers, "The Pastry A.I. That Learned to Fight Cancer," *New Yorker*, March 18, 2021, https://www.newyorker.com/tech/annals-of-technology/the-pastry-ai-that-learned-to-fight-cancer.
8. Suresh Sambandam, "Combining Human and Artificial Intelligence for a More Inclusive Work Environment," *HR Technologist*, November 12, 2019, https://www.hrtechnologist.com/articles/digital-transformation/combining-human-and-artificial-intelligence-for-a-more-inclusive-work-environment/.
9. Example: https://www.ibm.com/support/pages/node/627717.
10. Mimi Ọnụọha, "The Library of Missing Datasets," 2016, https://mimionuoha.com/the-library-of-missing-datasets.
11. *APA Dictionary of Psychology*, s.v. "interviewer effect," accessed October 13, 2021, https://dictionary.apa.org/interviewer-effect.
12. https://weallcount.com/.
13. Heather Krause, "Is the 'Interviewer Effect' Skewing Your Survey Results?" We All Count, January 30, 2019, https://weallcount.com/2019/01/30/an-introduction-to-the-interviewer-effect/.
14. Paul J. Lavrakas, *Encyclopedia of Survey Research Methods* (Thousand Oaks, CA: Sage Publications, Inc., 2008), https://dx.doi.org/10.4135/9781412963947.
15. Heather Krause, "Foundations of Data Equity" (presentation, We All Count, November 2020), https://weallcount.com/wp-content/uploads/2020/12/Data-Equity-Framework-Talk-November-2020.pdf.

16. Krause, "Data Equity."
17. "Black Census Project Results," Black Futures Lab, 2019, https://blackcensus
.org/?mc_cid=7dc380cde6&mc_eid=2f391118d6.

Chapter 15: DEI Principles to Live By

1. Kurt Andersen, *Evil Geniuses: The Unmaking of America: A Recent History* (New York: Random House, 2020).
2. D'Vera Cohn and Paul Taylor, "Baby Boomers Approach 65—Glumly," Pew Research Center, December 20, 2010, https://www.pewresearch.org/social-trends/2010/12/20/baby-boomers-approach-65-glumly/.
3. Jack Kelly, "Baby Boomers Are Leaving the Workforce to Live Their Best Lives in a Silver Tsunami 'Great Retirement' Trend," *Forbes*, October 1, 2021, https://www.forbes.com/sites/jackkelly/2021/10/01/baby-boomers-are-leaving-the-workforce-to-live-their-best-lives-in-a-silver-tsunami-great-retirement-trend/?sh=574143f1260b.
4. Kristen Bellstrom and Emma Hinchliffe, "Companies With More Women in Leadership Performed Better in the Pandemic," *Fortune*, July 14, 2021, https://fortune.com/2021/07/14/companies-with-more-women-at-the-top-fared-better-during-the-pandemic/; Anna Meyer, "New Report: Companies With Diverse Boards Out Performed Their Peers During the Pandemic," *Inc.*, July 13, 2021, https://www.inc.com/anna-meyer/diversity-board-directors-covid-pandemic.html.

Acknowledgments

This book is grounded in the experiences of those who have been willing to tell their stories. I am grateful to every survey taker and interview participant who has trusted GEN, and me, with your story. This wouldn't have been possible without you.

Thank you to Michael Campbell, Adaobi Obi Tulton, Dawn Kilgore, and the rest of the team at Wiley for seeing the possibilities in this book and championing the message. Because of you, I had the opportunity to write the book I wanted.

I owe a debt of gratitude to the brilliant writers, thinkers, and experts I have learned from—especially Dr. Iris Bohnet. Her work in behavioral economics and gender equality shaped my own thinking around designing bias out of the workplace. I am grateful to have learned from Ijeoma Oluo's research and writing. *So You Want To Talk About Race* may be the most dog-eared book on my shelves. I want to thank Ruchika Tulshyan for sustaining a focus on the workplace experiences of women of color; I continue to learn from her writing. I have also leaned on the work of Paul Farmer, Atul Gawande, E.F. Schumacher, and Amartya Sen, whose works reliably elucidate the gaps between good intentions and meaningful impact.

I want to recognize the University of Washington's Evans School for being a partner in our foundational research, and Dr. Karin Martin, specifically, for facilitating our collaboration with the Evans School Student Consulting Lab. Thank you to Dr. Hala Annabi at the University of Washington's Information School for expanding the research on the talents that individuals with autism bring to the workplace.

I am also grateful to the earliest advocates and supporters of GEN for championing a systemic approach to equity. Dr. Kristin Hull, thank you for chasing me down outside our first conference together, for leading Nia in becoming the first GEN-certified organization, and for our continued friendship. Misia Tramp, you were one of the first believers, the loudest voice telling me "to give it a bloody go," and a true ambassador. Thank you. Randall Lane, your guidance and sponsorship early on was invaluable. The early supporters of this approach have been beacons for showing others what is possible—Dorothy Bullitt, Ray Carney, Leslie Decker, Laura Espriu, Lydia Frank, Gay Gabrilska, Megan Gaiser, Krissy Goff, Kristin Graham, Archis Gore, Dr. Gerry Herbison, Liz High, Hilary Laney, Christopher Malsbury, Sandra Masiliso, Kate Mills, Gracian Nolasco, Joy Turner, Sol Villarreal, Lila Williams, Dr. Joseph Williams, and David Wolf—thank you all for being early advocates, connectors, and supporters.

Aparna Rae and Nicole DeKay, thank you for being co-conspirators in insisting on integrity in data. I'm thankful we found each other.

Finally, this would have been impossible without the people in my life who support me. Jannel Anderson, Mackenzie Berg, Matt Brain, Colin Cureton, Jessica Lind Diamond Green, Pat Green, Amanda Helfer, Margaret Kutcher, Sean MacDonald, Jenifer Sapel, Shonita Savage, and Tyler Wisdom—thank you all for being there for me, buying me a meal or a coffee or a drink when I needed it, reminding me that rest is resistance, stepping in as emergency data entry support and proofreaders, pulling me out of my writing hole for bike rides and walks, and making me laugh. You are my partners in storm chasing and re-grounding. Thank you.

To the two people I'll never know how to thank enough—my parents. No matter what I've been working on, you two have always been my first and last readers. You've believed in me through every revision of life I've been working through, and every time this got hard, I reminded myself whose daughter I am. Thank you for always encouraging me, through your own example, to ask what else is possible. I love you. Thank you.

About the Author

Sara Sanford is the founder of GEN and the architect of the GEN Certification, the first gold standard for intersectional gender equity in US businesses, which has now expanded to certify businesses globally. She has provided consultation to leaders in business and government on equity strategy and communication. Her insights make her an internationally sought-after advisor to Fortune 500 companies, associations, NGOs, and foundations. She is a popular TED speaker and has been interviewed by the *New York Times* and featured as a subject matter expert on television and radio. A graduate of Carleton College and the University of Washington, she lives in Seattle.

Index